D1592637

DATE DUE

THE TRADITIONAL AND NATIONAL
MUSIC OF SCOTLAND

THE
TRADITIONAL AND
NATIONAL MUSIC
OF SCOTLAND

by

FRANCIS COLLINSON

Routledge and Kegan Paul
LONDON

First published in 1966
by Routledge and Kegan Paul Ltd
Broadway House, 68–74 Carter Lane
London, E.C.4

Reprinted 1970

Printed in Great Britain
by Western Printing Services Ltd, Bristol

ISBN 0 7100 1213 6

Dedicated to

HER MAJESTY QUEEN ELIZABETH
THE QUEEN MOTHER

With Her Gracious Permission

Contents

songs, the *keening* and the dirge—an example of the mourning song—the minor pentatonic scale, description of by Necker de Saussure—funeral airs resembling piobaireachd tunes

Plates

Preface

THE urge to write this book has arisen partly from my desire to present in tangible form the outcome of a number of years spent as a founder member of the School of Scottish Studies, of which I was invited by the University of Edinburgh to take charge of musical research at its inception in 1951, and of which I am privileged now to be an Honorary Research Fellow. There has also been present however that perpetual urge to achieve something, patently desirable, which has never been done before; for, curious to relate, no book has ever appeared which has been devoted entirely to the traditional and national music of Scotland in all its aspects, though many have been written upon some particular facet of it—Gaelic song, for instance; the songs and ballads of Lowland Scotland (books on the ballads being almost *ad infinitem*), the fiddle music, the bagpipes and their music etc. etc.; and some of these are very good. Dr Henry Farmer went some way indeed towards supplying the want, in his excellent *A History of Music in Scotland*, published in 1947; but he is as much concerned with the music of the Church, the 'sang-schule', and the concert-room, as with the music of the folk; and though many of the relevant facts concerning Scotland's traditional, and more particularly *national* music are to be found in his pages, they are necessarily stripped to the bare essentials, so as to leave room for a mine of other musical information.

It is perhaps only when one brings it all together into one book that the astonishing colour and variety of Scotland's music becomes apparent—the music of the Highlands, of the Lowlands, of the Western Isles, and of the Borders, each with its own characteristics and flavour; the music of its singers, its pipers, its fiddlers, and the last surviving fragments (or reconstructions of them) of the music of its ancient harpers. Nor must we forget the not inconsiderable contribution of song, pipe-music and fiddle-tunes accredited to the composers of Scotland's 'fairy population'!—whatever the true source of it may be—

which is still believed in in parts of the country, or at least cautiously left as an open question. Finally there is the music that Scotland has fallen heir to, in Orkney and Shetland—one of the beneficent results of a slight difficulty of payment of the dowry of Norway's Princess Margaret at her marriage to Scotland's King James III in 1469.

This book, as its title implies, is basically about music. To present the music of Scotland, particularly of Gaelic-speaking Scotland, in its true historical background however, it is necessary to take notice of a number of other subjects—Gaelic history for example, including the fictitious 'histories' of Ossian and Cú Chulainn; and the Gaelic poetic metres, of which those of the ancient classical poetry were numbered in hundreds, according to the standard authority (it was, in the main, poetry intended to be sung). Necessary, too, to wrestle with the endless pitfalls of Gaelic orthography, of which little appearing in print earlier than the present century appears to hold good, and that little of small help to the non Gaelic-scholar. Here is the appropriate place to say that my own knowledge of Gaelic is limited solely to such acquaintance as the recording, transcription and study of Gaelic song has brought, an acquaintance restricted by the formidable difficulties of the language, and curtailed by much time necessarily devoted to the music of the rest of Scotland as well.

Such subjects, and others involved in these pages, are beyond the normal scope of the musicologist—even of the Scots folk-musicologist, and I have deemed it necessary accordingly to seek advice of my specialist friends and of my colleagues of the School of Scottish Studies, and to ask them to read and comment on my text. Some of their comments, as is perhaps only to be expected, disagree with what I have written, and I owe it to the reader to set down their observations, which I have done in the form of footnotes. I am sure the reader will find these instructive and of interest, even when they are not directly concerned with music.

It remains to thank all those who have helped me in my task. First I must record my gratitude to Professor Sidney T. M. Newman, M.A., D.Mus., F.R.C.O., F.T.C.L., Dean of the Faculty of Music, Edinburgh University, for his help and encouragement in these studies in Scots music over a long period of years, which have made the writing of the book possible.

I have to express my most grateful thanks to my friend J. L. Campbell of Canna, D.Litt., LL.D., for keeping me on the rails throughout the Gaelic portions of the book, and for a great many valuable comments and suggestions. I have to thank him also for the generous use of his sound-recordings of Gaelic songs; and finally for the careful reading and correcting of the proofs of the chapters concerned.[1]

My warm thanks are due to Basil R. S. Megaw, B.A., F.S.A., F.M.A., Director of the School of Scottish Studies, Edinburgh University, for permission to use transcriptions of the School's sound-recordings, and for placing the technical and other facilities of the School at my disposal. I have also to thank my colleagues of the School and others of Edinburgh University lecturing staff for their continuous and ungrudging help throughout the preparation and writing of the book, and for providing me with texts and translations from the Gaelic; also for correcting and commenting on the proofs of the parts concerned with their own special subjects. These include:

Hamish S. Henderson, M.A., Senior Research Fellow (Scots Folk Song Texts), John MacInnes, M.A., Research Fellow (Gaelic Song Texts), Anne Ross, M.A., F.S.A., F.S.A.Scot., Research Fellow (Custom and Belief), Alan J. Bruford, B.A., Research Archivist, Gillian Johnstone (Music Transcriber), Fred Kent (Technician and photographer), R. Morton (Draughtsman/Illustrator) and other members of the School, some of whom prefer to remain anonymous; and the Rev. W. Matheson, M.A., Lecturer in Celtic, Edinburgh University, for providing me with recordings of Gaelic songs collected or remembered and recorded by himself, for generously making available to me information from his own researches for a forthcoming book by himself on the ancient Scottish harper and song-poet Rory *Dall* Morison; also for reading and correcting and making valuable comments on my text and on the proofs.

I have also to thank R. L. C. Lorimer, M.A., sometime Scholar of Balliol College, Oxford, for reading and commenting on the proofs of the chapters on the bagpipes and their music, and for much information on this subject.

My grateful thanks are due to the following:

For permission to use transcriptions of recordings (i.e. music, text, and/or translations):

Professor J. H. Delargy, D.Litt., LL.D., for the Irish Folklore Commission; Séamus Ennis, formerly of the Irish Folklore Commission; Calum Johnston, Isle of Barra, on behalf of his sister the late Annie Johnston, and for the use of Gaelic songs recorded by himself; Mrs

---

[1] For various reasons, technical and otherwise, I did not find it practicable to submit the proofs of the musical examples, for supervision of the Gaelic titles or of the text underlying the music, to my Gaelic-scholar friends. I must therefore accept full responsibility for any mistakes in the Gaelic which may appear in these.

Margaret Prance (grand-niece of Francis Tolmie); Mrs Katherine Douglas, Isle of Skye; James Ross, M.A., formerly of the School of Scottish Studies, Edinburgh University.

Also to all the singers of the songs quoted throughout the book, whose names appear in the musical examples, or their executors.

For permission to quote from the published works of the following:

(Authors) Henry G. Farmer, M.A., Ph.D., D.Litt., Mus. Doc. (*A History of Music in Scotland*); Margaret Fay Shaw, Isle of Canna (*Folksongs and Folklore of South Uist*); Prof. Otto Andersson, Finland (*The Shetland Gue*; *Ballad Hunting in the Orkney Islands* etc.); I. F. Grant, LL.D. (*The Macleods—The History of a Clan*); Dr Donal O'Sullivan, Dublin (*Carolan*); Dr William and Norah Montgomerie (*Scottish Nursery Rhymes*; *Sandy Candy*; *The Hogarth Book of Scottish Nursery Rhymes*; and the former, for *articles and pamphlets quoted*); The executors of Alexander Carmichael (*Carmina Gadelica*).

(Owners of copyright) Messrs Oliver & Boyd, Edinburgh (*Carmina Gadelica*); The English Folk Dance and Song Society (*The Tolmie Collection of Gaelic Songs*); W. & R. Chambers Ltd. (*Father Allan's Island*) Paxton & Co. Ltd., Music Publishers (*Songs from the Countryside*); Dr L. Vargyas, and Dr B. Rajeczky, Budapest (*Studia Memoria Belae Bartok Sacra*).

For permission to use pictures or photographs for illustrations and/or for other help:

The National Museum of Antiquities of Scotland (and for much help from the Keeper of the Museum, R. B. K. Stevenson); The Scottish National Portrait Gallery; The Ministry of Public Buildings and Works; The Trustees of the British Museum; The National Library of Scotland; Edinburgh University Library; Edinburgh Central Public Library; The Clan Macpherson Association; The Mitchell Library, Glasgow; The Highland Folk Museum, Kingussie; Ilay Campbell, Argyll (owner of the picture, 'Highland Dance'); and other owners of pictures whose permission has been obtained through the Scottish National Portrait Gallery.

Scotland's Magazine; Lafayette Ltd. (Glasgow), photographers; Tom Scott, Edinburgh, photographer.

For information on Scots songs, ballads, and tunes:

Cedric Thorpe Davie, O.B.E., F.R.A.M., A.R.C.M.; Miss Grant, Balvenie House, Dufftown; John Hewie, Jedburgh; John Byers, Newcastleton (author of *Liddesdale*).

For information on the bagpipes:

Seumas MacNeill (Senior Lecturer in Natural Philosophy, Glasgow

University; Principal The College of Piping, Glasgow); J. M. A. Lenihan; Lyndesay G. Langwill, Edinburgh; William A. Cocks, Co. Durham.

For information on Scots fiddle music:

James Alan Rennie (author of *Romantic Strathspey*); Alec Grant, Dufftown.

For information on the Harp:

Mrs Hilda Campbell of Airds, Hon. Life President, *Comunn na Clarsaich* (The Clarsach Society); General Sir Philip Christison, Bt., G.B.E., C.B., D.S.O., M.C., D.L., F.S.A. (Scot.), President, *Comunn na Clarsaich*; Mrs H. J. Wilson, A.R.A.M., Hon. Secretary, *Comunn na Clarsaich*; Miss Jean Campbell, T.D., L.R.A.M. (Council, *Comunn na Clarsaich*); George Davidson, Aberdeen; I. F. Grant, LL.D., Mrs M. J. Watt, Banchory, Aberdeenshire; Miss Barry Milner, Plockton; Miss Russell-Fergusson; Carl Dolmetsch, Haslemere; Mrs P. K. F. Hood, Battle, Sussex.

For information on the music of Orkney:

Dr Hugh Marwick, Orkney; Wm. Ronald Aim, Orkney; Archie P. Lee (B.B.C., Glasgow).

For information on the music of Shetland:

Tom Anderson, Lerwick, Shetland.

For other information and help:

Miss Ethel Bassin, Edinburgh.

So many kind friends have helped me in my task that my fear is that someone may have been inadvertently omitted. If this should be so, I beg that he or she will accept both my gratitude and my apologies.

FRANCIS COLLINSON

Innerleithen, 1966

Traditional and
National Music Defined

FIRST let us define the terms of our title and set down what exactly we mean by the 'national and traditional' music of Scotland. It is perhaps too much to hope that every reader will agree with the writer's own definition, but at least this should provide a compass bearing on his ideas on the subject which may help to clarify some of the following pages.

The traditional music will naturally include all the indigenous *folk-music* of Scotland—the Border and 'Child' ballads (still sung by the folk of Aberdeenshire and the north-east—the tinker folk especially), the bothy ballads, which originated in the farm bothies of the same district, and which linger on, even to the extent of having become 'mechanized' with the tractor taking the place of the horse as one of the subjects to sing about; it will include also all the anonymous Gaelic labour songs and lilts from the Hebrides—waulking songs for the shrinking of the cloth, rowing songs, milking, churning, reaping, corn-grinding, spinning, and 'dandling' songs, as well as the laments and love songs, the pibroch songs and fairy songs and sung 'ports' for dancing; it will include likewise the songs of the coal-miners and of the Glasgow streets. It should *exclude* the obvious importations of English folk-song of which there are or were a great many floating about in Scotland, introduced either in the ordinary traffic between the two countries of people who sing and pick up songs, or by the itinerant ballad-sellers of an age not so very long gone. But some of these, like the English folk-song of 'The Turtle Dove' which was transmuted by Scotland's national poet Robert Burns into 'My love is like a red red rose' have become so enshrined in our national heritage of song that it would be impossible and unthinkable to exclude them.

Scottish song cannot however be limited to folk-song. 'Scots wha ha'e' is not a folk-song, but the literary creation of Robert Burns set to a traditional tune—the old air of 'Hey tuttie-tattie', of which popular though unverifiable tradition has it that it was the tune of Robert the Bruce's march at Bannockburn. 'Auld Lang Syne', as it is everywhere sung, is a literary metamorphosis and amplification of an older song of the same title, again by Robert Burns, which isn't even sung to its own proper traditional tune but to another air, 'The Miller's Wedding', substituted by the Edinburgh music publisher George Thomson. These two songs were composed, or 'patched' from old ones, *expressly for publication*, and so may be appropriately called national rather than traditional songs. Nevertheless they do possess an element of the traditional in that both poems were written to anonymous traditional tunes.

This leads one to say that much of what is accepted as *traditional* in Scots music is of *known* authorship. In the case of the songs, both Lowland and Gaelic, the known element is usually the authorship of the words, which are generally directed to be sung to a named traditional air. The songs of Allan Ramsay, Robert Burns, Lady Nairne, Jean Elliot, Sir Walter Scott in Lowland Scots; and of almost any of the well-known Gaelic poets such as Alexander MacDonald (Mac Mhaighstir Alasdair), Robert ('Rob Donn') Mackay, and Duncan Macintyre ('Donnchadh Bàn') come readily to mind.

In the case of the earlier Gaelic poets such as Mary Macleod and Iain Lom, as indeed with many of the later ones also, both the words and the tunes of their songs have been recovered from *oral tradition* alone—some of the poems within the past hundred years or so, and some of the tunes in very recent times. In this sense, of being recovered from oral tradition, they must certainly be allowed to be 'traditional'.

With instrumental music it would seem to be enough, to merit the title of 'traditional', that it should have been passed by ear and not by the printed copy, from one player to another, or, among the pipers, from pupil to master, even where the authorship is known. The pipe music of the MacCrimmons and the fiddle music of Niel Gow and William Marshall are alike accepted as part of the general corpus of the traditional music of Scotland as much as are the countless anonymous tunes for these instruments. Such a song as 'Caller Herrin'' on the other hand, which was written by Lady Nairne about the end of the eighteenth century to a published harpsichord composition of Nathaniel Gow, son of Niel, should perhaps more properly be called 'national', for neither the words nor the tune are traditional; and it first saw the light of day as a printed song, to be sung in the fashionable Edinburgh drawing-rooms. Nevertheless, as Gow's harpsichord piece is based on the traditional street-cry of the Newhaven fisher-lassies calling their wares in the streets of Edinburgh, there is perhaps just sufficient of the traditional element for the song to qualify for that label, though that is open to argument.

The composition of Scots music both vocal and instrumental by no means of course stopped at the end of what we may call the 'traditional' period, which may be said to coincide roughly with the end of the eighteenth century. New words have continued and still continue to be written both to traditional and to composed airs, many of which have found a permanent place in Scotland's national music. Of those of which both the words and the tune have been composed, perhaps the most popular are the songs of Robert Tannahill and R. A. Smith, poet and composer respectively,[1] of whom both lived into the nineteenth century; and there has been a trickle of song writing in Lowland Scots— and a minor deluge in Gaelic, which continues to the present day. Pipe tunes have been turned out by the hundred under the acknowledged names of their composers, mostly pipers in the Highland Scottish Regiments. One of the most prolific composers of fiddle tunes of all time, Scott Skinner, who died in 1927, was composing reels and strathspeys for the fiddle into his old age.

One cannot call any of this music 'traditional', for it has been written for and disseminated by the printing press and not by oral or aural transmission. It must therefore rather be called *national*. Folk-song is however in a different category. It still continues healthily to evolve in Scotland, notably among the berry-pickers (most of them tinker folk) of the fruit-growing districts of Perthshire; and all of it, because of the circumstances of its composition and of its dissemination alike, may be accepted as a part of Scotland's *traditional* music which is still in the process of formation, paradoxical though this may sound!

Finally one would not wish to deny the masterly Scots songs of Francis George Scott an honoured place among the national music of Scotland; but these come into the category of Art Song, and though the roots of many of them may lie in the gapped scale systems of the older traditional Scots music, as Art Songs they fall outside the scope of this book.

---

[1] The popular 'Jessie the Flower o' Dumblane' was written and composed by that team. Tannahill wrote it to supplant the traditional bawdy song 'The Bob o' Dumblane'. (Hamish Henderson.)

CHAPTER I

The Native Idiom

H AVING attempted in our introduction to define and differentiate the terms *traditional* and *national* in the music of Scotland, we can now combine them under the general heading of Scots music, of which we must first set out to examine its characteristics. That it possesses a strong and unmistakable native idiom is obvious from the most casual acquaintanceship with it; and the question at once arises, 'What is it that makes the "Scottishness" of Scots music?' It is a question that cannot be answered without some resource to technical terms, but it is one which can hardly be shirked in any book on Scots music that is to make sense.

First and foremost among the factors that go to make this Scottishness is the use of the *gapped scale* as the basis for very many Scots tunes. Of these, there are two main species, the five-note or *pentatonic scale* with its two gaps within the octave:

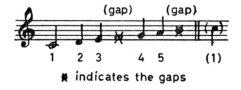

𝄪 indicates the gaps

and the six-note or *hexatonic scale*, which theorists mostly agree has been evolved by filling in one of the gaps in the five-note scale:

Here the minim shows the filling in of one of the gaps. The gap still remaining is indicated by the sign ⊗.

Each of these two types of scale may be regarded as the prototype of a group, which can be formed by the process of 'inversion'; that is, by transferring the bottom note of the scale to the top so that each note of the scale becomes the lowest or 'keynote' or 'final of the mode' in turn. This may be demonstrated with the pentatonic scale thus:

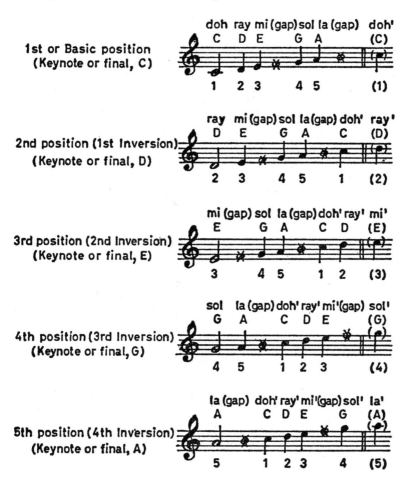

The interesting point about these five positions of the pentatonic scale as far as the resultant music based upon them is concerned is that each of them has its own particular sound and flavour. Tunes constructed upon the first or basic position for instance have much of the characteristics of a major key, owing to the presence of both the major third and sixth reckoning upwards from the keynote. For an example we need go no further than the air of 'Auld Lang Syne' (or to give the air to which this is sung its proper name, 'The miller's wedding') :

AIR

THE MILLER'S WEDDING

(Auld Lang Syne)

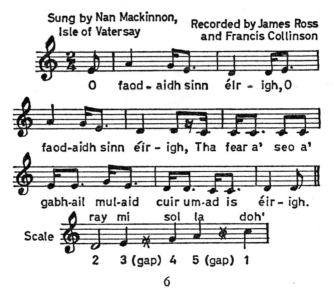

Should auld ac-quaint-ance be for-got, and

ne-ver brought to mind? Should auld ac-quaint-ance

be for-got, and days o' lang___ syne?

Scale

doh ray mi (gap) sol la (gap) (doh')
1   2   3   4   5   (1)

Tunes constructed upon other positions of the scale may sound either minor, major or indeterminate according to their individual contours. The second position of the scale for instance does not have either a minor or major third from the keynote, yet the following little Gaelic tune constructed upon this position sounds more major than minor, because of the strong flavour of C major in bars 5 and 6:

Sung by Nan Mackinnon, Isle of Vatersay

Recorded by James Ross and Francis Collinson

O faod-aidh sinn éir-igh, O

faod-aidh sinn éir-igh, Tha fear a' seo a'

gabh-ail mul-aid cuir um-ad is éir-igh.

ray mi sol la doh'

Scale

2 3 (gap) 4 5 (gap) 1

6

O FAODAIDH SINN EIRIGH

Translation by James Ross:

O we may rise,
O we may rise,
There is a man here sorrowing,
Clothe yourself and rise.

Note. The tune of this song used to be played by the piper on the morning after a wedding, to waken the newly-wedded couple.

On the other hand, the Lowland air of 'Andro and his Cutty Gun', which is in the same mode, has more of a minor flavour than a major. This is the more remarkable as the middle section, like the tune above, also veers towards C major; but by the time this is arrived at, the minor feeling of the air is firmly established:

ANDRO AND HIS CUTTY GUN

Blythe, blythe and mer-ry was she, Blythe was she but and ben, and well she loo'd a Haw-ick gill, and laughed to see a tap-pit hen. She took me in and sat me down and hecht to keep me law-in' free, but cun-ning car-lin that she was, she gar'd me birl my baw-bee.

An air constructed upon the third position, that is, the *second inversion*, of the pentatonic scale may be seen in the well-known tune of 'Roy's wife of Aldivalloch'.

ROY'S WIFE OF ALDIVALLOCH

Roy's wife o' Al-di-val-loch, Roy's wife o' Al-di-val-loch

Wat ye how she cheat-ed me as I cam' ow'r the braes o' Bal-loch.

Scale   mi   sol   la   doh' ray'
3   4   5   1   2

Tunes constructed on the fourth position, that is, the *third inversion* of the pentatonic scale, are rare, but do exist. Here is one from the recordings of the School of Scottish Studies, a tune for the old sinister ballad of 'The False Knight upon the road':

THE FALSE KNIGHT UPON THE ROAD

"What's up-on your back?" said the false knight upon the road, "My

ban-nocks and my books," said the wee boy, and there he stood.

Scale   sol   la   doh' ray' mi'
4   5   1   2   3

(The above song sung by Nellie Macgregor, Aberdeen; recorded by Hamish Henderson.)

Tunes constructed upon the fifth position, i.e. the *fourth inversion*, of the pentatonic scale exist in plenty. 'My tocher's the jewel' is a typical example:

MY TOCHER'S THE JEWEL

O meik-le thinks my love o'— my beau-ty, and meik-le thinks my— love o'— my kin, but lit-tle thinks my love I— ken braw-ly my toch-er's the jewel has charms for him. It's a' for the ap-ple he'll nourish the tree; It's a' for the hin-ney he'll cher-ish the bee. My lad-die's sae meik-le in love wi' the sil-ler, he can-na hae love to spare for me.

Scale as here sung   Scale transposed to key of C
la doh' ray' mi' sol'   la, doh ray mi sol
5   1   2   3   4   5   1   2   3   4

Folk-musicologists are generally of the opinion that the pentatonic scale is vocal rather than instrumental in origin; and certainly it is one of the easiest scale-wise divisions of the octave to sing in accurate intonation without the aid of instrumental accompaniment. Further division of the octave, as in the six- or seven-note scale, necessitates the use of the semitone; and though one might think that everyone is used to the sound of a semitone in modern times, the fact is that it still remains an unstable and fluid interval in the musical vocabulary of the traditional singer who sings without accompaniment, of whatever nationality, as all students of folk-song know from experience.

The Six-Note Scale

Most musical theorists agree as has been said, that the six-note or hexatonic scale has been evolved from the five-note by the filling in of one of its two gaps with an intermediate note. This means that each position of the five-note scale may be turned into two different six-note scales by the insertion of an intermediate note in either of the two gaps (see page 5).

As each of the two gaps in the pentatonic scale consists of the interval of a minor third (i.e. three semitones) any intermediate note within the gap must either proceed by the step of a semitone followed by two semitones (i.e. a full tone) or *vice versa*, by a tone followed by a semitone. Not all the combinations possible by this procedure are used in folk-song; and of those which are found, a good number will be seen to duplicate each other in the sequence and size of their intervals. It would be tedious and over-technical however to enumerate these here. Suffice it to say that, as with the pentatonic scale, tunes constructed upon these six-notes scales have their own distinctive flavour, which roughly speaking is either major or minor, or to be more exact *modal* (an important distinction). They have something of the qualities of both the five-note scale and the seven-note, which we presently have to discuss.

As with the five positions of the pentatonic scale, Scots airs may be found on all the fourteen different hexatonic scales, and indeed these six-note tunes, as has already been observed, are more numerous than five-note. It would add unnecessarily to the bulk of the book to give examples of them all in staff notation. 'The Flowers of the Forest' (old tune), 'O send Lewie Gordon Hame', 'O whistle and I'll come to you my lad', 'Gala Water', 'Whistle o'er the lave o't', 'John o' Badenyon', 'Lassie wi' the lint white locks', 'Auld Rob Morris', 'Ca the Yowes to the Knowes', are all hexatonic tunes in various inversions of the scales.[1]

The Seven-Note Scales: the 'Church Modes' in Scots Song

The next step in the evolution of the Scottish musical scales is, logically, to fill in the remaining gap in the six-note scale (or what comes to the

[1] It should be observed however that various printed editions of Scots tunes are by no means uniform, and what appears as a gap in the scale in one collection may be filled in with an editorial passing note in another. This of course applies to pentatonic and hexatonic scales alike. The versions of the tunes quoted above are all taken as far as possible from definitive sources. The same lack of scalic uniformity may be observed of course, in recorded versions of the same folk-tune by different traditional singers.

For further discussion of the hexatonic scales and their classification, cf. *The MacCormick Collection of Waulking Songs* by J. L. Campbell and Francis Collinson (The Clarendon Press, 1969).

same thing, *both* gaps in the pentatonic scale) with an intermediate note.

Although a great many different seven-note scales could theoretically be formed by the various possible permutations with their inversions, in the filling in of the two gaps of the pentatonic scale by the steps of either a semitone or a tone, in practice these seven-note scales are limited to seven—in Scots music as in the folk-music of many other nations. These seven scales correspond to the seven possible inversions of the *major scale*.

Here is the scale resulting from the filling in of the *first gap* of the pentatonic scale in its basic position by the step of a semitone, and the *second gap* by the step of a tone, i.e.:

Readers will readily recognize this as the ordinary major scale.

These seven scales, formed by the successive inversions of the major scale, will be found to correspond in the sequence of their intervals to the seven 'Church' or '*Ecclesiastical*' Modes. This is a fact the more remarkable in that the correspondence seems to be fortuitous, for the Church Modes have other theories for the process of their formation (too abstruse to be discussed here). It is a similarity that is of primary importance in the classification of folk melodies, for it provides an existing system of nomenclature of the seven scales which is, or should be, readily understood by every musician.

As the seven scales corresponding to the Church Modes form the constructional basis of so much folk-music, Scottish and otherwise, it is desirable to say something about them, even at the risk of becoming rather technical for the general reader.

First, the ordinary major scale of *doh ray mi fah sol la te (doh)* which for our purpose we can call number one of the seven, goes, in the Church Modes, by the name of the Ionian Mode. It should not be necessary to quote more than the names of some of the many Scots airs constructed on a scale which is of such familiar and everyday usage in music in general. 'My love she's but a lassie yet', 'Bonny wee thing', 'Kind Robin Lo'es me', 'The bush aboon Traquair', 'Busk ye, my bonny bride', 'Corn rigs', 'The Birks of Invermay', 'Cam' ye by Atholl?', 'Logie o' Buchan', 'Will ye go to the ewe-buchts', 'Duncan Gray', and 'The weary pund o' tow', are but a few.

When we invert the major scale or scale of the Ionian Mode in the same way as we did the pentatonic by transferring the bottom note to the top, so that the note D now becomes the lowest note or keynote or 'final', we get the scale *ray mi fah sol la te doh* (ray):

This scale corresponds to the Dorian Mode in the Church modes, and may conveniently go by the same name in folk-song. Its most noticeable characteristic is the major sixth in an otherwise minor scale. This becomes clearer if we set the scale in the key signature of D minor, for the sixth, B, will then require a natural in front of it:

As a basis for tune construction, the Dorian Mode is rare in Lowland Scots music, but common in Gaelic. An example, one of the few to be found in Lowland Scots, may be seen in the second strain of the air of 'The wee wee man'. The first strain is hexatonic. (Scale opposite.)

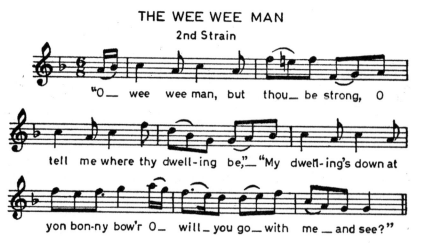

[1] The numbers refer, as in the similar diagrams of the five-note scales, to the original position of the notes in the *basic uninverted position* of the scale, which in the seven-note scale forms the major or Ionian mode.

Dorian mode (transposed)

Even this tune is not really true Dorian in character, for by far the greater part of the tune lies in the key of F major, and it is only the final cadence on the two Gs that brings it within the classification of Dorian. This is a common species of mixture of modes which we will examine in greater detail a little further on. Much more characteristic of the Dorian Mode is the following typical example from a Gaelic song:

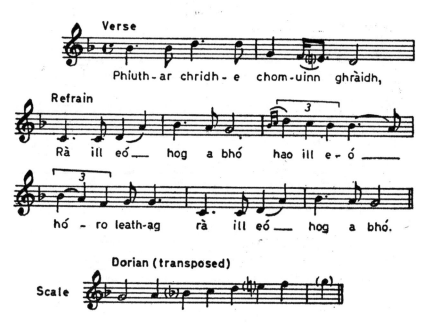

Translation:

> Dear sister, darling companion
> Rà ill eó, hog a bhó,
> Hao ill eó, ho ro, leathag
> Rà ill eó hog a bhó
> (These refrain vocables meaningless)

A second inversion of our scale will bring the note E to the bottom as keynote or 'final'. This is the Scale of the Phrygian Mode:

The outstanding characteristic of this mode is the intial step of a *minor second* in a minor key. If we set the key signature of E minor (one sharp) at the head, we would have to indicate the second note of the scale, F with an accidental *natural* sign.

There are a few Scots tunes in this mode. A good example is the air of 'The bridegroom greets when the sun gaes down', which is the air to which Lady Anne Lindsay wrote her song of 'Auld Robin Gray':[1]

AULD ROBIN GRAY

The tune of 'On Ettrick's Banks' is another example of this mode, though curiously enough the earliest printed version of the tune, in 'Orpheus Caledonius' 1733, suppresses the characteristic minor second

[1] The better-known, though vastly inferior tune to which 'Auld Robin Gray' is often sung, was composed by an English clergyman!

and so changes the scale to Hexatonic, with the second degree gapped; and one has to go to the later editions such as Oswald's Caledonian Companion (1743) for the modal version.

The next inversion of the seven-note scale brings us to the very rare Lydian Mode, of which Cecil Sharp said he never found it in English folk-song (*English Folk-song, Some Conclusions*, page 54. Novello, 1907). Its characteristic is the interval of the *augmented fourth* in an otherwise major scale:

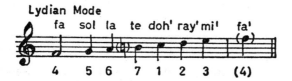

It does exist in both Lowland Scots and Gaelic melody, though the writer has so far found but two examples of it, one in the waulking-song-type of tune of *'Smi'm shuidh air creagan a' Chiuil* and one in a tune for the ballad of Tam Lane, both from the School of Scottish Studies collections:

'S MI'M SHUIDH AIR CREAGAN A CHIUIL

Translation:
Sitting on Creagan a' Chiùil
(Refrain) E ho hi hi, etc. (meaningless)

15

TAM LANE

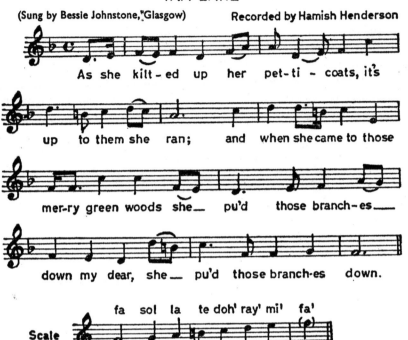

(Sung by Bessie Johnstone, Glasgow)   Recorded by Hamish Henderson

As she kilt-ed up her pet-ti-coats, it's up to them she ran; and when she came to those mer-ry green woods she— pu'd those branch-es— down my dear, she— pu'd those branch-es down.

With a further inversion of the seven-note scale we arrive at the Mixolydian Mode:

Here the characteristic is a minor seventh in an otherwise major scale. Transposed up one tone, this is the mode in which the scale of the Scottish Highland bagpipe is cast:

[1] In bagpipe staff notation the key-signature, by convention, is always omitted. F♯ and C♯ are always to be understood if they occur in the tune. The third and seventh from the keynote A in the Scottish bagpipe are 'out of tune' by concert standards.

Here is a typical mixolydian Scottish bagpipe tune:

A SHEAN BHEAN BHOCHD
(The Poor Old Woman)
Glengarry's March

'Waly Waly', (Scots version), 'I ha'e laid a herring in saut' and 'Lady Cassilles lilt' are examples of song airs in this mode.

The next inversion of the seven-note scale with A as the lowest note, gives us the Aeolian Mode:

This is one of the commonest of the seven-note scales in Scots song. It has the characteristics of a minor key in common with the Dorian and Phrygian modes, but has a *major* second and a *minor* sixth. 'The Laird of Cockpen' is a typical Aeolian Scots tune:[1]

---

[1] It is of course in this case sung a fourth lower than the scale as set out above.

17

THE LAIRD OF COCKPEN

The Laird of Cock-pen, he's proud and he's great, His

mind is ta'en up wi'the things o' the State, He wanted a wife, his

braw house to keep, but fa-vour wi'woo-in' was fash-ious to seek.

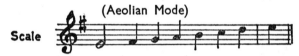

Scale (Aeolian Mode)

Finally, with the last of the seven possible positions of the seven-note scale, we come to the debatable Locrian Mode:

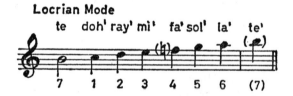

Locrian Mode

This mode was considered inadmissible to the Church Modes, owing to its imperfect fifth; and it existed as a mode only in theory.

Nevertheless a case exists, though not an unshakable one, for at least one Scots tune being considered as in the Locrian Mode,[1] namely, 'The Souters of Selkirk', a somewhat remarkable melody:

[1] The writer has only found one example of the Locrian Mode in the whole of English folk- and traditional song. This is the tune 'The Woods so Wilde' in the *Fitzwilliam Virginal Book*.

THE SOUTERS OF SELKIRK

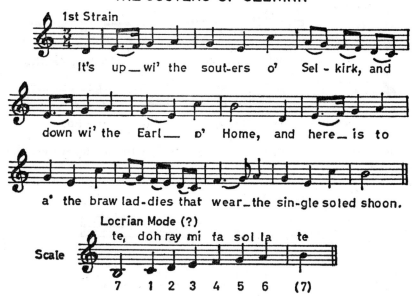

It must be said however that except for the actual cadence on B, the melody lies in the key of C major. The tune therefore belongs to that class (and it is quite a numerous one) of which 'The wee wee man' quoted above, is an example, where the cadence seems to be at variance with the rest of the melody. With the 'Souter's o' Selkirk' it cannot be denied that the final note B has the feeling of an ending on the seventh of the major scale of C, rather than of a final B in the Locrian Mode.[1]

In the folk-music of most countries, it is a constant and practically invariable rule that a melody ends upon its keynote or modal 'final', so that the last note of a tune can be reckoned as the keynote, upon which the scale of the tune may be calculated and classified. In this however the music of Scotland may be said to be unusual in that this rule does not always hold; and there are numerous cases in which it would hardly be possible in the context of the melody to accept the last note as the final of the mode. A good example of this is to be seen in the well-known tune of 'The Campbells are Comin'. There is no need to quote more than the ending of the first of the two strains, as the cadences of both strains are the same:

[1] It should be added that 'The Souters o' Selkirk' is almost certainly an old Border pipe-tune, and it may well be that the last note of the tune was originally B flat and not B natural, in conformity with the minor seventh of the bagpipe scale.

THE CAMPBELLS ARE COMIN'

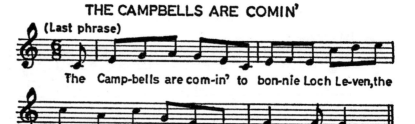

The Camp-bells are com-in' to bon-nie Loch Le-ven, the

Camp-bells are com-in', o - ho, o - ho.

If now we take the last note E as the final of the mode, we get the following scale:[1]

Phrygian Mode

This is the Phrygian Mode, which we have described above. But there are positively *none of the characteristics* of the Phrygian Mode in the tune. The Phrygian is one of the modes with a 'minor' flavour, whereas the tune of 'The Campbells are Comin' is definitely major. Again the note F in the tune has here none of the pathetic qualities of the minor second of the Phrygian Mode, but obviously has the feel and sense of the fourth degree of the major scale of C. It is obvious therefore, that the tune ends, not on the final of the Phrygian Mode, but on the third of the scale of C major.

Other Scots airs will be found to end on other degrees of the scale which similarly cannot be accepted as the final of the mode for classification purposes. 'The Collier's Bonnie Lassie' ends plainly on the fifth of the scale; so does the air of 'Here's a health to ane I lo'e dear'. This air, curiously enough, in its *original* form ends regularly on the keynote; but Robert Burns in his song added an evocative 'Jessie' at the end of both strains which demanded two additional notes, and either Burns himself or his editor added the two notes to the tune in publication, with a resultant ending on the fifth of the scale instead of the keynote. It is an interesting example of how a melodic irregularity can come about in a traditional air through the caprice of a poet; for Burns was musician enough to know very well that those two extra syllables might well interfere with the formal correctness and authenticity of the air.

[1] The note B will be found in the second strain of the tune, thus completing the seven notes of the scale.

HERE'S A HEALTH TO ANE I LO'E DEAR

Here's a health to ane I lo'e dear;____ Here's a

health to ane I lo'e dear, ____ Thou art sweet as the smile when

fond lov-ers meet, and soft as their part-ing tear, Jess-ie.

Ionian Mode

Scale

(a) Final of the mode
(b) Last note of the tune

The melody in its original form ends on the note C at the word 'tear'.

THE NATIVE IDIOM (*Continued*)

With the arrival of the seven-note scale in the evolutionary scheme, we find ourselves on common ground with English and other folk-songs. Yet the tunes of Scotland are always distinctive and unmistakable. We must therefore obviously look for further characteristics in Scottish melodies besides the scalic ones, and see if we can discover what it is that makes for distinctive Scottishness in music which is constructed upon the same scale material as that of other countries.

Firstly of course, it must be said that an air in the seven-note scale may have much of the flavour of one in a gapped scale if one of the notes of the scale occupies an unimportant position in the melody, occurring perhaps as an unaccented passing note and perhaps no oftener than once within the compass of the tune. Such a note is technically said to be 'weak'. These are special cases however and will not provide the whole explanation.

Perhaps the commonest and most noticeable feature of many Scots airs apart from scalic construction, is that they so often begin in one key and end, so to speak, in another. The most frequent instance of this is to find a tune commencing in a major key (or a major-type gapped scale) and ending in the relative minor. 'Green grow the rashes-o' is a typical example:

GREEN GROW THE RASHES - O

There's nought but care on ev'ry han' In ev'ry hour that passes-o; what

sig-ni-fies the life of man, an' 'twere na' for the lass-ies - o?

Green grow the rash-es - o; green grow the rash-es - o; The

sweet-est hours that e'er I spend are spent a-mang the lass-ies o,

Scale

(a) Last note of the tune
(b) Final of the mode (Ionian)

There are numerous examples of this same scheme of keys in Scots airs. 'O puirtith cauld', 'O for ane-an'-twenty Tam' and 'Gin I had a wee house' are a few of them.

Sometimes instead of ending on the relative minor, a tune will suddenly and unexpectedly come to rest on the *second* degree of the scale in which the main part of it is cast—i.e. 'Tullochgorum', 'Jenny Dang the Weaver' and 'Lassie wi' the lint-white locks'—

LASSIE WI' THE LINT-WHITE LOCKS

(Last phrase of the tune)

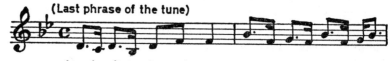

Lassie wi' the lint-white locks; Bonnie lassie artless lassie

wilt thou wi' me tent the flocks? Wilt thou be my dear-ie-o.

Scale

(a) Final of the mode
(b) Last note of the tune

The classification of such melodies is always something of a puzzle to the folk-musicologist. To allot them to the mode indicated by their last note is to give them a label which is often quite uncharacteristic of the main trend of their melody. Yet such have been the rules of systematization of folk-tune since the days of Ilmari Krohn of Finland and of Bela Bartók in the early years of this century; and it would be something of an upheaval to try to alter it. The best one can usually do is to adhere to the rule in spite of the contradiction of the tune itself, and qualify the individual case as it requires.

Such contradictory endings to tunes are however only one of the characteristics of Scots melody. Sometimes the Scots character may emerge from no more than a brief but unmistakable melodic turn or 'thumbprint'. Take the following phrase from 'My Nanny O' for instance:

MY NANNIE O

Be - hind yon hills where Lu - gar flows, 'Mang

"Thumbprint"

muirs and moss - es ma - ny o.

Equally unmistakable is the 'thumbprint' in 'My Nannie's Awa' ('modern' though this tune is said to be):

MY NANNIE'S AWA'

Now in her green man-tle blythe Na-ture ar-rays, and

"Thumbprint"

list - ens the lamb-kins that bleat ow'r the braes.

Such 'thumbprints' are particularly common in the lighter music ('*ceòl eutrom*') of the Scottish bagpipe, particularly in the pipe-marches e.g.:

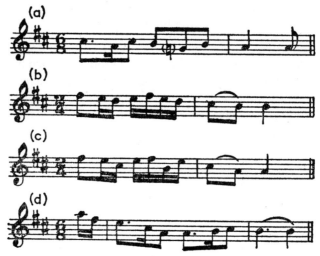

Perhaps the commonest of all these thumbprints—practically to the extent of being a cliché—is the sequence of a melodic figure on a major triad followed by the same or other figure on the major triad a tone lower—the unfailing standby of the music halls when a bit of 'Scotch' music is in requirement! This however derives legimately enough from the scale of the bagpipes (see page 16) in which the triads of A major and G major, the tone below, are both to be found, and so quite rightly may be placed in sequence when desired. The well-known pipe-tune of 'The Inverness Gathering' consists almost entirely of this formula:

THE INVERNESS GATHERING

Curiously enough, the fiddle, although technically unrestricted to any particular scale, is influenced quite a great deal in Scots music by the bagpipe scale, and by this sequence of triads in particular. Many of the early fiddle tunes of course were simply borrowed from the existing pipe-music, and to this day many Scots fiddlers play very little else but pipe-tunes (and use the musical ornamentation appropriate to piping technique in doing so) but even apart from this, we find the formula persisting in the music of such true composers for the fiddle as Niel Gow. His 'Mrs Moray of Abercairny's Strathspey' is typical:

The formula is rare in vocal music, being in fact not very easy to sing, but it may be seen in such songs as 'Tullochgorum' in which the words have been set to a tune which is obviously instrumental in its origin:

TULLOCHGORUM

O Tul-loch-gor-um's my de-light; it gars us a' in ane u-nite, and

on- y sumph that keeps up spite, in con-science I ab-hor him; For

blythe and mer-ry we'll be a', blythe and mer-ry, blythe and mer-ry,

Blythe and mer-ry we'll be a' and make a hap-py quor-um; For

blythe and mer-ry we'll be a', as lang as we hae breath to draw, and

dance till we be like to fa' the reel o' Tul-loch-gor - um.

A piper of the writer's acquaintance once referred to this particular progression as 'the *double tonic*' obviously in the sense of the tonic or 'keynote' being shifted between the two 'keys' of the true tonic key and the 'key' or triad one full tone lower. The term has no basis of authority as far as the writer is aware, but it is a convenient one for the purpose, and he proposes to use it in this sense throughout the rest of the book.

One may find also a variation of the same formula in the sequence of a *minor* chord followed by the major triad on the tone below (a sequence of chords also to be found in the bagpipe scale). It may be seen in the fiddle-tune of 'Coutie's Wedding':

Grace-notes and melodic decoration are of the essence of Scots music in all its varieties, though of course these are to be found in the folk-music of most countries. Grace-notes may vary in Scots music from the simple single decorative note springing from the next note above or below the principal note, to the most complicated roulades and melismata of pibroch, and even of the vocal music of certain specific areas of the Highlands and Islands, notably in the Isle of Lewis in the Hebrides, of which the following is a specimen:

ORAN NA LEANABH ÒG

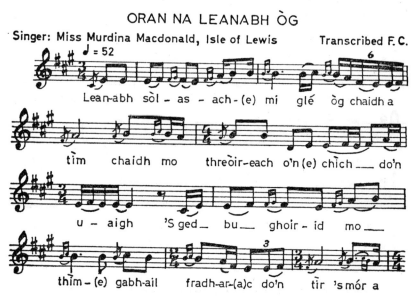

th'ag-am (e) ri ____ inns' (e) do'n   t-sluagh

Hexatonic

Scale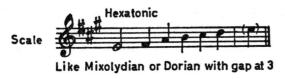

Like Mixolydian or Dorian with gap at 3

Translation: ORAN A LEANABH OG

A happy child am I who left life very early: I was led from the breast to the grave. Though my time was short observing the world, I have much to tell to the people.

Occasionally a downward grace-note may leap from a wide interval above the principal note. Here is an extract from the 'diddling' of the tune of a ballad, of which he had forgotten the words, by an Aberdeenshire tinker, and which he attested as being the tune of 'Sir Hugh of Lincoln' or 'The Jew's Daughter'. Here one of the grace-notes leaps from the unusual height of a whole octave and a fourth, i.e. an *eleventh*, above the principal note:

Air of SIR HUGH OF LINCOLN
or THE JEW'S DAUGHTER

Recorded by Hamish Henderson
Singer: Willie Whyte, Aberdeenshire   Transcribed F.C.

Da-di   ay   ri deed-ie - um dlo ho;   Da-di

ay   ri ra-ri tam da-di deed-le tum. *etc.*

These widely-spaced falling grace-notes, though seldom of as large an interval as this, are characteristic of a number of Lowland and Scottish Gaelic singers. They probably derive from the bagpipe, of which both the style and the music have a widely-pervading influence on much Scottish traditional music.

The tune in part quoted above is identical with one which the same singer sang to the ballad of Tamlane. John Leyden, in his introduction, written in 1801, to his edition of *The Complaynt of Scotland*, notes that 'The air of Tamlane is extremely similar to that of "The Jew's Daughter."' This similarity, here confirmed in the singing of this Aberdeenshire tinker has apparently never been found by other collectors until now. For the Tamlane version see page 16.

Finally, to turn from melody to rhythm, there is the Scots Snap—or as it is more often horribly called, the 'Scotch snap'.

This is the rhythmic figure of a semi-quaver followed by a dotted quaver, i.e. ♫. It is particularly characteristic, and is one of the staple rhythms, of the Strathspey; but it appears in every form of Scots music. Sometimes, particularly in Gaelic vocal music, the first note may be shortened to a demi-semi-quaver, being then followed by a doubly dotted quaver:

O'n ta - ca so an dé __

There has been no more maligned and vilified Scottish musical idiom than this. Let us take a few remarks about it from some of the current musical reference books. In *Grove's Dictionary of Music* (fourth edition 1940) we read:

> In the hands of Hook and the other purveyors of the pseudo-Scottish music which was in vogue at Vauxhall and elsewhere in the eighteenth century, it (i.e. the Scots snap) became a senseless vulgarism, and with the exception of a few songs such as 'Green grow the rashes', 'Roy's wife' and 'Whistle o'er the lave o't' and the strathspey reel in which it is an essential feature, its presence may generally be accepted as proof that *the music in which it occurs is not genuine.* (!!!)

(Italics and exclamation marks are the writer's.) Elsewhere in the same work we read:

> Beethoven appears to have been under the impression that the Scotch snap was characteristic of all Scottish music, whereas really it only belongs to the Strathspey, the reel, and the Highland fling.

In the *Oxford Companion to Music* likewise we find (fourth edition):

> No Scottish song earlier than the eighteenth century seems to have the snap, and the question of its provenance is at present difficult to answer.

The fact is of course that the few musical manuscripts earlier than the eighteenth century containing Scots tunes which have come down to us, are almost all written in tablature for Court types of musical instruments such as the lute (to the technique of which the 'snap' is alien) and for such un-folk-like instruments played with the bow as the Lyra Viol or the Viola da Gamba, in none of which we necessarily find the native folk idiom.

While a few of the remarks quoted about the snap may be to some extent justified, particularly regarding its use in the hands of alien imitators of Scots music, such statements as that the music in which the Scots snap occurs is not genuine, are such wild nonsense that it becomes necessary to step aside and debunk the debunkers. From a long study of Scots music, the writer can state categorically that *the Scots snap is the very life-blood of Scots musical rhythm,* in both instrumental and vocal music. This is particularly so in Gaelic music, as the following typical examples from Gaelic songs may show:[1]

(a) Ragh-ainn e ho ro a hò
Fhir a chin duibh, ho ___ ho.___

(b) 'S toigh leam cruinn - eag dhonn nam bò

(c) Tha m'fhear-ann saibh-ir, o hó ho ro hi ro, nam
b'aill' leat mi, tha m'fhear-ann saibh-ir o hó.

[1] William Matheson (Lecturer in Celtic, Edinburgh University) makes the reservation however that the 'Scots Snap' is not typical of Gaelic vocal music if this means an unnatural shortening and lengthening of syllabic values.

That Robert Burns the poet, who probably knew more about Scots songs and song airs than any man before or since, realized the native force and rightness of the 'snap' is shown by his choice of words to go with it. He sets the snap in the dance tune of Invercauld's Reel with the words:

O   Tib-bie   I   hae seen the day *etc.*

The old Scots name of 'Tibbie' matches the snap perfectly. Again, in writing a new song, 'Blythe blythe and merry was she' to the old tune of 'Andro' and his cutty gun (cf. page 7) Burns resets the snap at the original word 'cutty' with the similar 'snap' rhythm of Glen*turit*.:

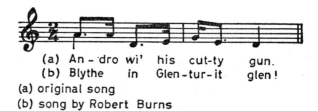

(a) An – dro wi'   his   cut-ty   gun.
(b) Blythe   in   Glen-tur-it   glen!
(a) original song
(b) song by Robert Burns

For an example in contemporary performance, here is one from the recording of a present-day folk-singer in Aberdeenshire:

TAM LANE

Singer: William Whyte   Recorded by Hamish Henderson

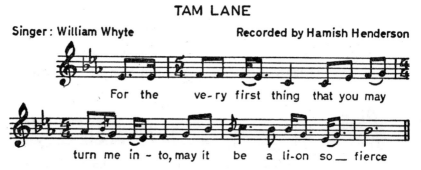

For the   ve-ry first thing   that you may

turn me in - to, may it   be   a li-on so__ fierce

Such sweeping condemnation of this genuine Scottish musical characteristic has not been without its stultifying influence. In published versions of both Gaelic and Lowland songs for the concert platform or competition festival, we are liable to find that the snap has been 'tastefully' ironed out.[1] Competitors who may have inherited their own orally

---

[1] William Matheson observes that this 'ironing out' often consists of putting the long note before the short when it should be the other way round.

transmitted versions of the songs, are forced to sing against their in-
stincts the refined versions of the book, or lose marks. Perhaps the best
comment on this comes from an American collector, Amy Murray, a
trustworthy observer and collector who studied Gaelic songs and singing in the Isle of Eriskay in 1905, and even earlier in Skye. In her book,
Father Allan's Island, she notes the same snatch of melody firstly as she
overheard it sung by a girl in the scullery of the Hospital at Dalibrog in
South Uist in the Hebrides (a), and then as it was sung in its official
published version at the local competition festival a few days later (b):

It is high time that the 'Scotch Snap' was restored to respectability
and given its rightful place again in Scots music!

These then are some of the characteristics that go to make the
Scottishness of Scots music. As a postscript, it may be of interest to add
that the credit for the 'invention' of Scots music used to be ascribed by
musical antiquaries of the nineteenth century to King James the First of
Scotland! This amusing fancy seems to have arisen from the writings of
an Italian poet, Tassoni, who, writing about the year 1620, refers to
'James King of Scotland, who . . . of himself invented a new kind of
music, plaintive and melancholy, different from all other.'

We know that James the First (who probably acquired much of his
artistic accomplishments in England, during his long if not unduly
harsh captivity there in his youth) was an accomplished musician and
apparently something of a composer; but that he 'invented' Scots music,
with its long evolution of gapped scales, its peculiar lilts and cadences,
and its characteristic and often rugged rhythms in Lowland Scots and
Gaelic alike, is a suggestion that can only raise a smile.

CHAPTER II

Gaelic and Lowland Scots Song

IT requires no more than a glance at the songs of Scotland to be aware
at once of a major cleavage—the division caused by Scotland's two
languages, Lowland Scots and Gaelic. In theory a non-musical division, in practice this cleavage has the effect of dividing the song melodies
of Scotland into two separate streams largely independent of each other.

There has, it is true, been a small amount of desultory borrowing of
song airs from the opposite language culture by both sides; but this has
been at the literary rather than at the folk level. The borrowing of
Gaelic tunes for Lowland songs has been the work of a relatively small
number of song-writing poets, of whom Allan Ramsay, Robert Burns,
Lady Nairne and Sir Walter Scott have been the leading figures.

On the opposite side of the picture, the borrowing of Lowland Scots
airs for Gaelic songs, though not unknown, has been meagre also in extent. The Book of Fernaig, a manuscript collection of Gaelic poems made
about the year 1688, ascribed to Duncan Macrae of Inverinate, is said to
contain songs sung to Lowland tunes, which Professor William J.
Watson[1] thinks might have been introduced into the Gaelic areas by
drovers and by Highland soldiers who took part in Montrose's campaigns (1644–5) and subsequent wars in England and Scotland.[2] Among
the Lowland tunes specified in the various Gaelic anthologies as airs for
the songs therein—usually with the direction *air fonn* (to the tune of)—
are such airs as 'The lass of Paties Mill', 'Wat ye wha I met yestreen',
'Tweedside', 'Through the Wood Laddie', etc. There are also a number of political poems set to such tunes as 'When the King comes into
his own', and 'Let History Record'.[3] The songs to these tunes are by

[1] Professor of Celtic, Edinburgh University, 1915–1936.
[2] Cf. *Bàrdachd Ghaidhlig*; Professor W. J. Watson, p. xxxii.
[3] *Highland Songs of the Forty-five*; J. L. Campbell, Oliver and Boyd, Edinburgh, 1933.
The tune, though mentioned, is not reproduced. J. L. Campbell observes that he has
never found it, and adds to the writer—'Alexander MacDonald gave it as the air of the
poem in question in his first edition (1751).'

such Gaelic poets as Alasdair Mac Mhaighstir Alasdair (Alexander Macdonald), Iain MacCodrum, Rob Donn (Robert Mackay) and William Ross; all poets of the eighteenth century.

These Lowland tunes were doubtless sung in highly Gaelicized versions, probably difficult to recognize as the same airs—as were the 'Long Tunes' for the singing of the Psalms in Gaelic, which, developed from the printed tunes of the Reformation Psalter, can now only be related to their originals by the skilled musicologist.[1]

(a)

ALLT-AN-T-SIUCAIR
(The Sugar Brook)

By Alasdair Mac-Mhaighstir Alasdair (Alasdair MacDonald)
(born early 18th century 'lived to a good old age')
As collected from a traditional singer in North Uist, by William Matheson.

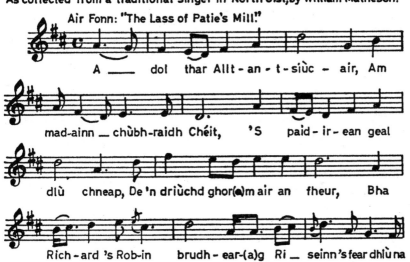

Air Fonn: "The Lass of Patie's Mill."

A ___ dol thar Allt-an-t-siùc-air, Am

mad-ainn ___ chùbh-raidh Chéit, 'S paid-ir-ean geal

dlù chneap, De 'n driùchd ghor(e)m air an fheur, Bha

Rich-ard 's Rob-in brudh-ear-(a)g Ri ___ seinn 's fear dhiù na

---

[1] William Matheson holds however that the appearance of tunes in the other language culture to that to which they are generally thought to belong is not always a case of simple borrowing of tunes from Highlands by Lowlands or vice-versa, but that the tunes may have existed in both traditions for a very long time. Thus when Alexander Macdonald cites the tune of 'The Lass of Patie's Mill' as the tune for his song '*Allt-an-t-siucair*' he is merely identifying a Gaelic tune by the name in which it appears in Lowland Scots musical publications. (Few tunes, if any, appear in Gaelic song collections of that period.) Mr Matheson sings the Gaelic version of the tune of 'The Lass of Patie's Mill' as above, and it may be compared with the Lowland air as it appears for the first time in print in *Orpheus Caledonius* (1733). (This is one of the airs ascribed by James Oswald to David Rizzio, Secretary to Mary Queen of Scots—Cf. 'James Oswald' in Glen's *Early Scottish Melodies*, p. 246.)

bhéus, 's goic moit air cuth-aig chùl-ghuir-(i)m 'S gùg-

Scale: Ionian mode

gùg aic air a' ghéig.

The Literature of the Highlanders, N. MacNeill (Eneas Mackay, Stirling 1892)

Free translation by Dr Anne Ross:

Crossing the Sugar Brook on a fragrant May morning,
Closely clustered white beads of dew on the [green] grass,
Richard and Robin Red-breast were singing—
One making a bass [to the other]
The blue-backed cuckoo proudly bobbing,
And cuckooing on the branch.

(b)   THE LASS OF PATIE'S MILL

from Orpheus Caledonius (1725)

The Lass of Pat-ie's M = = = = = ill, sae

bon-y blith and gay, in spite of all my

ski = = = = = ll she stole my heart a-way.

When ted-ding of the hay, bare-

head-ed on the Green, Love 'midst her locks did

play, and wan-ton'd in her e'en.

★ written so in the original edition.

34

Scale

This division of the song music of Scotland by its two languages resembles that of the sister country of Ireland, which has songs both in Irish Gaelic and in English. The many songs in the English language are of course a later growth (though some of them are doubtless based on the older Irish Gaelic melodies). They are the heritage of an alien culture imposed by invasion and colonization.[1] This has been lucidly expounded by Dr Donal O'Sullivan of Trinity College, Dublin, who in his excellent book *Songs of the Irish* crisply describes some of these so-called 'Songs of Ireland' in the English language as being '*as far removed from Ireland as from Araby*'.

In Scotland of course, the two languages of Gaelic and Lowland Scots have existed side by side from long before the days of remembered song.

THE EARLY GAELIC SONG MUSIC

We could equally well deal first in this book with either Gaelic or Lowland Scots song. That we have chosen to start with Gaelic is simply for the reason that we can date a certain amount of the Gaelic vocal music as belonging to a period earlier than anything comparable in Lowland Scots.

The fact that we find our earliest traditional songs and ballads in the Gaelic tradition may be ascribed to two causes: firstly to the extraordinary persistence of folk-memory in the Gael, and secondly to the fact that most Scottish Gaelic verse is meant to be sung;[2] of which the result is that much of the earlier verse, of the vernacular type at least, has tended to survive with its melody still 'adhering' to it (though the tunes of the more esoteric poetry of the professional bards all seem to have been lost).[3]

So it happens that, incredible as it may seem, we may still hear the

[1] Dr J. L. Campbell points out to the writer that there were Norse settlements in Ireland from the tenth century and English ones from the twelfth, and that Norman French was spoken there after 1172. It cannot be said, therefore, that Gaelic was the sole indigenous tongue in Ireland.

[2] One cannot say that *all* Gaelic verse is meant to be sung. Hogmanay ballads for example, were often simply recited, and today not everyone who can recite Ossianic ballads can sing them. (Information from J. L. Campbell.)

[3] John MacInnes, Research Fellow, School of Scottish Studies, Edinburgh University, observes: 'With the disappearance of poets composing in the literary language,

songs and lays of Ossian sung from oral tradition in the Gaelic parts of Scotland (now mostly confined to the Islands of the Hebrides)—a poet traditionally though inaccurately ascribed to the third century A.D.[1]

What is precisely meant by the Ossianic Lays or Ballads needs a little explaining. They have nothing *directly* to do with the famous 'Ossian' of James Macpherson which aroused the tremendous controversies of the eighteenth century—not, at least, in the form in which he wrote Ossian, for his epic poems of Fingal and Temora (extending to six and eight 'books' or parts respectively) are now recognized to be literary compositions of his own, based rather loosely upon a number of ancient ballads or folk-poems which he collected in the Highlands both orally and in manuscript, and of which he made a *mélange* without much regard for either names of persons or places, or of time-sequence. The date of his tours of the Highlands to collect the poems was 1759-60.

It is these ancient ballads themselves, which we may still find sung in the Hebrides, with which we are concerned here. These embrace several separate and distinct layers of folk material. Of the different folk[2] strata with which they are concerned, there is first the Ulster Cycle of tales of the Irish hero Cú Chulainn and his warriors;[3] then there is the Arthurian Cycle, that widely-spread cycle of tales of which Tristan and Isolde is the best-known example, of which at least one ballad, '*Am Bròn Binn*',[4] is still sung.[5] Finally there are the Ossianic ballads proper, concerned with the huge folk-cycle of Fionn and his band of heroes the Fian or

---

[1] The writer is informed by a Gaelic colleague however that modern scholars regard Ossian and his fellow heroes as fictitious characters.

[2] John MacInnes queries the use of the word folk here and says: 'The Ulster Cycle as we have it in the MSS is a literary cycle, though in some form or other it may have existed orally before it was written down.'

[3] A Gaelic colleague of the writer's says: 'Cú Chulainn's role in the Ulster Cycle is that of principal warrior to his uncle Conchobhar Mac Nessa, King of Ulster. Cù Chulainn is sometimes referred to as "The Irish Achilles". Hero of great deeds from his early youth, he was slain while still a young man defending Ulster *single-handed* against the combined power of the rest of Ireland. The social scene in the Ulster Cycle is quite different from that in the Ossianic, e.g. chariot fighting, which is standard in the Ulster Cycle has completely disappeared in Ossianic. Broadly speaking one might say that the state of society reflected in the Ulster Cycle corresponds roughly to that found by Caesar in Britain. The Ossianic Cycle is obviously later and seems to have already displaced the Ulster Cycle in popularity in early medieval times. Cù Chulainn is generally regarded as a mythological figure.

[4] William Matheson has since observed however that there is little evidence for an Arthurian cycle in Gaelic, and that *Am Bròn Binn* is the sole example.

[5] The writer has heard and helped to record it.

---

some poems at least were "vernacularized" and transmitted by the ordinary people. J. L. Campbell says that the tunes to which the Ossianic ballads are sung may well represent those associated with Bardic verse.

Fingalians, and with Ossian, Fionn's son, the warrior poet who sang of their deeds.

For the history of Fionn we are dependent upon Irish sources. He is mentioned in Irish manuscripts of as early as the sixth or seventh century and succeeding centuries, in verse genealogies, poems, anecdotes and stories. It was not till the ninth century however[1] that what were hitherto only scraps of tradition and stray references, began to develop into a saga.

Up to the twelfth century, this material was chiefly the province of Irish historians, who used it for a (pseudo) scheme of Irish history, a scheme which went back to the Tower of Babel or thereabouts! In this scheme, Cú Chulainn was allotted to the first century A.D. and Fionn to the third century—dates which, however, have no real validity.[2]

In the earliest form of the tradition, Fionn was reputed to be a demi-god, and descended from the gods. In later tradition he became the great warrior-hunter, national hero and saviour of Ireland in the wars with the kings of Lochlainn. By then he had come to be regarded as a mortal man—who eventually died the death of a mortal. His followers, the Fian or Fingalians, were tough warriors who were said to be either 'sons of kings who had quarrelled with their fathers, landless men (dithir) or men expelled from their clan (éclaind), men proscribed, or men who seized this means to avenge some private wrong by taking the law into their own hands'.[3] Modern authorities however give it as their opinion that the Fian were conscripted soldiers of one of the early vassal races of Ireland. The Fionn cycle is in fact, in this view, the hero-lore of a subject race, not a ruling one.[4]

It was about the beginning of the twelfth century that the stories of Fionn and his Heroes began to be turned into verse ballads,[5] a form thought to be borrowed from monastic tradition, as may also have been the kind of music to which they are sung.[6] The composition of these ballads, begun in the twelfth century, continued in an ever-growing accumulation of folk-lore till at least as late as the middle of the eighteenth century;[7] from all of which it will be seen that the concept

[1] Information taken from the notes to *Duanaire Finn* (Irish Texts Society).
[2] Cf. *The Gaelic Sources of Macpherson's Ossian*, by Derick S. Thomson.
[3] Note quoted by Neil Ross in *Heroic Poetry from the Dean of Lismore* (Scottish Gaelic Texts Society) from the writings of Kuno Meyer.
[4] Cf. Eoin MacNeill's notes to *Duanaire Finn*, Vol. I, p. xxxii.
[5] The earliest ballads extant are in the *Book of Leinster*—about 1160 A.D. (Information from John MacInnes.)
[6] Information extracted from Gerard Murphy's notes (ibid.), p. lxxxvi.
[7] Gerard Murphy, ibid., p. lxxxviii.

of Fionn became purely folkloristic, to be added to by the storytellers and ballad-makers at will.[1]

These ballads and tales of Ossian, though Irish in origin,[2] have always been as popular in Scotland as in Ireland. How this came to be so is a question for the Celtic scholar. It may be simply that, as a good story is popular everywhere, the Irish stories of Fionn and Ossian his son were the very material for the Highland storyteller at the ceilidh. They were 'written for the people, not the learned few' (though this was presumably after the Irish Historians had finished with them). They were already composed *in the Gaelic* and so ready to hand, even allowing for the differences in the Irish Gaelic, which in earlier days were not so great as now, and which in any case, in the manner of oral transmission, were doubtless soon ironed out.[3]

At least one of the ballads seems to be a Scottish composition—the '*Duan na Muilgheartaich*' (see page 43).[4] 'The Lay of Fraoch', also quoted in these pages (page 45) seems to be a Scottish creation *as a ballad*. It is known in a prose version in Irish manuscripts as early as the eighth or ninth century.[5]

Being a folk-lore cycle not accurately based upon history, the Ossianic[6] ballads permit the widest anachronisms. Thus Ossian himself, though traditionally accredited to the third century, is made to converse with St Patrick, who commenced his mission in the fifth, which would make Ossian over two hundred years of age when these versified conversations took place. As they have come down to us, most of the Ossianic ballads seem to express the struggle of the Gaels with the Norsemen.

[1] Some of the authors of the ballads are mentioned by name, e.g. in the Book of the Dean of Lismore. (Information from William Matheson.)

[2] William Matheson observes: 'It is wrong to distinguish between Scottish and Irish tradition here. There was *one* tradition, common to all Gaels.'

[3] MacNeill thinks that the Fenian sagas reached Scotland from literary sources (*Duanaire* Vol. I, p. xxiv).

[4] Cf. Reidar Christiansen, *The Vikings in Gaelic Tradition* (Oslo 1931).

[5] *Táin Bó Fhraoích*.

[6] A Gaelic colleague points out to the writer that the term *Ossianic* ballad is of Lowland Scots usage probably arising out of the 'Ossian' of Macpherson. The Gael prefers to call them Heroic Ballads, as the Gaelic ballads are not all concerned with the Ossianic or Fionn cycle. Though anachronisms arise within the cycle, the Gael keeps the different cycles distinct from each other. Macpherson introduced personages from the two cycles into the same ballad stories. He mixes up the periods and makes Cú Chulainn in his chariot *meet* Fionn as an ally, who with his warriors fought on foot.

John MacInnes observes however that the term 'Heroic Ballads' is only used by the Gael when speaking or writing in English, and that there is no technical term equivalent to 'Heroic Ballad' in Gaelic. These compositions, he observes, are known as *Duain* (plural of *Duan*) or *Laoidhean* (plural of *Laoidh*).

Many of the tales of the Norse invasion, as recounted in the ballads, introduce elements of the supernatural.

As far as our study is concerned, there can be little doubt that some of these ballads as still sung in the Highlands of Scotland, were composed as early as the twelfth century. It is instinctive in the Gael to use old existing tunes for the composition of new songs, and however old the ballads are, some of their tunes are probably older still. Some of the Ossianic ballad tunes have a remarkable resemblance to ecclesiastical chant, as we shall see in a moment.

The metre of the ballads, which are usually of four-line stanzas, is *syllabic*—that is, with a regular number of syllables to the line according to the metrical scheme of each particular ballad, but without any regularly recurring stress as in modern poetry, such irregular stresses as do occur being no more than the natural stresses of the words themselves.

Such syllabic poetry of irregular stress was the form taken by the old classic Gaelic verse of the professional Bards. The metres as used by the Bards were many and complicated, with strict rules about the arrangement of internal and end-rhymes, the use of alliteration and assonance, and the number of syllables to a line. Professor W. J. Watson in his *Bàrdachd Ghàidhlig* makes mention of 'over three hundred varieties of metre *known to us*',[1] implying that there may have been more.

The training of the professional Bard was, as might be expected from this, long and arduous, demanding the memorizing both of the rules of the poetic craft and of great numbers of actual poems and tales. There were degrees of bardship, each succeeding degree requiring the memorization of a greater number of poems or tales, of which the highest degree required the holder to be able to repeat from memory three hundred and fifty, many of them of great length. The bardic student used to memorize in darkness as an aid to concentration, and the late seventeenth-century writer Martin Martin describes how the students of the bardic colleges used to shut both doors and windows of the room where they met for daily study, wrap their plaids round their heads, and lie with eyes closed and with a large stone on the belly, for a whole day, memorizing poems and the rules of poetry.

The Ossianic ballads are a less strict, more vernacular form of this poetry, in which many of the rules of versification are relaxed.[2] Correct

---

[1] The writer's italics.
[2] John L. Campbell has observed to the writer that the Heroic Ballads might rather be called a corrupt form of the older bardic poetry, for it is certain (a) that the reciters do not now understand many of the words, and (b) intelligible modern words have

syllabification is observed, but the rhyme scheme is simpler, and alliteration and consonance need not be used.[1] The subject is of course rather one for the Celtic scholar than the musician, but as most Gaelic poetry was composed to be sung, it is one with which the student of Gaelic music is forced to some extent to grapple.

It is stated by many authorities that the Heroic ballads were in former times sung to the accompaniment of the clarsach or Celtic Harp. Unfortunately the form which this accompaniment took is completely lost to tradition, and there are no written examples of it.[2]

The Heroic ballads, as has been said, can still be heard in the Hebrides. Here is one which the writer collected in company with the noted folk-song collector Margaret Fay Shaw in 1954. It is the 'Lay of the Smithy', 'Duan na Ceardaich',[3] which tells of how Fionn, with his son Ossian and his grandson Oscar and three others of the band of the Fian fall in with a 'monstrous smith' who possesses magical powers in the forging of weapons (presumably a Celtic equivalent of Vulcan). He agrees to make weapons for them on condition that these must be tempered in human blood, for which the band must draw lots to choose the victim. The lot falls upon Fionn himself. Fionn however finds the smith's mother, an old hag, and persuades her to go to the smithy. The smith, who is crouching behind the closed door waiting for Fionn, thinks it is Fionn who approaches, and as the hag enters the smithy, he plunges the sword through her body.

Some versions of the ballad, one of which is to be found in *Duanaire Finn*, run to over forty verses. Two tunes are given here. The first was recorded by the writer and Margaret Fay Shaw[4] at Lochboisdale in 1955.

[1] Neil Ross, *Heroic Poetry from the Dean of Lismore*, p. xx. (Scottish Gaelic Texts Society, an edition in which the writer understands Professor J. C. Watson also had a considerable part).

[2] The word *cruit* occurs in the original Gaelic of the ballads, and this has generally been translated as 'harp'. The *cruit* and the harp are however different instruments.

[3] Some of the heroic ballads are termed *duan* and some *laoidh* (lay). It would seem that musically speaking the *duan* is of a more recitative form than the *laoidh*, which is generally more of a song type of melody than a chant. This may be seen in the example of 'Laoidh Fhraoich' (p. 45). Both however are in the irregularly stressed syllabic metres. For a fuller discussion of the lay 'Duan na Muilgheartaich', cf. Reidar Christiansen's *The Vikings in Gaelic Tradition*, p. 215.

[4] Author and editor of *Folksongs and Folklore of South Uist*, Routledge and Kegan Paul, London, 1955.

---

at times been substituted for unintelligible old ones. In the Ballad of the Sea Hag ('Duan na Muilgheartaich') for example, the expression *mor-thimchioll* used is not understood today, but it is good classical Gaelic.

DUAN NA CEÀRDAICH
(The Lay of the Smithy)

Singer: Miss Penny Morrison, Iochdar, S. Uist.
Recorded by Margaret Fay Shaw and Francis Collinson.
Music transcribed by Gillian Johnstone, School of Scottish Studies.

Fionn Mac Cumhail m'ainm baist-idh Chan eil ag-u
or-(o)m ach sgeul-a Bha mi uair__ mi u-all-ach
ghobh-ar Aig Righ Loch-lainn a's a' Gheil-(i)bh-inn

Tha mis-e cuir mar gheas-u oir-(i)bh-se, Bho sibh luchd
freasd-al mo cheàrd-ach 'S an con-al-an uar-(e)
craic-inn 'S a dhion o dhor-us mo cheàrd-ach

Approximate translation:[1]

Verse 3. Fionn Mac Cumhail[2] is my name. You only know me by reputation.
I herded goats in my time for the King of Lochlann in Gealbainn.

Verse 5. I put spells on you, as you are a folk dependent upon the work of the
smith (i.e. for arms) to follow me to the door of my smithy.

---

[1] These texts are somewhat corrupt and recourse has had to be made to existing
translations by J. F. Campbell of Islay and others.

[2] The name of the speaker should here be Lonn mac Liobhan, the smith of the tale,
who speaks in answer to a question from Fionn Mac Cumhail as to who he is.

DUAN NA CEÀRDAICH
(another tune)

Singer: Mrs Archie Macdonald, South Uist.
Recorded by Calum Maclean, School of Scottish Studies.
Music transcribed by Gillian Johnstone.

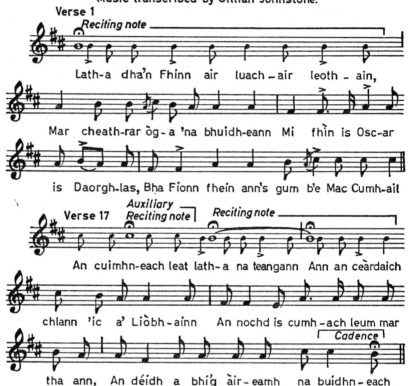

Approximate translation:

Verse 1. One day the Fiann were out on the plain of rushes, four valiant men of the band, I myself, and Oscar and Daorglas. Fionn himself was there, the son of Cumhal.

Verse 17. Do you remember the day of straits in the smithy of the children of Liobhan? Tonight I am dispirited after the enumeration of the company.

In the first verse of this second tune, and in a number of the succeeding verses not shown in the example, it may be noticed that only four out of the complete pentatonic scale of five notes are used. The fifth note, E (number 4 in the numerical sequence) appears however in verse 17 i.e.:

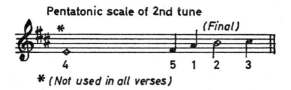

Pentatonic scale of 2nd tune

(Final)

4   5   1   2   3

* *(Not used in all verses)*

Amy Murray gives another more extended version of the tune of this ballad, which covers two stanzas of the poem instead of one as above, and which begins similarly with a reciting note.[1]

Here next is the tune of the Monster Sea Hag of Norway, '*Duan na Muilgheartaich*' mentioned above, also recorded by the writer and Margaret Fay Shaw at Lochboisdale. The lay tells of how the Monster Sea Hag, 'the bald, russet-yellow Muilgheartach, of blue-black face and tufted tooth like a rusted bone', sailed from Norway to avenge the death of her mate, the Smith of the Oceans (*Gobha nan Cuan*), whom Fionn and his band had killed in a raid. After unsuccessfully trying to pacify her with bribes, the Fiann fought and killed her. The King of Norway, furious at her death, sent a large war-fleet to avenge her. The armada looked so formidable as it approached the coast that the Fiann again tried to buy off the foe. The offer was a second time refused, and a terrific battle ensued. The Fiann won the day and the Norsemen were driven off.

DUAN NA MUILGHEARTAICH
(The Lay of the Monster Sea Hag)

Singer: Miss Penny Morrison, Iochdar, S. Uist.
Recorded by Margaret Fay Shaw and Francis Collinson, 1953
Music transcribed by Gillian Johnstone.

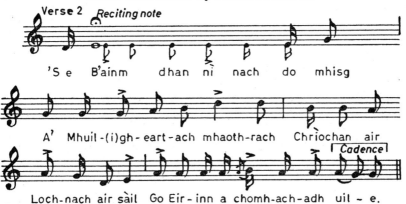

[1] Cf. *Father Allan's Island*, p. 100, by Amy Murray (Moray Press, Edinburgh, 1936).

43

Approximate translation:[1]

Verse 2. The name of that creature—
   Was the bald russet Muileartach
   From Lochlann's bounds, coming on brine,
   To fight all Ireland.

Verse 11. There was dew [i.e. of blood?] on the points of the spears
   By Mac Cumhail of the sides so white;
   The side of her shoulder was on the ground;
   There was a shower of her blood on the heather.

It is remarkable how many features in these tunes correspond to Latin plainsong. Firstly there is the reciting note on a monotone; secondly, the approach to this reciting note from above or below, corresponding to the 'intonation' of plainsong (in plainsong the approach is from below); thirdly, that in a number of verses, as shown in the second tune for the 'Lay of the Smithy', use may be made of only a part of the scale (here the pentatonic) as do many of the plainsong melodies or 'tones' in the music of the Church, which only use a part of the complete seven-note scales of the Church Modes;[2] fourthly, the descending cadence at the end of the verse or sometimes of the ballad, which one also finds as an essential part of plainsong.

Though most of the tunes of the lays have this chant-like quality, they do not however all begin with a reciting note. Here is a particularly beautiful one without this feature, sung by the late Duncan Macdonald

[1] The Gaelic text is corrupt, and the translation follows a different and more intelligible version.

The '*Duan na Muilgheartaich*' seems only to have been recovered in Scotland, not in Ireland.

[2] Other interesting examples of this incomplete use of the scale in Ossianic chant may be found in Mrs Kennedy Fraser's *Songs of the Hebrides*, Volume 2, introduction, pp. xi and xii.

of South Uist. This is 'The Lay of Fraoch' ('*Laoidh Fhraoich*')[1] which tells of the jealousy of Meadhbh (*Maeve*). Fraoch, whom she desires for her own lover, is in love with her daughter Fionnabhair. In the madness of her jealousy she plots to encompass Fraoch's death. She feigns sickness and persuades him that the only thing that will cure her is the fruit of a magical rowan tree which grows on an island in the loch, but which is guarded by a fierce monster. Fraoch, unafraid, offers to get the fruit, and swims across to the island. By good fortune he finds the monster asleep, and so is able to return unscathed with the rowan berries. Meadhbh, foiled in her design, then says that nothing will now avail her but a sapling pulled from the root of the tree; and Fraoch swims across to dare the monster a second time. This time however the pulling up of the sapling awakens the sleeping monster. It attacks Fraoch, and seizes one of his hands in its jaws. Fraoch finds to his dismay that he has come without his knife, but Fionnabhair, who has been watching from the shore of the loch throws him a knife set in gold. A desperate struggle follows between man and beast in which Fraoch succeeds in killing the monster; but his hand is bitten off in the struggle, and he dies of his wounds.

He is buried in a nearby meadow, called ever afterwards the meadow of Fraoch; and a cairn, The Cairn of the Hand, is heaped over his grave, beside which Fionnabhair is left to mourn and keen his loss.

Here is the tune. The bar-lines merely indicate the lines of the poem, and it is in free rhythm.

THE LAY OF FRAOCH

Collected by Wm. Matheson from the singing of Duncan MacDonald, S. Uist.

Transcribed F.C.

Verse 1 as sung (in free rhythm)

Laidh eusl-aint-e throm, throm,—air nigh-ean Odh-uich nan corn fi-al, Chuir-eadh leath' fios air Fraoch, 'S dh fhios-raich an laoch ciod e (a) mi-an?

---

[1] *Laoidh Fhraoich* is mentioned by Pennant in his *Tour in Scotland.* Cf. under Loch Aw (Awe).

45

Verse 3 as sung

Fraoch mac Feadh – aich nam ar-(a)m geur,

Thàin – ig e o'n bhéist — gun fhios, 'S ult – ach leis d'an

chaor – an dhear – (a)g, Dan bhall an raibh Mai 'na tigh.

Scale — Pentatonic

3 4 5 1 2 (3)

3rd position

(The text transcribed by the writer with the aid of the text as printed in *Leabhar na Feinne*; ed. J. F. Campbell of Islay.)

LAOIDH FHRAOICH (THE LAY OF FRAOCH)

Translation by Frances Tolmie. (Tolmie Collection No. 86)

1. There came an overpowering illness to the daughter of Odhuch of the generous drinking-horns, who sent a message to Fraoch; and the hero asked what was her desire.

2. She declared that she would never be well unless she were to receive the full of her tender palms of rowan-berries from the little cold pool (or lake) but that no other was to pluck them than Fraoch.

3. 'A fruit gathering like that I have never done', said Fraoch son of Idad of keen-edged weapons, 'and though I have never done the same, I will go and gather the rowan-berries for Maive.'[1]

Perhaps the most fascinating of these survivals of ancient folk-tales in sung verse is to find a ballad from the Arthurian cycle of romances. Such is '*Am Bròn Binn*', 'The Sweet Sorrow', recorded twice by John L. Campbell in the Hebrides and twice by the School of Scottish Studies—once from one of our most prolific folk-singers, Miss Annie Johnston of Barra, and once on the mainland of Scotland from a tinker, blind Alec Stewart of Lairg.

The ballad has been identified by the late celebrated Celtic scholar Dr George Henderson as one of the Sir Gawain stories. A knight, Fiosfalaich (in some versions the King of Britain) dreams of a beautiful

---

[1] The third verse of the translation by Frances Tolmie does not correspond to verse 3 of the text as sung here, and is merely included to convey the story.

woman. He determines to go in search of her, and sets off in a swift vessel with his gillie and his dog. After voyaging for 'seven weeks and two months' they come to a harbour with a castle of white stone nearby. There he finds the lady of his dream. She is in the power of the lord of the castle, the *Fear Mór* (great man) whom they plot to beguile to his undoing. While the knight hides himself the lady (in some versions named Helen) persuades the *Fear Mór* to lay his head in her lap while she sings to him with the harp. By her singing she lulls him to sleep. Then taking the sword from his girdle she kills him; and so she is free to depart with her knight.

Dr George Henderson identifies Fios-falaich with Sir Galahad, and his full discussion of the lay may be read in an article contributed by him to *A Festschrift to Professor Kuno Mayer*. Here is the tune of '*Am Bròn Binn*' as collected by J. L. Campbell:

AM BRON BINN

[*for Scale see overleaf*]

47

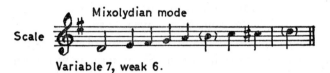

Scale — Mixolydian mode

Variable 7, weak 6.

The note values are approximate and are dictated solely by the prosody values of the word syllables.[1]

Translation:

The King of Scotland saw in a dream
The woman of fairest hue under the sun.
He would rather be beloved of her
Than to converse with a man like himself
Fios-falaich spoke to Fiann;
'I shall go seek her for you
I and my servant, and my dog
The three of us, to seek the woman.'[2]

From the musical point of view, it is noteworthy that although many, and probably indeed most of the tunes of these heroic ballads, Fenian and Arthurian, are in the pentatonic scale, the six-note and seven-note scales were in use at this early period also, and we find a number of them cast in both these scales.

It would of course be rash to draw conclusions from resemblances to ecclesiastical music in these chants or tunes which may merely be due to features which are apt to occur in any kind of primitive chanting—the approach to a reciting note, the reciting note itself, and a falling cadence at the end; but it would seem to strengthen the possibility at least of some of the Ossianic chants having been borrowed from the church.

It is possible too, however, that a number of the tunes may have been borrowed from the music of the old bardic poetry, which was also syllabic and without regular stress, but with much stricter rules of versification.[3] We cannot tell, for none of the tunes for the old bardic poetry has survived as such, though tunes for popular syllabic poetry of a later date have come down to us, for example the tune for '*Oran na Comhachaig*' on page 60.

[1] The Tolmie Collection (No. 90) gives a version to a different melody with chorus refrains of the waulking-song type. This was probably used for waulking the cloth, to be described later. A text of twenty verses is given.

[2] The translation does not follow exactly the text as here sung.

[3] Cf. *Heroic Poetry from the Book of the Dean of Lismore*, Introduction. (Scottish Gaelic Texts Society.)

William Matheson observes: 'What is more likely is that the chants of the ballads were simply the same type of chants as were sung to the syllabic metres in general; and these ultimately derived (like the metres) from the Latin hymns of the Church.

The ballads in performance have not got quite the smooth flow of Latin plainsong, but this is mainly on account of the fact that Gaelic is a more strongly stressed language than Latin. In some ways the Ossianic poetry has rather the quality in performance of quick-moving operatic recitative, for it is usually sung at a fast pace.

Undoubtedly the whole subject of the music of the Heroic Ballads and other syllabic Gaelic poetry is one which presents fascinating possibilities for further study.

The reader will find a number of Ossianic chants in the introductions to Mrs Kennedy Fraser's *Songs of the Hebrides*. These are interesting, as are further Ossianic tunes not here quoted, in the Tolmie Collection. Patrick Macdonald gives eight Ossianic tunes (numbers 115–122). These are unfortunately without their texts, and are moreover forced into regular modern rhythms between bar-lines. There are also a number of so-called Ossianic and Fingalian airs scattered through the fiddle-tune collections of Fraser of Knockie and Niel Gow; but these must be regarded as of doubtful authenticity, and there is not much to be gleaned from them for the purposes of serious study.

As a postscript, it may be amusing to quote an account by Alexander Pope, Minister of Reay in Caithness, written in 1763, of an old Highlander who, when singing the Ossianic Ballads (or one of them at least, 'Duan Dhiarmid') always used to remove his bonnet as a mark of veneration for these ancient Heroes and for Ossian their bard, who commemorated their deeds in song. He says:

> There is an old fellow in this parish that very gravely takes off his bonnet as often as he sings 'Duan Dearmot' (The Lay of Diarmid). I was extremely fond to try if the case was so, and getting him to my house I gave him a bottle of ale, and begged the favour of him to sing 'Duan Dearmot'; after some nicety he told me that to oblige his parish minister he would do so, but to my surprise he took off his bonnet. I caused him stop, and would put on his bonnet; he made some excuses; however, as soon as he began, he took off his bonnet, I rose and put it on. At last he was like to swear most horibly, he would sing none, unless I allowed him to be un-covered; I gave him his freedom, and so he sung with great spirit. I then asked him his reason; he told me it was out of regard to the memory of that Hero. I asked him if he thought that the spirit of that Hero was present; he said not; but he thought it well became them who descended from him to honour his memory.

One cannot generalize as to whether this was a custom among the Highlanders when singing the Ossianic Ballads—it would naturally only apply to the singing of them out of doors, when the bonnet would normally be worn.[1] It is in interesting contrast to the piper who, to this day, before he will consent to play *pìobaireachd* (pibroch) insists, for the same reason, on *putting on* his bonnet, as a mark of respect to the *ceòl-mór*, the *great music*, of the pipes, and the masters who composed it.

Finally, it may perhaps not be inappropriate to conclude this description of the Ossianic ballads by saying that these are not something extracted from old manuscripts; they are still sung in Scotland today.

After the Ossianic ballads with their accretions of incident, real or fanciful, from the Norse invasions, there seems to be an extraordinary gap in the folk material as remembered by the Gael; for the next songs we have are of the seventeenth century—a gap of about three hundred and fifty years, even if we accept the incidents of the ballads as extending to the close of the Norse campaigns.

This gap has evoked comment from almost every writer on Gaelic song. It is remarkable for instance that there are no songs or ballads on the Scottish War of Independence, with its heroic leaders Wallace and Bruce, and its epic victories of Stirling Bridge and Bannockburn, in which the Highlanders played a brave part. Nor, to look forward a couple of hundred years or so, are there any Gaelic songs about Mary Queen of Scots, whose glamour was surely of the essence of song, and whose impact upon the Highland clans was far from negligible.[2] The only dateable poem preserved orally in this long period of emptiness seems to be an incitement at the Battle of Harlaw,[3] the battle which broke the power of the Lords of the Isles in 1411.[4] This was composed by one of the last of the professional Bards, Lachlan Mór MacVurich, family Bard to Clanranald. There is also a bagpipe piece, 'Pìobaireachd Dhomhnaill Duibh' celebrating the first battle of Inverlochy 1431.

[1] Colleagues of the writer disagree with him and state that the bonnet was worn indoors except at meals.

[2] John MacInnes observes: 'Though Gaels fought at Bannockburn, it is questionable if a victory over the English leaders by non-Gaelic families meant much to the national pride of the Gaels. This however depends on one's interpretation of Scottish history.

John L. Campbell adds: 'Apart from the heroic verse, the oral tradition of folk-song seems to be closely associated with the clan system that arose out of the breakdown of the Lordship of the Isles at the end of the fifteenth century. This was followed by a period of extreme confusion and many stirring deeds, in clan fights and civil wars, so perhaps it is not surprising that older themes were forgotten. The Lordship itself was celebrated in bardic verse.' (See W. J. Watson, *Scottish Verse from the Book of the Dean of Lismore*.)

[3] William Matheson says however that this incitement is of doubtful authenticity. The bagpipe piece is also of doubtful and probably later date.

[4] Nevertheless the Battle of Harlaw was regarded as a victory by the MacDonalds of the Isles.

After this long hiatus, the first songs to which we can assign a period with any certainty are the 'Great Songs' (*Orain Mhóra*) of the vernacular poets of the seventeenth century—songs of eulogy of the great Highland Chiefs of the day who were the patrons or clan chiefs of the poets in question, enlarging upon their power, their princely hospitality and their prowess in battle.

With these and all the countless songs that follow, great and small, 'mór' and 'beag', we find a fundamental change of metric construction. Gone is the old syllabic metre of irregular stress of the ballads and of the professional trained Bards; and in its place we find the familiar regularly stressed metre of modern poetry[1] and a corresponding style of music in which they were sung[2] In this, as far as the stature of the music is concerned, there was an undoubted loss as well as gain; for though we have many a fine song in the new genre, there is a nobility about some of the Ossianic tunes which is not always present in the other genre, particularly in some of those being currently manufactured, though these of course have little or nothing in common with the typical seventeenth-century eulogistic song.

The earliest examples which have come down to us of this system of stressed metre, except for one or two stray pieces, are from the two seventeenth-century poets Mary Macleod of Skye and Iain Macdonald ('Iain Lom') of Lochaber.[3] They were both completely untrained in

[1] John MacInnes criticizes this statement however as being too sweeping. It is of course a question for the Gaelic scholar rather than the musician.

[2] The composition of songs in *syllabic* versification (often invaded by 'stress timing') survives here and there to the present day—though a Gaelic colleague of the writer's is inclined to think that the composers of them have not been aware of this as a conscious exercise.

[3] John L. Campbell is of the opinion that too much has been made (i.e. by commentators) of Mary Macleod and Iain Lom as *innovators* in Scottish Gaelic verse. It is true, he observes, that they are among the earliest modern Gaelic poets whose names are known to us, but they were composing in what seems to have been already a well-established popular tradition. Nor is it the case that their verse is the earliest known in stressed metres. Cf. '*Tàladh Choinnich Oig*' (lullaby for the young Kenneth, son of Colin Mackenzie of Kintail) in *Folksongs and Folklore of South Uist* by Margaret Fay Shaw, composed for a child born in 1569; and the song to Mac Iain 'ic Sheumas in connection with the battle of Carinish, fought in 1601.
A contemporary of Mary Macleod who has received little if any notice [i.e. by the writers on the subject] was Nic Iain Fhinn, the Barra poetess, who is said to have made several waulking songs connected with the Mac Neils of Barra, including '*Beinn a' Cheathaich*' (Kisimul's Galley), see p. 71.
The reader is therefore recommended to keep this reservation in mind. The writer's late colleague at the School of Scottish Studies Calum Maclean (died 1960), in an article published posthumously in the *Transactions of the Gaelic Society of Inverness* (Vol. xxxix–xl, 1942–50) says of Mary Macleod and Iain Lom: 'They wrote in the vernacular, although they owed much to the Bardic Schools, for their poetry is in

bardship—indeed it has been said that there is no evidence that Mary Macleod could either read or write. Yet she has been described as 'the inimitable poetess' of the Isles, and as the most original[1] of all our Gaelic poets.

It must be said indeed that the very perfection and mastery of this style to be found in the works of these two poets lead Gaelic scholars to believe that they themselves could not have originated it, but that it must have been in use for some time and ready to their hand; and that the two systems, the new and the old, probably co-existed for some considerable time—one authority puts it at from one to two hundred years. It is suggested further that of these two separate strands of poetry which were being woven independently at this period, the stressed metre, i.e. the 'new style', not being based upon the Latin model of the Church, was the more truly indigenous of the two.[2]

[1] 'But this is owing to a (wrong) belief that she invented new techniques.' (William Matheson.)

[2] Indeed John MacInnes says in a note to the writer: 'The earliest Gaelic verse was rhythmical; melodies of stress-timed verse had therefore an even older origin, but they must have been modified in the course of transmission through many centuries.'

Another Celtic scholar and colleague of the writer's suggests that a third strand of song poetry, in addition to the native syllabic and stressed metres, existed also at that time in the numerous songs of an international type which had become incorporated into Scottish Gaelic song, and which went by the name of *amhran*. The writer disclaims the specialized knowledge to discuss this, but it seems to him that there may be a possible parallel to these in Lowland Scots song, in the numerous songs of the Court, mostly of French origin, which came flooding into seventeenth-century Lowland Scotland, and which appear in the early collection of Scots songs along with the true traditional songs of the country. The term *amhran* seems to be now used to denote a particular class of Gaelic verse metre—the 'lyric' or 'song' metre. Cf. Professor W. J. Watson, *Bàrdachd Ghàidhlig*.

William Matheson says in a note to the writer: 'The type of metre and tune in question [i.e. of these Amhrain] is of international character. Variants are liable to turn up not only in the Lowlands of Scotland, but also in Ireland, England and on the Continent. This probably reflects the cosmopolitan and peripatetic character of those who practised this kind of verse (and music) in the middle ages. But Seán Ó Tuama in his recent book *An Grá in Amhráin na nDaoine* gives good reason for believing that the themes favoured in verse of this kind originated in France. It is therefore likely that the verse forms and type of tune come from there also. Their appearance in Ireland is probably connected with the settlement of Norman families there in the twelfth century.'

Oran, the Scottish Gaelic word for a song, is another form of the word *amhran*. *Amhran* is regular in Irish and in some Scottish dialects, e.g. Sutherland.

---

spirit and content much the same as that of the Schools. But the extent to which they are indebted to oral tradition and literature is much greater. Their songs and poems must in many cases have derived their form from earlier songs and poems, which have been lost because they did not find their way into manuscripts. Many of these songs must have lived on even after the days of Iain Lom and Màiri Nighean Alasdair Ruaidh (Mary Macleod) and are now lost.'

Mary Macleod (Màiri Nighean Alasdair Ruaidh, i.e. Mary, daughter of red-haired Alasdair)[1] was said to be related to the Chief of the Clan Macleod. The date and place of her birth and of the wanderings in exile of her early life are subjects of tradition and guesswork. She is generally thought to have been born at Rodel in Harris, though the Isle of Pabbay, Harris, is also claimed as her birthplace. Estimates of the date of her birth vary widely. A reasoned estimate by Professor W. J. Watson, however, based upon the personalities to whom her poems were addressed gives circa 1615 for the date of her birth and about 1707 for her death.[2]

Her life was one of wide vicissitudes. At the early age of possibly eleven years she was employed as nurse in the household of the Chief of the clan Macleod at Dunvegan, who was at that time the great Rory Mór (he of the enormous drinking horn). It is said that she herself claimed that in the course of her life she nursed five Lairds of Macleod and two of the Lairds of Applecross.

Her first song, now lost, was one she made to amuse the children at Dunvegan.[3] A little later however she composed a song which displeased her employer, and so provoked him that he refused to have her at Dunvegan, and sent her, some say, to Mull under the charge of a relative of his own, others say to a succession of places including the Isle of Scarba and the Isle of Pabbay in Harris. Neither the name of the song nor that of the Chief who dismissed her seems to be known, though the date of her dismissal, which was after the death of Rory Mór, must on that account have been after 1662[4]. The cause of her dismissal is also a matter of guesswork. It has been suggested that her song contained an overpraising of the Chief's uncle and cousin, perhaps to the fancied disparagement of himself: a Chief was, as indeed he had to be in those times, sensitive to the eulogy of a relative who might well be regarded as a possible rival for his own position. Francis Tolmie offers the alternative suggestion that the song may have overpraised, not a possible rival, but the Chief's own children, bringing the fear that it might cause ill luck to them. Anyone who has seen the power of Highland superstition will agree that at least this is not as absurd as it sounds.

Mary Macleod's fortune turned again however with the composition of another song: '*Luinneag Mhic Leòid*' (Macleods' Lilt). This time she

---

[1] Or *Alexander*, as the Gesto *Collection of Highland Music* has it.
[2] *Bàrdachd Ghàidhlig*, p. xxxiv.
[3] The song has not survived and some authorities are inclined to characterize the story as mere hearsay.
[4] 'Mairi Nighean Alasdair Ruaidh', *Transactions of the Gaelic Society of Inverness*, Vol. xxii, 43.

praised the right person in the Chief himself—and in no small measure.
The song so moved or flattered the Chief that he sent a boat to bring
her back to Dunvegan. Such is the power of song—at least in Gaelic
Scotland. He did, however, take the precaution of making a condition
of her reinstatement that she would promise to compose no more
songs!

The poetic Muse however proved to be too strong to be suppressed
by the dictates of a Highland Chief, and shortly after her return we find
her composing another song, and one which again incurred the wrath
of her Chief. When challenged with it, she made the now classic reply
that 'it wasn't a song, it was only a croon (!)' Sufferers of 'pop' music
on the radio will be only too ready to grant the distinction.

What concerns us most in this book, of course, is the *tunes* of Mary
Macleod. It is a common practice, as the writer has seen for himself in
the field, for the Gaelic composer of song poems, as it was for the
Lowland song-writers (as shown in the songs of Burns, Lady Nairne
and Scott) to take an existing tune as the spring-board for the composition of a new song, and to use that tune for it afterwards. There is a
curious tradition regarding Mary Macleod however that she was not
possessed of a particularly good ear for music;[1] and the late Rev.
Kenneth Macleod used to tell of a tradition that there was another
woman who used to *compose the tunes* for Mary Macleod's songs,[2] and
who, according to the extract quoted below, always accompanied her
on her travels.[3] The picture of this two-woman song-composing team,

[1] The same was said about both Burns and Scott. In the case of Burns at least, this
was sheer nonsense.

[2] William Matheson comments: 'I have heard this tradition in South Uist, but it
applies only to the provision of the vocables for her waulking songs.' John MacInnes
adds that 'something like this was also said about Mairearad Ni Lachainn—a Mull
poetess'.

[3] Information from J. L. Campbell, who also contributes the following extract
from the note-books of Father Allan Macdonald, the famous priest-folklorist-folk-
musician of Eriskay (1895–1905).

'Mairi Nighean Alasdair Ruaidh (i.e. Mairi Macleod) though popularly so called
was not "Mairi" at all, but Fionnaghal. The delusion crept in owing to a certain
"Mairi dhubh nan òran" (Dark Mairi of the songs) always accompanying her, who
sang her songs for her and committed them to memory, as Fionnaghal herself was
defective both in memory and singing. Rev. Alexander Campbell frequently told me
that he had a grand aunt who was named after Nighean Alasdair Ruaidh, and consequently named "Fionnaghal". This poetess lived for some time in Eriskay at the
spot where Prince Charlie afterwards landed, when he first set foot in Scotland. The
site of the house is that now occupied by a house of two sisters McInnes at Coil(l)eag
a' Phrionnsa.' (II 15, written perhaps in 1892).

Rev. Alexander Campbell (1820–93) was a retired priest, a native of South Uist,
from whom Fr Allan got a lot of local tradition.

wandering about among the islands of the Hebrides, sometimes in semi-exile as far as their patrons were concerned, is a strange one.

Whoever it was who composed the airs for Mary Macleod, it was a person with a strong gift for melody, for they are striking tunes. Some of them have a wide melodic compass, a characteristic which here is an integral feature of the melody, and not just arising as in so many of the Lowland Scots song-airs of the printed collections, through the addition of a second strain to the melody (often in an awkwardly higher tessitura than the first!).

Here is a fine example from the Tolmie Collection (number 43). This is 'Cumha Mhic-Leoid' (Lament for Macleod). According to Miss Tolmie, this was sung at the bedside of her Chief, Macleod of Dunvegan, when he pretended that he had died. The Macleods seem to have been rather fond of this kind of pastime, for it is said that when one of them lay sick and dying he sent for Mary Macleod and said that he would like to hear the lament which she would doubtless compose for him. The poetess complied by improvising at his bedside another song since become well known—*An Talla am bu Ghnàth le Mac Leòid* (Macleod's Wonted Hall).

CUMHA MHIC - LEOID

(Lament for Macleod)

by Mairi Macleod (Mairi nighean Alasdair Ruaidh)

[*for Scale see overleaf*

Like Aeolian or Phrygian with gap at 2

Translation by Frances Tolmie:

In the state in which I am this night, I am satiated with sore weeping; without
rest, without peace or joy.

With health uncertain, and of recovery there being no hope, my gladness is
for ever gone.

For Macleod, beloved, is in a fine woollen shroud, with no covering to his
side but boards.

It was with thinking on thee that my body has been in acute suffering, and the
lashes worn away from my eyes.[1]

The other of the two representative poets of this emergent stressed
metre, the Lochaber Bard Iain Lom (pronounced *lowm*—the word
meaning bare—said to have been called so because he was bare in the
face and without a beard).[2] He is probably best known outside Gaeldom
as the man who cut off the heads of the seven murderers of the heir to
the House of Keppoch to which he himself belonged, which now
appear carved in stone at the Well of the Heads (*Tobar nan Ceann*) on
the road to Fort Augustus as it skirts the shore of Loch Oich. The story
is that MacDonald of Keppoch sent his two sons to be educated abroad
and entrusted their affairs while they were away, to their cousins. They
took advantage of the absence of the heir and his brother however to
establish themselves in the saddle of power and authority of the Keppochs
which, though they were but a branch of their great Clann Domhnaill
(MacDonald), was considerable, to the extent of commanding three
hundred men in the field.

On the return of the heir and his brother to claim their birthright, the
seven cousins foully murdered them. Iain Lom, who was himself a
member of the Keppoch family, did not rest until he had brought
vengeance upon the murderers. Receiving aid from a kinsman in North
Uist, he succeeded in capturing and putting all seven of the murderers to
death. The poet himself cut off their heads, washed them in the well,
and carried them as a grim trophy of vengeance to the Chief of his clan
at Glengarry. The date was 1663.

[1] Other tunes to the songs of Mary Macleod are to be found in Mrs Kennedy
Fraser's *Songs of the Hebrides*, Introduction to Vols. II and III.

[2] Cf. *Sàr Obair*.

Another version of the reason for his nickname of 'Lom' is said to be that he was
'bare' in the sense of being *plain-spoken* and cutting in speech.

A song exists by Iain Lom on the subject of this tragedy, 'Mort na Ceapaich' (Murder of Keppoch) of which the words are given in Sàr Obair nam Bàrd,[1] and what is likely to be two slightly differing variants of the traditional tune in Patrick Macdonald's and Simon Fraser's collection of Highland Airs under the title of 'Cheapuich na fasoch' (Keppoch desolate). This is typical of the kind of scattered and haphazard documentation to be found in the songs of this early Gaelic period.

CEAPACH 'NA FÀSACH (Keppoch desolate)
MORT NA CEAPAICH (Murder of Keppoch)

Air from Patrick MacDonald's Collection

Slow

'S tearc an diugh mo chùis ghàir-e   Teachd ___ 'sna

raid-ibh so 'niar;   'G amh-arc fonn In-bhir-Làir-e

'N dèidh a stràc-adh le sìol   Tha Cheap-ach 'na fàs-ach gun

aon àird oirr-e 's fiach,   's léir ri fhaic-inn a

bhraithr-ean,   Gur trom a' bhàrc oirnn an t-sìon

Note. The fitting of the words to the air by the writer is conjectural.

Iain Lom had already come into the limelight as the man who eighteen years before, had guided Montroses's lieutenant Alasdair MacColla in his famous outflanking march at Inverlochy in the mid-winter of the year 1645. MacColla, upon catching sight of the Campbells under the Earl of Argyll lying unsuspectingly in flank in front of him, offered the poet in gratitude the reward of the place of honour at his side in the battle; but Iain Lom, who, in spite of his prowess in the affair of the Tobar nan Ceann, was of a canny nature, made his famous reply, 'If I

[1] See also the definitive Orain Iain Luim, Songs of John Macdonald, Bard of Keppoch, edited by Annie M. Mackenzie (Scottish Gaelic Texts Society, 1964).

go along with thee today and fall in battle, who will sing thy praises tomorrow?' MacColla saw the force of this and replied, 'Thou art in the right, John'; and arranged for him to view the fight from the more convenient vantage point of the castle of Inverlochy. From this grand-stand view of the battle, Iain Lom was able to compose one of his most remarkable poems, 'The Day of Inverlochy', a song which is still sung in the Highlands. The following is a version of it collected by the writer and his colleague James Ross in the Isle of Vatersay in 1959.

BLÀR INBHIR-LOCHAIDH (The Field of Inverlochy)
by Iain Lom

Singer: Nan Mackinnon, Isle of Vatersay   Recorded by James Ross and Francis Collinson

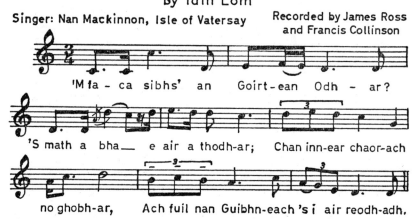

'M fa - ca sibhs' an Goirt-ean Odh - ar?

'S math a bha __ e air a thodh-ar; Chan inn-ear chaor-ach

no ghobh-ar, Ach fuil nan Guibhn-each 's i air reodh-adh.

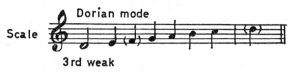

Scale — Dorian mode

3rd weak

BLÀR INBHIR-LÒCHAIDH (THE FIELD OF INVERLOCHY)

Translation of the opening two verses by John Stuart Blackie:[1]

1.   Did you hear from Cille-Cummin
          How the tide of war came pouring?
       Far and wide the summons travelled
          How they drove the Whigs before them!

2.   From the castle tower I viewed it,
          High on Sunday morning early,
       Looked and saw the ordered battle
          Where Clan Donald triumphed rarely, etc., etc..

[The verse here transcribed is verse 20 in Mackenzie's *Sàr Obair*.]

[1] The full translation in verse is to be found in *The Book of Highland Verse*, Edited Dugald Mitchell (Alex. Gardner, Paisley, 1912).

The scale by the 'rule of the last note', is Dorian, but one feels the note C as a strong secondary centre. This is an example of the mixed modes mentioned on page 13 (*passim*) and 20.

An interesting and in some ways a more arresting variant of the tune has been collected by J. L. Campbell, and is set down for comparison. The five-eight rhythm, though regular throughout the song, gives a feeling of rhythmic freedom which allows the prosodic values of the words full play. In this respect, although the metre of the poem is of regular stress, the musical effect is redolent of syllabic verse.

LATHA INBHIR-LOCHAIDH
The day of Inverlochy

Sung by Ruairi Iain Bhain, Barra

Collected by John Campbell
Transcribed by Seumas Ennis

By courtesy of the Irish Folk-lore Commission, and of the collector and transcriber.

Before taking a quick glance at a few of the other Gaelic poets (which for our purpose means song-composers) of the seventeenth century, who are of particular interest from the musical point of view, mention should be made of one remarkable survival of a *sixteenth*-century song[1] 'Oran na Comhachaig' (Song of the Owl) because curiously enough it has retained its popularity as a song to the present day. It is attributed to Donald Macdonald of Lochaber, better known as Domhnull mac Fhionnlaigh nan Dàn (Donald son of Finlay of the poems). Composed in the decrepitude of extreme old age, it is in the form of a dialogue between himself and the owl. It is some seventy stanzas long, of which shorter excerpts appear in current song books under the title of 'Craig-ghuanach' (Lightsome Crag). Here is the transcription of a recording of the singing of it by Angus MacLellan of South Uist,[2] to a tune which he learned from Alasdair MacDonald who came from North Uist as a cattleman. The tune is in the free rhythm typical of the tunes to poems in syllabic (as opposed to stressed) metre. The song is generally sung to a more modern-sounding stressed metre tune, but this is much more likely to be the style of the original tune of the song, and it is not impossible that it may be a survival of the original tune itself.

ORAN NA COMHACHAIG
Song of the Owl

Recorded by John L. Campbell

Singer: Angus MacLellan, South Uist.

Transcribed F. C.

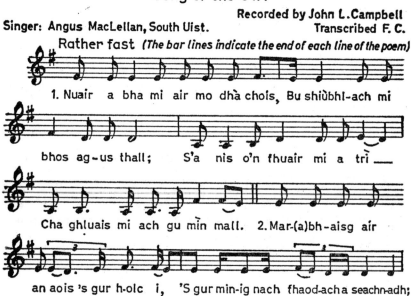

Rather fast *(The bar lines indicate the end of each line of the poem)*

1. Nuair a bha mi air mo dhà chois, Bu shiùbhl-ach mi bhos ag-us thall; S'a nis o'n fhuair mi a trì ___ Cha ghluais mi ach gu mìn mall. 2. Mar-(a)bh-aisg air an aois 's gur h-olc i, 'S gur min-ig nach fhaod-ach a seachn-adh;

---

[1] William Matheson dates the song as 1580–1620.

[2] Angus MacLellan, now aged ninety-six (in 1965), is the teller in Gaelic of *Tales from South Uist* and of *The Furrow Behind Me* both translated by J. L. Campbell and published by Routledge and Kegan Paul.

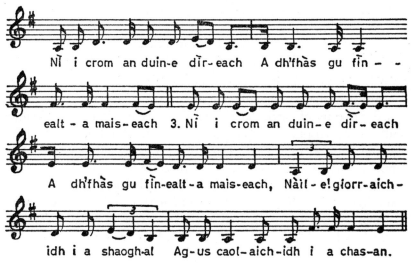

Nì i crom an duin-e dìr-each A dh'fhàs gu fìn - - ealt-a mais-each 3. Nì i crom an duin-e dìr-each A dh'fhàs gu fìn-ealt-a mais-each, Nàil-e! gìorr-aich-idh i a shaogh-al Ag-us caol-aich-idh i a chas-an.

(Said to be composed by Donald Macdonald of Lochaber in sixteenth or early seventeenth century.)

Note that the second half of stanza 2, beginning 'Nì i crom an duine', etc. is repeated as the first half of stanza 3 *to the first part of the tune*. This is a common but rather remarkable feature of Gaelic narrative song. Another tune to this song, in stressed metre and regular rhythm obviously not contemporary with the poem, is given in the Gesto Collection.

Further verses:

> 'S a Chomhachag bhochd na Stròineadh
> Nochd is brònach leam do leaba
> 'S ma bha thu ann ri linn Dhunnchaidh
> 'S beag ioghnadh leam ge troma t' aigne.
>
> 'Ach 's mise cho aoise dha'n darach
> A bha thall ud as a' Chòirnich
> 'S ioma linn a chuir mi romham
> 'S mi Chomhachag bhochd na Stròineadh.

From Professor Stuart Blackie's translation:[1]

(*The Hunter*) When I had two legs to walk on,
> I scaled the Ben light-footed and strong,
But now that I am fitted with three
> Softly and slowly I trail me along.

O poor old owl of the Strone,
> Hard is your bed this night in my room,
But if that you be as old as Clan Donald,
> You had cause enough in your day for gloom.

[1] Professor Blackie's translation though conveying the idea of the song differs from the text as sung here.

(*The owl*)   I am as old as the oak on the moor,
By many a wintry blast o'er blown;
And many a sapling grew to a tree,
Ere I became the old owl of the Strone, etc.

Of the other numerous Gaelic poets named in the collections as flourishing in the seventeenth century besides the two we have mentioned, three are of particular interest from the musical point of view: Roderick Morrison, '*An Clàrsair Dall*' (The Blind Harper); John MacKay, '*Am Pìobaire Dall*' (The Blind Piper) and Lachlan Mac-Kinnon, '*Lachunn mac Thearlaich Oig*' (Lachlan son of young Charlie).

Roderick Morrison,[1] harper to the Macleods and contemporary of Mary Macleod at Dunvegan, was both harper and poet. A few of his songs exist. They are mostly of the order of eulogies or laments for the Chiefs of Macleod, though a song of his also survives about the regular convivial meetings of the Highlanders of which the highlight was always the drinking of a dram 'to the next merry meeting', and to the anticipated good quality of the dram which it would furnish in its turn. The *Clàrsair Dall* had a particular reason for composing the song, which was that he feared he might be robbed by some of the lawless clansmen around him in the place where he lived, Tota-Mór in Glenelg. He therefore invests them in the song, to quote John Mackenzie, with all the attributes of honour, honesty and good neighbourliness, as a result of which they acted towards him in the character in which he painted them.

The tune is in Patrick Macdonald's Collection, No. 166, and is also to be found in a different variant in the Angus Fraser Manuscript in Edinburgh University Library. Three other tunes to the songs of the *Clàrsair Dall* are known and are to be found in the Angus Fraser Manuscript. The tune of the well-known song '*Hi oró's na hóro eile*' is also attributed in the Gesto Collection to the *Clàrsair Dall*, but again one cannot say if he composed it. Like so many of the Gaelic poets he is known to have used existing tunes for at least some of his songs, and as one cannot be certain that any of them are his own composition it would not serve any useful purpose to set them down here.

John MacKay, '*Am Pìobaire Dall*' (The Blind Piper) or as he is often called, John Dall MacKay, 1666–1754, piper to Mackenzie of Gairloch, is better known as a composer of pibroch than of song airs. Two at least of his songs are still sung. One of the best-known song poems is the 'Lament for Corrienessan', of which the tune has been learnt by William Matheson in South Uist. It is in free-rhythm syllabic metre:

[1] *c.* 1660–1712/13 (William Matheson).

LAMENT FOR CHOIRE AN EASAIN
(Am Piobaire Dall)

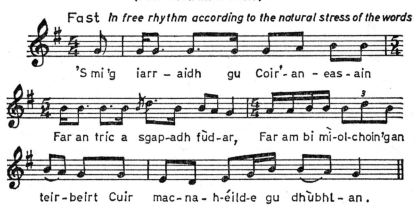

Fast *In free rhythm according to the natural stress of the words*

'S mi 'g iarr – aidh gu Coir'- an - eas-ain

Far an tric a sgap-adh fùd-ar, Far am bi mì-ol-choin'g an

teir – beirt Cuir mac-na- h-éild-e gu dhùbhl – an.

Translation by Dr Anne Ross:

> And I longing for Coir'-an-Easain,
> Where powder was often exploded,
> Where the hunting dogs would be used to incite them,
> Setting the stag at defiance.

Lachlan MacKinnon, a contemporary of *An Clàrsair Dall*, a native of Skye of whose songs a few have been preserved in print, is worth a passing mention because he is described as a fiddle player as well as a poet. It is of interest to find evidence of a fiddle-playing tradition so far to the west of Scotland, and at that date, as of course it is best known as the instrument *par excellence* of the North-east. The tune of his song, 'Latha Siubhail Sleibhe dhomh', is to be found in Patrick MacDonald's *Highland Airs*, No. 128.

One cannot close the chapter without mention of a name which does not appear among the bards—the name of MacCrimmon; for it was Patrick Mór MacCrimmon who composed what is musically the finest lament in song of them all—both words and music if tradition is correct. It is, to be sure, the ground or 'urlar' of a pibroch, but it was conceived as a lament for the great Rory Mór Macleod. It was one of a class of songs known as 'pibroch' songs, though whether it came first as a song, or whether the words were added afterwards to the pibroch ground, it is impossible to say. Sufficient it is that here is the touch of a master. Here it is in the form, slightly different from the rhythm of the pibroch version, in which it is usually sung:

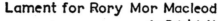

TOG ORM MO PHÌOB

Lament for Rory Mor Macleod

by Patrick Mor MacCrimmon

Translation:

Give me my pipes
And I shall go home
For I am sore grieved
Alas that this should happen

Give me my pipes,
I am sore grieved
For Ruairidh Mór
For Ruairidh Mór.

This is how the song is usually sung, though the rhythm is of doubtful accuracy. The rhythm of the pibroch, as it has come down to us in the notation of the nineteenth-century piper Angus Mackay whose father studied with the MacCrimmons, is more subtle—and more truly Gaelic. (It is probably the correct rhythm of the song also.) Here is the pibroch notation, but without the piper's grace-notes for clearer reading, to which the writer has conjecturally fitted the words:

64

MACLEOD OF MACLEOD'S LAMENT

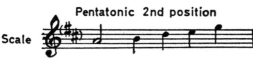

It is interesting to notice how, by avoiding the C sharp and the F sharp of the bagpipe in his choice of scale the tune gives the impression of a minor key rather than of a major.

The word *orm* is pronounced as two syllables by the insertion of a vowel sound between the r and the m, i.e. 'or-(o)m'. This extra vowel sound (which is apparently a fairly late development and is not counted metrically) making the second syllable, is known to Gaelic scholars as a *svarabhakti* vowel.

This is a typically Gaelic rhythm, with the figure ♪♩ ♪♩., in which the short note comes on the beat, but with a persuasive rather than a hard accent.[1] Here one sees the genesis of what, at a faster and sharper tempo, becomes the Scots snap.

In concluding this chapter it must be said that the whole subject of the early Gaelic poets is fugitive and thinly documented, at least as far as the music of the songs is concerned. It is in such a sphere as this that the age-old tradition of the Gael becomes manifest, of using the medium of memory rather than the notebook or the printed page as a means of preserving his folk-lore and music. We are still dependent for knowledge of the tunes of the songs of the seventeenth century (not to mention those of the Ossianic ballads) on present day research in the field.[2] These gaps in our knowledge of Gaelic song are slowly being

[1] William Matheson observes: 'Also typical of the Gaelic rhythm in certain metres is the fact that the stressed syllable coincides with the long off-beat.'

[2] J. L. Campbell adds: 'We can today (though the job has been left to the last possible moment) still record many of the airs to which poems composed in the seventeenth century were sung: these are likely to have persisted, otherwise the songs would have

filled by the publications of the Scottish Gaelic Texts Society, but we still await a definitive work on the songs of the Gaelic poets—and indeed on Gaelic songs in general—in any way comparable to the numerous annotated collections of the songs of Lowland Scotland.

---

been forgotten. Sometimes we may be able to check them against versions printed by Patrick Macdonald or Simon Fraser, but we can do no more.'

CHAPTER III

The Gaelic Labour Songs

THE songs which we have been considering in the last chapter, though of known authorship as regards the poems, are generally accepted as traditional in the sense that they have been disseminated by oral means from singer to singer as with traditional folk-song, and not by the printed page. The tunes, as we have seen, are mostly either truly traditional or of uncertain origin.[1]

Now we come to that great sea of truly traditional Gaelic music, the labour songs and all the songs related to them.

The term labour song covers a wide variety of species. As a rough first classification these may be divided into two main classes—songs for the communal task, in which strongly marked and compulsive rhythm induces synchronization of effort or movement; and songs to beguile the solitary occupations of the womenfolk in house or byre—churning, spinning, weaving and the like—and persuasive soothing songs to cajole the cow, that erstwhile sharer of the roof-tree in the black houses of the Hebrides, to give her milk.

Of the communal type of labour song, by far the commonest is for the shrinking or 'waulking' of the newly woven cloth. The waulking of the cloth was a frequent task in the old days, and it required many songs for the work of shrinking a piece of cloth to the proper consistency, so much so that we find songs which were apparently composed

[1] J. L. Campbell observes: 'The songs that have been here considered *are* traditional in the sense that they have been recovered from oral tradition solely, nearly always, if not always after the deaths of the composers. The only distinction between them and the rest of the oral tradition is that they are ascribed to authors. None of them were in print before the publication of Ronald MacDonald's *Eigg Collection* in 1776. This was the first printed anthology [i.e. of Gaelic songs].

'Out of sixteen poems ascribed to Mary Macleod, four were only recovered in Lochaber by D. C. Macpherson about a hundred years ago. Better versions of these have been recorded in the Outer Isles since.'

The writer himself would add that the first collection of the *airs* of Gaelic songs was that by Patrick Macdonald, published 1784.

for other tasks such as rowing or reaping, impressed into its service to swell the numbers.[1]

The manner of waulking the cloth has often enough been described. From six to twelve women sit round a narrow table—which as often as not is a barn door taken off its hinges and laid on trestles or other supports for the purpose. The web of newly woven cloth, which has been steeping in a tub of special solution—in the old days hot urine was used—is taken out and laid wet on the table; and the two ends of the cloth are sewn together so as to form a continuous band. The women grasp the cloth with both hands and pass it slowly round the table in a leftwise motion, that is, sunwise (*deiseil* is the Gaelic word) with a rhythmic thumping. The direction of movement is significant, for the importance of performing all circular movements or progressions in a sunwise direction is deeply rooted in folk belief. The actual four-movement sequence by which the cloth is made to travel round the table seems to differ slightly in different islands. As the writer remembers seeing it, it was as follows; *one*, the cloth is grasped in front of the sitter and thumped on the table where it lies; *two*, it is pushed outwards towards the centre of the table and thumped on the table at the end of the stroke; *three*, it is brought back to the first position close to the sitter, again with a thump; *four*, the cloth is passed to the left with a final thump and there released. The cloth is grasped afresh in front of the sitter, and the sequence is repeated endlessly for as many times as there are verses to the song.[2] The first and third thumps are more strongly accented than the second and fourth,[3] making a vigorous, strongly accented rhythm, a rhythm which becomes strangely mesmeric in its insistence. After a minute, or so, this THUMP, thump, THUMP, thump, THUMP, thump, THUMP, thump, becomes as exciting as an African drum beat. Then the leader begins to sing, and the chorus

[1] J. L. Campbell observes: 'The waulking song is the commonest labour song today, because the handloom making of tweed has been kept up in the Isles; whereas the rowing and reaping songs have gone out, as no one now reaps with the sickle, and boats have engines—but it was the reaping and rowing songs that struck the earlier visitors to the Highlands, e.g. Johnson, Boswell, Pennant—they were then heard far oftener.'

[2] Margaret Fay Shaw in her *Folksongs and Folklore of South Uist* gives a different routine of movements, and Amy Murray in her book *Father Allan's Island* (the Isle of Eriskay) one which seems to be different again.

[3] Since writing this, further research has disclosed that the accentuation of the thumping of the cloth may be varied in different songs, resulting in different musical patterns, thus clearly showing that though the thumping is primarily functional, its rhythmic aspect forms an important element in the musical performance of the song. This is discussed more fully in *The MacCormick Collection of Waulking Songs* by John L. Campbell and Francis Collinson (Clarendon Press, 1969).

chime in with the refrain. The leader tells the story of the poem and often follows on to take the first part of the refrain herself, and the chorus chime in with the rest of the refrain, the whole melody unwinding itself into a cyclical tune suited for endless repetition. The accents of the thumping coincide with the accents of the music to start with, but many of the tunes are cunningly constructed with an extra beat to the last bar to throw the accent on the *off-beat* the second time round, like a Gaelic 'rock-and-roll' rhythm, a feature that adds spice to the music and the performance. The women sing these songs with a curiously incisive, rather harsh quality of chest-voice that is characteristic of the waulking and which one does not readily hear in their other songs.

In former times the waulking of the cloth was done with the feet, by sitting on the ground and agitating it with kicking movements. From this type of waulking it is said that the menfolk were barred!

Though the waulking of the cloth is becoming rarer as methods of shrinking the cloth by machinery oust the manual process, the womenfolk of the islands are beginning to realize the interest and value of the songs.[1] They meet together for the pleasure of singing them for their own sake, either holding a long scarf or other light piece of cloth with which to simulate the movement of the web of cloth as they sit round the room in ordinary fashion; or as they do in the Isle of Lewis, actually seated at the waulking table with a dry finished piece of cloth instead of the wet unshrunk web, to copy more exactly the traditional movements and rhythm. The social singing of these songs with the singers holding handkerchiefs between them continues in Cape Breton to this day, as the writer has himself witnessed in the exhibition performance of a song-team from there.

Gaelic scholars are not agreed about the age or period of composition of the waulking songs. One of our foremost Gaelic scholars is of the opinion that the words of most of them (which he considers to have been largely extemporized), date, on the evidence of their subject matter, from the seventeenth century or the middle of the sixteenth at earliest, but that the tunes, or at least the tune-types, are much older; in fact the inference is that the same process has been at work as has been already described, of taking older airs as a framework on which to hang new words. Others hold that the words are the older of the two[2] and that

[1] In Barra and Uist they *have* realized it since 1920 or so. (J. L. Campbell.)

[2] J. L. Campbell observes: 'This would not necessarily make the tunes less old than the words.' William Matheson says: 'I don't think we should speak of "tunes" at this date at all. These people could extemporize *music* just as they could *words*.' The writer

they are poems of literary creation of a previous period which have been adapted to labour use by setting them to melodies of the waulking type—sometimes by procrustean methods which result in the normal accents of words being displaced—wrenched accent being the technical term.[1]

One can admittedly find isolated cases of an older song adapted to labour use which is known to have existed previously in its own form and right. There are examples of this in several of the more popular Ossianic ballads such as the 'Lament for Diarmaid', 'Ossian's Warning to his Mother', and the Arthurian ballad of '*Am Bròn Binn*' already mentioned, which have been re-set to waulking tunes with refrains that are obvious accretions; but such examples would seem to be too few to prove a theory. It is of course a discussion for the Celtic scholar and one on which the writer would not presume to venture an opinion.

The musical characteristics of the waulking song tune, though it displays a variety of minor differences of form, is constant in its basic conformation to the requirements of the task, in possessing a short (sometimes very short) verse sung alone by a leader, followed by a longer refrain sung by the body of the workers. The verse may consist of one or perhaps two lines of a long poem, which may take up as little as one bar of music, while the refrain may be anything up to twelve bars or so in length. Sometimes, rather oddly, the single line of the poem may be broken in the middle by the refrain, irrespective of the curious grammatical results that often ensue.

In the refrain of the waulking song we meet with the characteristic nonsense syllables common to many types of Gaelic song. There is a regular and recurrent vocabulary of these, of which the following are typical:

Hi ri hoireann o (pronounced *hee thee hothen-o*)
Horo eile; horo hua; horo nàilibh (pronounced *nàalif* (long vowel))
  holo ghealladh e (pronounced *iallachie*) hŏrō hug abhi.
Fal-u-il-o fal-u-oro; E ho i iu rabho, hem i ho, etc., etc.
hur-a-bhi hō-ro.

One finds the same sort of thing in Lowland Scots song in such refrains as '*linten adie toorin adie*', '*Durrum-a-doo a daddio*' or '*Hey Willie*

[1] William Matheson observes: 'There is a tendency to confuse the age of specific songs and the age of the class of song to which they belong. Most of the specific songs are seventeenth century; but this *class* of song must have existed from a much earlier period. Early specific examples have just faded from popular memory with the passage of time.'

is however inclined to be sceptical of this. Tunes are troublesome things to extemporize.

Wallackie noo noo noo', etc., but while in Lowland Scots such refrains are more or less 'throw aways' in Gaelic they *are* the song, quite as much as the verse lines that tell the story; so much so that it is by the meaningless syllables of the refrain that a singer will remember and identify a song, and particularly the tune of it, and not by that part of it which makes sense and tells a story, the verse lines. They form in fact, as a kind of by-product, a rough mnemonic system for tune finding, somewhat akin to the pipers' *'canntaireachd'*, but in a much less exact form, and more in the way that the nonsense words *Lilli burlero bullen a la* immediately suggest their proper tune to the English-spoken person.

Here then is a typical waulking song melody of the simple kind with one line of verse and three lines of refrain, of which the leader or soloist takes the first line of refrain alone following the verse. The following will show more clearly the lay-out of verse and refrain and of soloist and chorus:

Verse (one eight-syllable line of poem taking up two bars of music):
　　　　Latha dhomh 's mi 'm Beinn a' Cheathaich.
Refrain (soloist) Far al il eò, ro ho bhi ó,
　　　(chorus) Hoireann is ó ho ró bhi o ho,
　　　　　　Hi rì horó ho bha, ó hug ó ro

BEINN A' CHEATHAICH

From the Isle of Barra – recorded from several different singers.

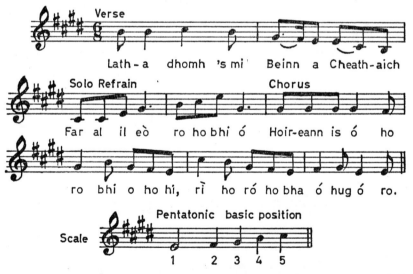

This song is of interest as being the original waulking song melody on which Mrs Kennedy Fraser based her song of 'Kishmul's Galley'. The notes will be found to be the same, but of different rhythm to Mrs Kennedy Fraser's song.

Translation by Annie Johnston, Barra.

1. One day when I was in Ben a Cheathaich,
2. I saw Mac Neil's Galley sailing.
3. She without rudder or stay or tackle;
4. Without means of restraining her speed;
5. Farquhar at the helm, brave deeds at his hand;
6. Young Roderick, the handsome heir;
7. And Neil the gloomy son of Roderick the Turbulent.
8. Joyfully would I take your ship—
9. Out from the country of the Macleans,
10. Into Kisimul of our fathers,
11. Where would be found a feast to be taken;
12. Wine-drinking from night to morning,
13. Piping charmingly on chanters,
14. And sweet harps being tuned in unison.

More complicated forms of the waulking song occur in which the soloist and chorus each enter twice within the round of the melody:

Verse (solo)   Di-Sathuirne ghabh mi mulad,
Refrain (chorus)   Na hao ri hiù a, hao ri hiù a;
Verse (solo)   'S ann Di-Luain a rinn mi 'n tuiream,
Refrain (solo—or chorus)   Na hao ri a bho libh o,
(chorus)   Hi o challa bhi hi ri hiu a hua.

DI-SATHUIRNE GHABH MI MULAD

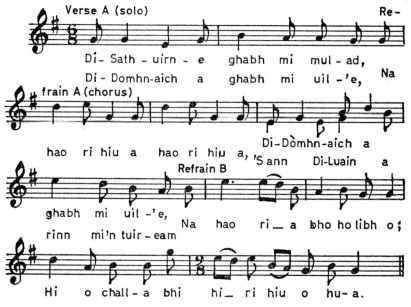

Scale

This is the tune to which Mrs Kennedy Fraser set words of her own, 'The Benbecula Bridal' of which the gist is of 'songs and piping and laughter'. Her English words were then turned into Gaelic by Kenneth Macleod, and both were published under this title (Gaelic, '*An Triall Bainnse*'). As will be seen from the translation below, the real words, which are of course still sung in the islands, are those of a lament. With all praise due to Mrs Kennedy Fraser for her great work in collecting and popularizing the songs of the Hebrides the world over, this is only too typical of the legacy of confusion which she and her collaborator Kenneth Macleod left to traditional Hebridean song, a confusion which will probably never be properly cleared up.

Translation:

> Saturday I felt the gloom come,
> Sunday it came in fulness.
> Monday dirge I was crooning,
> Busy hands I saw around you,
> Closing lips I loved to look on,
> Closing eyes that shone in beauty.

This song shows the frequent device mentioned above of a three-beat bar at the end of the melody, which reverses the accent the second time round. The accent (i.e. the louder of the two thumps) comes naturally on the first beat of every bar the first time; but by reason of the extra beat in the three-four bar at the end it comes on the second beat, that is the off-beat, the second time round.

It takes about half an hour to 'waulk' a piece of cloth to the right tightness and thickness for most ordinary purposes; but special qualities of cloth such as that for the clothes of the fishermen, which has to withstand the cold winds and wet conditions of their work, and so has to be of as close a texture as possible, take about twice as long. With the customary practice of singing each verse-line twice (which naturally doubles the length of the song), a waulking song can go on for as much as twelve minutes or so; and the women reckon the task by the number of songs it takes rather than in terms of minutes—which probably helps to conceal the fact that it is hard work! The songs vary in length, but it usually takes about nine songs to do a piece of cloth. Generally speaking, a round of waulking begins with songs of slow tempo, working up through those of moderate speed, to quicker songs. This is partly because the wet cloth at the beginning of the waulking is heavy to handle and gets lighter as it dries out with the squeezing and thumping, and partly because the singers warm naturally to their task and tend to

73

quicken the tempo involuntarily. For this reason we find waulking songs ranging from the slow song such as 'Griogal Cridhe'[1] (Beloved Gregor), the lament of the wife of the Macgregor killed before her eyes by armed men, to songs of gayer subjects suited to faster tempos, on such themes as—praise of the youth of the clans, hoisting the sails of a ship on which the beloved is sailing; mermaids, hunting of the deer or of the seals, songs about the cattle in the pastures or at the summer sheilings, satirical songs and flytings such as 'Cha déid Mór a Bharraidh bhrònach (Mór won't go to sorrowful Barra), the latter a boasting song between two poetesses from Barra and South Uist.[2]

The final stage of the waulking consists of the slapping of the cloth with the open palms of the hands to give it a nap or pile. The songs for this, òrain basaidh (slapping songs) they are called, are quick in tempo and light in mood, and often of an improvisatory nature. A favourite one is 'An long Eireannach' (The Irish ship) in which the name of each young woman in turn is coupled with that of a young man, as the one she would like to take with her on 'the Irish ship'. Such songs give opportunity also of poking sly but good-humoured fun at any non-Gaelic-speaking strangers who may happen to be present at the waulking, of which the writer himself has more than once been the victim! Another such song is 'Coisich agus faigh dhomh céile'[3] (Step out and get me a sweetheart)[3] in which the appropriate sweetheart for each girl is named in succession.

Here is an òran basaidh collected in the Hebrides by the writer and his colleague James Ross.

ORAN BASAIDH

Singer: Nan Mackinnon, Isle of Vatersay.

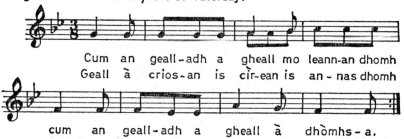

Cum an geall-adh a gheall mo leann-an dhomh
Geall à crios-an is cìr-ean is an-nas dhomh

cum an geall-adh a gheall à dhòmhs-a.

[1] A Gaelic colleague observes however that 'Griogal Cridhe' is properly a lullaby which may have been pressed into service as a waulking song. It appears as a waulking song in the *Tolmie Collection* (No. 41). For the song see p. 87.
[2] J. L. Campbell has recorded versions in Barra, Vatersay, and Cape Breton.
[3] Both songs are to be found in *Folksongs and Folklore of South Uist* by Margaret Fay Shaw.

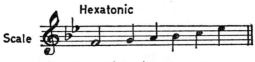

Like Mixolydian with gap at 6

TRANSLATION

May my lover keep the promise that he has made to me;
May he keep the promise that he has made to me;[1]
He promised me a belt, and combs and dainties
He promised to buy me a silken gown,
He promised that and much else besides.

Another song-type mentioned as being used at the waulking, but one which the writer cannot remember having heard is that used for wringing out the cloth, the 'òran teannachaidh (tightening song). Francis Tolmie gives three, of which the following is probably the one with most musical interest:

ORAN TEANNACHAIDH

Tolmie Collection No. 68

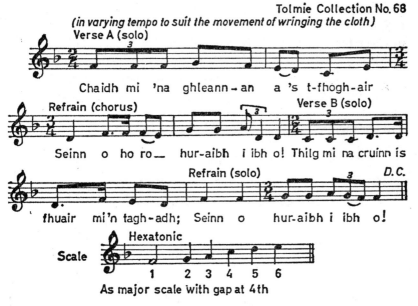

As major scale with gap at 4th

ORAN TEANNACHAIDH

Translation by Francis Tolmie:

Refrain: Sing O! huravi ivo
Verses: 1. In autumn I went to the little glen:
          I cast lots and won the best.

[1] Literally: Keep as a promise what my lover promised to me.

75

2. A young man I found, clever and wise;
3. A youth after whom there was no pursuit.
4. Thou goest to the hill, where barking is heard.
5. With thy greyhounds thy sagacious white dogs,
6. And thy terriers following them
7. Such is my beloved, and no wanderer, etc.

Other types of communal labour song

The reaping and the rowing song.

Besides the songs for the waulking of the cloth, which were the most numerous, there used to be songs for reaping and for rowing. Neither have survived in actual use, but many of the best of them have been gathered into the waulking repertory, which has helped to preserve them.

Fundamentally the task of reaping does not require a concerted movement on the part of the reapers; no doubt however they did wield their sickles in time to the music, if only to justify the use of a song! The reaping songs, like some of the rowing songs, are difficult to identify as such, for few of them refer directly to the task for which they were used, a feature characteristic of most Gaelic labour songs.[1] Here is one however for which we have the authority of Francis Tolmie, 'Oran Arabhaig' (song of strife). This is a taunting or boasting song (flyting) said to have been extemporized between a woman of the clan Macleod and one of the Clan Donald. According to Miss Tolmie, reapers singing this song have been known to become so worked up in their clan fervour as to cut themselves with their sickles! (accidentally of course).

REAPING SONG

Oran Arabhaig-Song of Strife

Singer: Margaret Gillies, Ebost, Bracadale, Skye. 1863

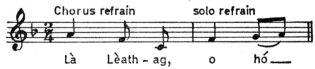

Là   Lèath - ag,   o   hó

---

[1] Out of forty-one songs used in the waulking of the cloth published in the *Tolmie Collection*, only one, 'Clò nan Gillean' ('The cloth for the young men') refers to either the cloth or to the process in hand. Referring to this fact that so few of the labour songs mention the tasks to which they are sung, some of the writer's Gaelic colleagues will not allow that they are labour songs in origin at all, but are more often than not simply ordinary chorus songs whose rhythm happened to be convenient or adaptable to a particular task. This may well be so; but it seems to the writer that, being found suitable for a particular task, they must almost inevitably have become labelled with the task in question.

Mhair-ear-ad chridh-e, o hó— Là Lèath-ag

o hó,— Nigh-ean nan Leòd-ach, o hó.—

Passage in the middle of the song

Eil—e la hó è hó; Eil—e la

hó è hó, Tha so fuar air, o— hó.

Translation by Francis Tolmie (Tolmie Coll. No. 74)

Macdonald poetess speaks:

Margaret dear, daughter of the Macleods, with yellow hair of golden hue, the year of thy marriage seems long gone by. Once, when I was sitting by the Sound of Rona, my face tuned towards Hirt (St Kilda) of big birds, a fellow came, boastful and pert, in velvet dress, with boots and spurs, and asked me—desiring conversation—what was the custom of Clan Donald—well known to me, befitting them; wine flowing, ale of third drawing poured from flagons. Not such as they, the race of Macleod, the race of the Mare, crippled and clumsy; feeding on chaff and coarsest grass, and black mill dust, devouring barley with soft water from the peat-bog, greeted only as 'Pru-seo-i',[1] with halters fastened round their heads, and withies upon their feet!

Macleod poetess[2] speaks:

Come! Come! Ye fled away, ye timid rabble! Remember the day of Glen-Healtuinn? Ye stood in the heather like hens; into the loch ye went like ducks, and like gulls went out to sea! Etc., etc.

[1] *Pru-seo-i*, a sound used when horses are called.
[2] J. L. Campbell observes: 'The Macleod poetess in the song is said to have been Mary Macleod. See K. C. Craig, *Orain Luaidh*; also version printed by J. C. Watson in *Gaelic Songs of Mary Macleod*, 1934.' Dr Campbell continues: 'but passages occur in *Tàladh Dhòmhnaill Ghuirm* (Notes, *op. cit.*, p. 112) and there is a lot of confusion here.'

Besides being an example of a reaping song, the song is a fair and interesting specimen of the Gaelic flyting song.[1]

Other reaping songs or melodies are to be found in the introduction to volume two of Mrs Kennedy Fraser's *Songs of the Hebrides*, page xiii.

The Iorram or Rowing Song

Among a sea-going island people like those of the Hebrides, the iorram (pronounced *irram*) or rowing song, must have been one of the most frequently heard songs in former days. It has now of course completely fallen out of use. Through being one of the earliest, perhaps indeed the first song type to have a regular rhythm—a feature imposed by the necessity of keeping the rowers in time with each other—it may well have formed an important landmark in the development of stress in Gaelic song and poetry, as Professor W. J. Watson in his *Specimens of Gaelic Poetry* (Bàrdachd Ghàidhlig) would seem to suggest, for he quotes as perhaps the earliest specimen of stressed metre known in Scottish Gaelic poetry, an iorram, dating, if tradition is correct, to well before 1500. Another standard verse-metre of iorram type which he codifies also, corresponds exactly to what he describes as the 'English' iorram 'Over the Sea to Skye' in the lines:

> Loud the winds howl, loud the waves roar,
> Thunderclouds rend the air.
> Baffled, our foes stand by the shore,
> Follow they will not dare!

This very popular song almost certainly has a Gaelic iorram as an original basis, and several versions of the supposed original have been collected.[2]

Like the reaping song the iorram is now often difficult to identify as such, because the words seldom refer to the act of rowing. A number of refrains contain the word 'iomair' meaning *row*, in such refrain-forms as 'iomair o ho', etc.; but this is rendered ambiguous by the fact that many iorram were impressed into waulking use, to the rhythm of which at a quicker pace they were also conveniently suited; and it so happens the word 'iomair' could also be interpreted as an exhortation to 'push' or drive the cloth round the table.[3] Here are two however in which the words of the songs do indicate that they are rowing songs:

[1] A fuller translation is given in the *Tolmie Collection* (*Journal of the Folk-song Society*, Vol. IV, p. 235). See also J. C. Watson, *Gaelic Songs of Mary Macleod*, p. 2.

[2] Since writing this the writer has received the following note from William Matheson: 'The Gaelic original of "The Skye Boat Song" is "*Cuachag nan Craobh*" (The Cuckoo in the Grove) with the two halves reversed.'

[3] 'A classification of Gaelic folk-song' by James Ross, *Scottish Studies*, Vol. I.

THE NESS ROWING SONG

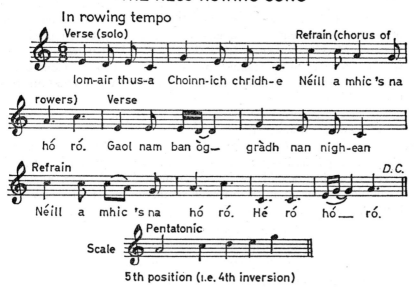

In rowing tempo

Verse (solo) — lom-air thus-a Choinn-ich chridh-e Néill a mhic 's na

Refrain (chorus of rowers) — hó ró. Gaol nam ban òg— gràdh nan nigh-ean

Refrain — Néill a mhic 's na hó ró. Hé ró hó— ró.

D.C.

Pentatonic Scale

5th position (i.e. 4th inversion)

There is a different tune for the 'Ness Rowing Song' in Patrick MacDonald's *Collection*, No. 65.

Verse: Row thou, dear Kenneth,
Refrain: Neil, son, *'s na hó ró*
Verse: Love of young women, maidens' darling!
Refrain: Neil, son, *'s na hó ró*
Hé ró hó ró

Iorram o'n 'Bhirlinn Chlann Raghnaill'

Sung by Ruairi Iain Bhàin
Recorded by J. L. Campbell

Transcribed by Séamus Ennis

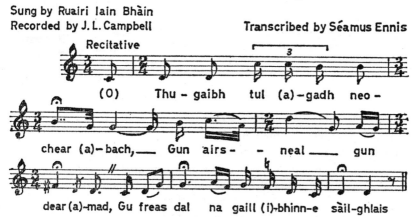

Recitative

(O) Thu – gaibh tul (a)–gadh neo–

chear (a)–bach,— Gun airs– – neal — gun

dear (a)–mad, Gu freas dal na gaill (i)–bhinn-e sàil–ghlais

By courtesy of the Irish Folk-lore Commission, and of the collector and transcriber

79

J. L. Campbell's notes on the Birlinn of Clanranald:

This iorram occurs in Alexander MacDonald's long poem *Birlinn Chlann Raghnaill*, 'The Galley of Clanranald', which was composed in the middle of the eighteenth century. The air was recorded by J. L. Campbell from Roderick Mackinnon, '*Ruairi Iain Bhàin*', on the Isle of Barra in 1937, and was later transcribed by Seamus Ennis of the Irish Folklore Commission. Another version of the air has been recorded from Angus John Campbell, Lochboisdale.

The iorram comprises the fourth section of the poem, and is introduced with these words (translated):

'*Then, after sixteen men had sat at the oars to row her to the sailing point, stout Malcolm, son of Ronald of the Ocean, called for a rowing song, and this was it.*'

The verse cited beneath the music is translated by the Rev. Angus and Archibald Macdonald in their edition of the poems of Alexander Mac-Donald, as follows:

> '*Let your spring be not awkward,*
> *But without languor or failing,*
> *To trust yourselves to the sea-grey tempest.*'

There are fifteen verses altogether in the iorram; each of them would have been sung twice.

Many iorrams are in three-four time, like this fine song in the *Tolmie Collection.*

IORRAM, IURAIBH O-HI, IURABH O-HU

Translation by Francis Tolmie (condensed):

Refrain: Iùraibh o-hì, Iùraibh o-hù.

Verses:
1. The place I behold, where last year I was staying
2. Though this year I no longer here abide
3. The slopes of Lochiel and of Kinloch-Luinnard,
4. Kinloch of the vessels and of fleets.
31. A greatly afflicted woman am I
32. John have I buried,

33. And Ruari, the brown haired youth, his locks in curls
34. At the temple on the hill.

Many of the iorrams which are written in three-four time in the printed
collections such as Mrs Kennedy Fraser's introductions to her *Songs of
the Hebrides*, are obviously in a slow six-eight time, with the complete
cycle of the 'in-and-out' of the oars taking up two bars of the three-
four rhythm (making one bar of six-eight). That is to say, the *pulse* is
equal to three crotchets—one bar of three-four time to each pulse. In
the case of the Tolmie example given above however, and other iorram
tunes similar to it, the musical content of each bar is so divided up that
the pulse must obviously be the crotchet, and there must therefore be
three pulses or *counts* to each bar. This is puzzling, for it is difficult to
see how the two-fold movement of the oars fits into the three pulses.
Possibly with the long oars required for a larger boat, particularly if
heavy-laden, the pull of the blade in the water took two counts, while
the pushing back of the oars above the water for the next stroke took
up the third. There were two kinds of iorram, one for the large boat
and one for the small, each of which had their proper Gaelic type-
name; and it is possible, though this is only a guess, that the two-four
and three-four rhythms may be the differentiating measure.

Other iorram tunes, but without words, may be found in the Gesto
Collection, in Patrick Macdonald's *Collection of Highland Vocal Airs*,
and in Fraser of Knockie's *Airs and Melodies peculiar to the Highlands of
Scotland*.

We have dealt with all the classes of communal labour songs known
to us. Before we go on to the songs for the *solitary* tasks, we should
perhaps mention the now obsolete quern song sung or chanted at the
grinding of the corn for meal, for this was a task usually or often performed by two women. The quern consisted of two round flat stones
of from about a foot to two feet in diameter, which were laid on one
another. The lower remained stationary while the upper was revolved
on it, the corn being ground between the two stones. The upper stone
had a hole near its edge for a wooden peg or handle with which to pull
or push it round. The process, as it has been described to the writer by
the late Miss Annie Johnston of Barra was for two women to kneel or
sit opposite to each other with the quern on the ground between them.
The peg was long enough for both of them to grasp it together, and as
one pulled the other pushed. The stones were heavy and the movements
were short and jerky. The tune fitted accordingly. Some of the quern
tunes are restricted in compass and chant-like. Here is an example from
the Isle of Barra which has rather more melody than many of them.

ORAN NA BRÀTHANN
Song of the quern

Singer: Miss Annie Johnstone, Barra.

(transcribed at an octave above pitch)

Brà brà bleith,   brà brà bleith,   Beil a' chailleach a' bhrà.

'S gheibh thu fhéin   am bonn-ach bràth-ann,   Cha bheil a chiall,

‖1. cha bhuin siod dhomh!   ‖2. 'S gheibh thu fhéin mac fir an taigh-e

Piu mosso

Beil - idh ag - us biadh-aidh,   biadh-aidh ag-us beil-idh!

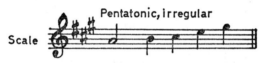

Scale — Pentatonic, irregular

(On the repeat of the tune for the second verse, cut from the end of the third bar to the second time bar.)

The *piu mosso* in the last four bars is interesting, and indicates the use of an occasional burst of speed, to vary the monotony of the task and keep the singers interested. The pull on the stones would come at each crotchet beat.

ORAN NA BRÀTHAN

Translation: 'Quern, quern, grind!
Quern, quern, grind!
Old woman, grind the quern
And you shall have the quern bannock.'
'I will not grind it indeed,
That does not befit me.'

'Quern, quern, grind!
Quern, quern, grind!
Old woman, grind the quern
And you shall have the goodman's son.'
'Faster I will grind and feed [the quern],
I will feed [the quern] and grind.'

Mrs Kennedy Fraser gives a number of quern tunes in the introductions to her volumes. There is also an interesting quern song contributed along with a number of other fine examples of Gaelic song, by Margaret Fay Shaw in a memorial collection to Bela Bartók, *Studia Memoria Belae Bartók Sacra* (Budapest, 1956):

QUERN SONG
Beil, a chailleach, a bhrà

Singer: Annie MacDonald, Lochboisdale.

Collected and transcribed by Margaret Fay Shaw

Translation: Grind the quern, old wife, grind the quern, old wife, grind the quern, old wife, a man is coming to ask for you! What clothing does he wear? He wears a tattered cloak, he wears rags, he has an old quern-skin(?) on! Grind the quern, old wife, grind the quern, old wife, a man is coming to ask for you!

Spinning Songs (Orain sniomh)[1]

A few of these are still sung in the Hebrides, although the task of spinning at home with either wheel or spindle has declined in Scotland

[1] W. Matheson observes to the writer: 'Spinning songs cannot be an old genre, as spinning wheels became common in the Hebrides only in the first half of the last century. In most cases they just used any song which was rhythmically suited for the purpose.'

almost to extinction among the ordinary folk. Here is a spinning song which the writer recorded a few years ago:

SPINNING SONG

Singer: Mrs Katherine Douglas, Kilmuir, Skye.

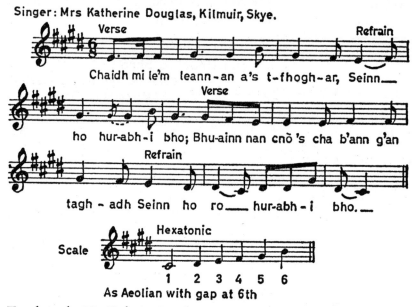

Chaidh mi le'm leann-an a's t-fhogh-ar, Seinn ho hur-abh-i bho; Bhu-ainn nan cnò 's cha b'ann g'an tagh - adh Seinn ho ro hur-abh - i bho.

Scale — Hexatonic

1 2 3 4 5 6

As Aeolian with gap at 6th

Translation by Mrs Katherine Douglas:

          I went with my love into the little glen,

(*Refrain*)   Seinn (sing) ho hurabhi bho; (meaningless)

          To gather nuts, and not waiting to choose them,

(*Refrain*)   Seinn ho hurabhi bho.

Margaret Fay Shaw gives three spinning songs in her book *Folk-songs and Folklore of South Uist*, one of which 'Cuigeal na Maighdin' (Distaff of the Maiden) is particularly attractive. Most of the spinning songs are in a swinging six-eight rhythm to match the spin of the wheel and the beat of the treadle.

Milking Songs (Orain Bhleoghainn)

These are still fairly plentiful, and are in common use by the women-folk of the crofts. Most of them are by way of being sung to the cow in terms of affection and praise at milking time—'O Bhólagan' (i.e. 'O little cow'), 'Gentle Cow', 'Darling of the cattle', etc. The following is a milking song in common use collected by the writer and his colleague James Ross 'Till an crodh, fair an crodh' (Bring back the cattle, guard well the cattle!)[1]

[1] Also used as a lullaby (information from John MacInnes).

84

TILL AN CRODH

Singer: Nan Mackinnon, Isle of Vatersay.

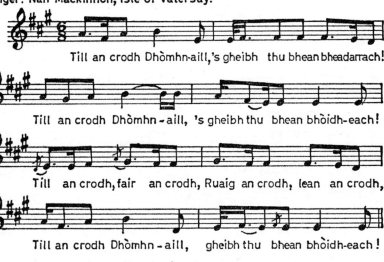

Till an crodh Dhòmhn-aill,'s gheibh thu bhean bheadarrach!

Till an crodh Dhòmhn - aill, 's gheibh thu bhean bhòidh-each!

Till an crodh, fair an crodh, Ruaig an crodh, lean an crodh,

Till an crodh Dhòmhn - aill, gheibh thu bhean bhòidh-each!

Scale   **Hexatonic**

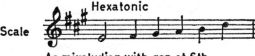

As mixolydian with gap at 6th

Translation:

> Turn the cattle Donald—
>   And you will get a lively wife,
> Turn the cattle Donald
>   And you will get a beautiful wife;
> Turn the cattle; watch the cattle;
> Drive the cattle; follow the cattle;
> Turn the cattle Donald—
>   And you will get a beautiful wife.
>
> See on each side cattle and sheep,
>   See on each side the wealth of MacIntosh;
>   Turn the cattle; watch the cattle;
>   Drive the cattle; follow the cattle;
> Turn the cattle my lad—
>   And you will get a beautiful wife.

Churning Songs (Orain a' chrannachain)
Milking songs lead naturally to churning songs, of which the following example was given to the writer by the late Annie Johnston of Barra[1]

---

[1] An arrangement of this song, with some difference of words, will be found in Mrs Kennedy Fraser's *Songs of the Hebrides*, Vol. I.

CHURNING SONG

♪=132 (Transcribed an octave higher than sung)

Am mais-treadh a bh'aig Muir-e, air ùr-lar a'ghlinn-e, A'
meud-ach-adh an im-e a' lùghd-ach-adh a' bhainn-e
Thig a chuinn-eag, thig! Blà-thach gu dòrn 's ìm gu uil-inn
Thig a chuinn-eag, thig! Tha glug a' seo, tha glag a' seo, tha
glag a' seo, tha glug a' seo; Tha rud na 's fheàrr na chòir a' seo, Tha
rud na' 's fheàr na fì-on ann. Thig a chuinn-eag, thig!
Blàth-ach gu dòrn 's ìm gu uil-inn, Thig a chuinn-eag, thig!

ORAN A' CHRANNACHAIN

Translation:

The churning which Mary did
At the foot of the glen,
Increasing the butter,
Decreasing the milk
Come, churn, come
Buttermilk to the wrist,
Butter to the elbow
Come churn, come!
There's a *glug* here,
There's a *glag* here,
There's a *glag* here
There's a *glug* here.
There is something better than is right here,
There is something better than wine.

86

Lullabies (Talaidhean or Crònain, i.e. croons)

Lullabies might be expected to be much the same in any racial culture. There is however a distinctive flavour both as to musical style and content in the Scottish Gaelic lullaby which makes it worth while giving an example or two.

In most of the Gaelic lullabies their purpose is plainly evident from their words and by the use of conventional vocables of soothing and endearment, characteristic of the Gaelic language such as 'O bà, O bà' (cf. Lowland Scots 'Baloo'), 'Mo leanabh' (my child), 'mo chéile' (my husband or wife, companion), 'Gille beag' (little boy), etc. and by the frequent exhortation of 'Dian cadalan' (go to sleep). Sometimes a Gaelic lullaby is interwoven with a lament for the death of the infant's father, of which the best known is 'Griogal Cridhe', the famous MacGregor lullaby already referred to. It is worth quoting, for it is one of the most pathetically beautiful examples of its kind in Gaelic song:

GRIOGAL CHRIDHE

Similar to version in Tolmie Collection No. 41.

Slow *(The dotted notes to be sung gently and without rigidity)*

Verse

'S iom-adh oidhch-e fhliuch is thior-am

'S lath-a na seachd sian, A sheall Griog - al

dhòmhs-a creag-an, Ris an gabh-ainn dìon;

Refrain

Och-an och-an och-an uir-idh, Och-an i-ri ó.

Och-an och-an och-an uir-idh, Caid-il thus-a, laoigh.

Scale

Hexatonic

1 2 3 4 5 6

As Mixolydian with gap at 4th

87

Translation:

> On many a wet night or a dry,
> And on a day of seven tempests,
> Gregor would find me a rock
> For shelter from the storm.

(*Refrain*)

> Ochan, ochan, ochan uiridh.
> Ochan uiridh o,
> Ochan, ochan, ochan uiridh,
> Sleep my little calf.

> I went up to the highest chamber
> And searched the room below,
> But could not find my beloved Gregor
> Sitting at the board.

> While the young women of the township
> Lie sleeping peacefully
> I lie by the edge of thy grave,
> Smiting my two hands.

Sometimes the Gaelic lullaby prophesies great deeds for the infant when he grows up. An example, though to modern ideas a preposterous one,[1] is the well-known '*Cagaran Gaolach*', in which the mother prophesies that the child will grow up to be a great 'lifter of cattle', like its father. Of one lullaby, '*Uamh an Oir*' (The cave of gold) both the tune and the story are taken from the pibroch and pibroch lore. It tells the story of a piper who enters a great cave or subterranean passage with the intention of exploring it to its end, expecting to find treasure. The sound of his pipes grows fainter as he penetrates further and further into the cave. Then suddenly, from the distance he is heard to cry, 'O that I had three hands, two for the pipes and one for my sword!' Then there was silence, the inference being that he had encountered some fierce monster guarding the 'treasure' and perished. This however belongs more properly to the subject of pibroch songs, to be dealt with in a later chapter.

As with the waulking songs, some of the lullabies seem to have served a dual purpose, that of being used for iorram (rowing songs) or rather, to put it a better way round, that some of the iorram were also used as lullabies. It can easily be understood that a song for the swing of

---

[1] A Gaelic colleague says: 'Cattle-lifting was of course an aristocratic occupation. Sheep-stealing on the other hand was plebeian and regarded as contemptible by Highlander and Borderer alike.'

the oars would suit equally well the slow rocking of an infant in its mother's arms. Here is one from the now uninhabited island of St Kilda, evacuated in 1930, which was described to the writer as a lullaby, but which was said to be used also as a rowing song. The words bear this out, referring to the rocking or tossing of the boat crossing from the main island of Hirta to the close-by Isle of Soay. It was brought to the Isle of Lewis by St Kilda fishermen and recollected for the writer by the late Nandag Macleod of Stornoway:

ST. KILDA LULLABY AND BOAT-SONG

Singer: Miss Nandag Macleod, Stornoway.   Noted by Francis Collinson

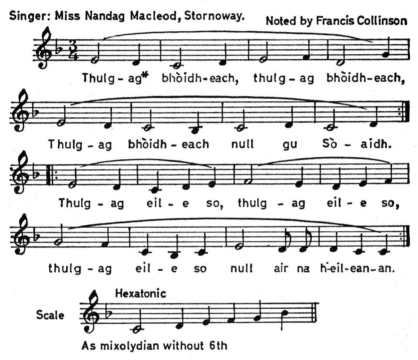

As mixolydian without 6th

Translation:

> Lovely *tulgag*, lovely *tulgag*,[1]
> A pretty pull [with the oars] over to Soay,
> This other *tulgag*, this other *tulgag*,
> Another pull here over to the isles.

'Thulgag' is customarily pronounced 'thul-a-gag', of which the musical performance would presumably be:

[1] *tulgag* means a 'jerk'—presumably a form of *tulgadh*, see 'Iorram of Clanranald', page 79.

89

Thul-(a)g-ag bhòidh-each

The extra syllable, which is known to language scholars as a *svarabhakti vowel*, could not however be detected in this singer's rendering.

One more lullaby, sung supposedly by a villainous foster-father in folk-tale, is worth quoting for the strange beauty of the melody. It was collected by the writer and James Ross in the Isle of Vatersay, but its place of origin was said by the singer to be the Isle of Mingulay, uninhabited since 1908:

Hó hó nighean donn, Gheibh mi 'n crodh leat

Singer: Miss Nan Mackinnon, Isle of Vatersay.

Translation:

Hó hó, brown maid,
Hó hó, brown maid,
Hó hó, brown maid,
I shall get cattle with you;
I'll seduce you,
I'll seduce you,
I'll seduce you,
When you are older.

This completes the catalogue of Gaelic work songs. It has been thought worth while to go into them in considerable detail, for many classes of them are unique to Scottish Gaelic culture alone and do not exist in the Lowland Scots tradition. The Lowland Scotswoman may well have sung at her work as she reaped the corn or churned the butter or spun the wool and flax, or shrank her newly woven cloth; but she possessed no specific songs for the purpose.[1]

CONCERNING GAELIC SONGS OF GENERAL TYPE

There are of course very many types of Gaelic songs besides the songs we have examined in this and the previous chapter. It would be impossible in such a book as this to examine and give examples of the myriad types of songs of a general nature. One can only enumerate a few of their themes, such as love songs and songs of disappointed love; songs of Homeland and of exile; of eulogy and of lament; soldiers' and sailors' songs; songs of battles, of victory and of lost causes; songs of Nature (a large section); humorous and satirical songs; all the subjects in fact which we may find as a theme for song anywhere.

Many of the songs have refrains; many have not, but are in the form of stanzas, of from four to eight lines, without refrain. Where a song has a refrain, more often than not it begins with it. This is a characteristic which we seldom find in Lowland Scots song, except where Lowland Scots words have been set to a borrowed Gaelic air.

Gaelic song refrains are to be found in a multiplicity of forms of from one line to six or eight or more. A very common form is that of three lines, of which the third is a repetition of the first, as:

> Tha m'inntinn trom, cha tog mi fonn,
> 'S e falbh nan tonn a shàraich mi,
> Tha m'inntinn trom, cha tog mi fonn.

> My mind is heavy, I cannot sing;
> Wave journeying has wearied me,
> My mind is heavy, I cannot sing.

Refrains may be entirely composed of meaningless vocables, as in the labour songs. More often, in songs of general use and theme, a refrain will have a mixture of meaningful lines and meaningless vocables,[2] as:

[1] Hamish Henderson, Senior Research Fellow, School of Scottish Studies, Edinburgh University, adds: 'See two songs in Ord's *Bothy Songs and Ballads*: "The Milking Song" and "The Quern Lilt". These are imitations by the Morayshire poet Robert Jamieson, but are probably based on collected fragments.' This hardly affects materially the writer's statement however.

[2] William Matheson observes: 'Refrains with some meaningful words seem to be of later date than those consisting entirely of meaningless vocables.'

> Bheir mi o hu o ho
> (sung three times)
> I am sad without you.

or:

> Rising today I am melancholy,
> Brown-haired girl of the cattle;
> *Hi ri o hu ho ho eileadh*,
> Brown-haired girl of the cattle.

Often we find a single 'horo' or other vocable syallable by way of interjection at the beginning or end of an otherwise meaningful line, as in the well-known 'Horo! My nut-brown Maiden', or '*Hi ri oro*, I am weary'; or '*Fire faire*, excellent is he', etc. Such matters however, particularly of verse forms, belong to the study of Gaelic rather than of music.

One or two individual types of song are worth a mention before we leave the subject. There is the common form of narrative song in eight-line stanzas, of which '*Mo Rùn Geal Og*' is an example. This may be heard in a recording by the fine traditional singer of Barra, Ruairi Iain Bhàin (Roderick Mackinnon), now no longer alive.[1]

Mention should be made too of the class of song with short verses and long chorus of meaningless vocables resembling those of the waulking song, but of a different origin, and not included in the waulking repertory. One of the best examples is the fine song of '*A Mhic Iain 'ic Seumais*', which may be dated at 1601, from its association with the Battle of Carinish, fought in that year. The song is said to have been improvised by the foster-mother of Donald 'son of John son of James' MacDonald, as she withdrew the arrows from his body and dressed his wounds on the field of battle. The foster-mother ordered her womenfolk to sing the chorus loudly so that his cries should not be heard by his followers to their dismay and discouragement while the fight was still in progress. The tune is a remarkable one and worth quoting in this fine version as sung by Calum Johnston of Barra. It has also been recorded from Ruairi Iain Bhàin.

A MHIC IAIN 'IC SHEUMAS
O John, son of James

Singer: Calum Johnston, Isle of Barra.   Recorded by John L. Campbell.
♩ = 69   Transcribed F. C.

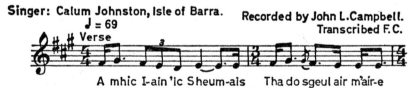

A mhic I-ain 'ic Sheum-ais   Tha do sgeul air m'air-e

---

[1] *Gaelic Folksongs from the Isle of Barra*, recorded by J. L. Campbell, issued by The Linguaphone Institute for the Folklore Institute of Scotland.

Air fail al ill leò, — Air fail al ill leò,

Latha Blàr na Féithe Bha feum air mo lean-abh,

Hi éil-e hé hò hi ri__ sa bhò rò ho hù o,

chall éil-ibh ò hi ri__ hò__ ro hi__ hò__hi.

Translation (F.C. from Tolmie):

          O thou son of John-son-of-James,
          For tidings of thee I am waiting,
(Refrain)   Air fail al ill leò, etc. (meaningless)
          On the day of the Battle of the Bog,
          [The aid of] my child was [sorely] needed,
(Refrain)   Hi éile hé hò, etc.

PUIRT-A-BEUL (Mouth-music)

Most people will have heard on the radio these Gaelic songs for providing, by vocal means, music for dancing; for the spectacle of dancing to mouth-music is now a common one on television. Few however even among folk-song collectors will have seen them used for this purpose in a true folk background, for though the singing of them for their own sake is widely popular, the use of puirt-a-beul for dancing, though it is a genuine enough tradition, seems always to have been a kind of marginal one. Puirt-a-beul never seems to have been used *extensively* for the dance, and the music of an instrument has always been preferred when it is available.

The word 'port' is defined in the Gaelic dictionaries as 'a tune played upon an instrument', and it was often used to denote in particular a piece of music for the Highland harp or clarsach, of which a few examples such as 'Rory Dall's Port', 'Port Athole', 'Port Gordon', etc. still exist in the form of song airs. A port-a-beul on this definition could therefore be described as a piece of instrumental music (i.e. for the pipes or fiddle) adapted for and sung by the voice.

This would of course imply that the tunes were first composed for the musical instrument and adapted later to vocalization; and such does indeed seem to be the case. It is of course impossible to be dogmatic about this, or to deny that puirt-a-beul *could* have existed before either the pipes or the fiddle were invented. The general opinion is however that as a form of music puirt-a-beul is of comparatively modern date— probably as late as eighteenth century.

James Ross in *A Classification of Gaelic Folk-song*[1] states it as his opinion that—'The *raison d'être* of this song type is the memorizing of dance tunes. . . . The practice of singing dance tunes such as strathspeys and reels appears to be of modern origin. . . . The puirt-a-beul are popularly supposed to have originated as a result of the religious opposition to musical instruments such as the bagpipes and the fiddle, which was at its strongest in the middle of the nineteenth century. . . . It is unlikely however that the mouth-music was widely used as an accompaniment to the actual dance. Its origin is more likely to lie in the desire of instrumentalists to perpetuate their favourite tunes after the destruction or banning of the instruments.'

Alexander Carmichael, gives a vivid account in his *Carmina Gadelica*[2] of this insensate destruction of musical instruments by the persuasion of the nineteenth-century revivalists or the compulsion of ministers and elders in the Highlands. He quotes a devastating conversation with a woman in the Isle of Lewis and reports her as saying 'The good men and the good ministers who arose, did away with the songs and the stories, the music and the dancing, the sports and the games that were *perverting the minds and ruining the souls* of the people, leading them to folly and stumblings' (the writer's italics).

'But how', Carmichael asked, 'did the people themselves come to discard their sports and pastimes?' 'Oh the good ministers and the good elders preached against them and went among the people and brought them to forsake their follies and return to wisdom. They made the people break and burn their pipes and fiddles. If there was a foolish man here and there who demurred, the good ministers and the good elders themselves broke and burnt their instruments.'

The writer himself has had experience of the stultifying effect of such religious bigotry in the Highlands in present times. In particular, a few

[1] *Scottish Studies*, Vol. I, 1957. Edinburgh.
[2] *Carmina Gadelica*, by Alexander Carmichael, Vol. I. Introduction p. xxx. Oliver and Boyd, Edinburgh, 1928.

years ago he went to an outlying district of the Isle of Harris which, he had positive information, was rich in both songs and folk tales. One of the modern revivalists who still periodically plague the west Highlands, had unfortunately been campaigning in that very district only a few weeks before; and when the writer got there, he met with a complete stone-wall of evasion and polite refusal even to discuss such things as the existence of folk-songs and tales. He was forced to come away empty-handed. Heaven alone knows how much priceless folk material must have been lost through these muddled and misguided men.[1]

This burning of the instruments reached its worst during the religious revivals of the early nineteenth century. There was an earlier period of Scottish history however when for more patriotic and desirable reasons the people of the Highlands may have set words to their pipe tunes as a means of preserving them, and without which many must have otherwise become forgotten. This was in the years following the collapse of the Jacobite rising of the 'forty-five' after the battle of Culloden. By a court order, following the Disarming Act of 1746, the bagpipe was deemed to be 'an instrument of war',[2] of which the possessor if discovered was liable to severe punishment, even to transportation and exile.[3] This period of suppression lasted for the best part of forty years.

Most puirt-a-beul have actual words, as distinct from the meaningless vocables of the labour songs, though such vocables are by no means non-existent. The words are as a rule, nonsensical, ludicrous, humorous or satirical, as in the well-known 'Brochan Lom':

BROCHAN LOM

Broch-an lom, ta-na lom, broch-an lom sùgh-ain;

Broch-an lom, ta-na lom, broch-an ta-na sùgh-ain,

---

[1] The writer must also put on record however the courtesy of the various Churches in the Highlands in allowing him to record their music, including the very beautiful congregational singing of the psalms in Gaelic in the protestant areas.

[2] Cf. Hume Brown; *History of Scotland*, Vol. III., p 261.

[3] One of the Jacobite prisoners tried at York for playing or being in possession of bagpipes, i.e. 'an instrument of war', was condemned and executed, November 1746. See *The Macleods* by I. F. Grant, p. 490 (Faber & Faber, London, 1959).

Broch-an lom, ta-na lom, broch-an ta-na sùgh-ain,

Broch-an ta-na ta-na ta-na, broch-an ta-na sùgh-ain.

Verse

Thug-aibh ar-an dha na gill-ean leis a' broch-an sùgh-ain,

thug-aibh ar-an dha na gill-ean leis a' broch-an sùgh-ain,

thug-aibh ar-an dha na gill-ean leis a' broch-an sugh-ain,

thug-aibh ar-an dha na gill-ean leis a' broch-an sùgh-ain.

Ionian Mode

Scale

BROCHAN LOM

The gist of the words in English is:

> Meagre porridge, meagre gruel,
> Meagre porridge, meagre gruel,
> (*repeated*)
> Thin porridge, thin, thin,
> Thin porridge like sowans
> (*three times*)
> Give bread to the lads
> With the sowans-like porridge,
> (*three times*)
> Meagre porridge, meagre porridge
> Thin porridge like sowans.[1]

[1] Sowans is a dish made by boiling the steeped husks of oats in water (*Chambers's Scots Dialect Dictionary*—there spelt *sowens*).

'MacThomas has a dirk' is a good example of the satirical port-a-beal. The wearing of a *biodag* or dirk, which is usually silver-mounted and topped by a cut cairngorm or other semi-precious stone, in distinction to the *sgian* or ordinary knife, implied a certain status; and anyone who wore one who was not adjudged to possess the necessary personal qualification was fair game for the satirist. There are several such dirk satires, all with the same underlying theme. Once the satire had been composed and set to a tune, it became sufficient to play the tune of it, even without the words, in the hearing of the victim of the satire, to commit a deadly insult. It is said that the subject of this particular satire was so infuriated at the tune being played in his hearing that he drew the said dirk and stabbed the piper with it, killing him. He is said to have stood trial for the deed and to have been acquitted, on the grounds that the avenging of such an insult was justified!

THA BIODAG AIR MAC THÒMAIS

97

Translation

Tom's son wears a dirk
There are buckles on his shoes
Tom's son wears a dirk
Though well would a knife suffice him.
A dirk clinks on him
Above the band of his trousers
Son of the awkward old man
Well would a knife suffice him!

In the following translations of port-a-beul words, we see a mixture of actual words and meaningless vocables:

DHOMHNUILL, A DHOMHNUILL!
(O Donald, Donald!)

O Donald, Donald, the wether has gone off to the moor,
O Donald, Donald, he has gone off with the tether.
  Hinn hainn hura-bhi,
  Isobel and Elizabeth,
  Hinn hainn hurrabhi
Calum's daughter and Donald!

Many puirt-a-beul words are simply settings of the well-known Scottish dance tunes. Here is a translation of the port-a-beul words of 'Gille-Calum' the tune for the Scottish Highland sword dance:

Gille-Callum two pennies,
Gille-Callum two pennies,
Gille-Callum two pennies
Gille-Callum half-penny.

His wife makes a wry mouth,
At the two pennies;
His wife makes a wry mouth,
And takes the half-penny.

The mouse bore a litter of sows,
She brought home a faggot of firewood,
A plate of meal, a hamper of heels (?)
Gillie-Callum half-penny!

Not all puirt-a-beul are in the rhythms of reel, strathspey or jig, and some of them would seem as if they must have been devised for dances which have become forgotten. In Nova Scotia the writer has seen the descendants of Scottish Highland stock perform step-dances around a row of lighted candles, which they extinguish one by one in the course of the dance with the sole of their foot, if possible without knocking the candle over. Superficially these dances resemble the tap-dance or soft-shoe dance of the popular musical theatre or music hall, but the dancers claim them to be traditional Scottish dances, brought over to Canada by their forefathers. Whether this is actually the case or not, the dances are, as far as the writer is aware, quite unknown in Scotland.

Alexander Carmichael describes or mentions the names of a number of all but forgotten Highland dances in *Carmina Gadelica* (vol. I, page 207) and says that 'the music was played by a piper or fiddler or sung as a port-a-beul mouth-tune, by a looker-on or by the performers themselves'. These include the curious ritual dance of '*Cailleach an Dudain*'[1] (Carlin of the mill-dust), '*Cath nan Coileach*' (The combat of the cocks), '*Turraban nan tunnag*' (Waddling of the ducks), '*Ruidhleadh nan coileach dubha*' (Reel of the blackcocks), and '*Cath nan Curaidh*' (Contest of the warriors).

Valuable research on the music of these dances and on the dances themselves has been done in the Hebrides, particularly in the Isle of Eigg by J. F. and T. M. Flett, who have published an informative article on the subject in the *Journal of the English Folk Dance and Song Society* (Volume VII, No. 2. 1953, 'Some Hebridean Folk Dances').

[1] The writer noted a tune for '*Cailleach an Dùdain*' on the Isle of Eriskay in 1951. As this is different from the tune collected by the Fletts, of whom see below, it may be of interest to include it here:

CAILLEACH AN DUDAIN
Noted by Francis Collinson

Port-a-beul words for '*Cailleach an Dùdain* from Alexander Carmichael's Manuscript now in Edinburgh Library, are reproduced by J. F. and T. M. Flett in their article in the *E.F.D.S.S. Journals* mentioned above and may be seen there.

Father Allan Macdonald, the folk-lorist of Eriskay says in his notebooks more than once however that it was danced to the pipes (information from J. L. Campbell).

Here is a port-a-beul tune from the Isle of Barra which on account of its striking and unusual cross rhythms could hardly have been intended for an ordinary reel, and may well have been used for some such dance as those mentioned above, and now forgotten:

Ruileadh cailleach, sheatadh cailleach

Singer: Calum Johnston, Isle of Barra

Ruil-eadh caill-each sheat-adh caill-each, Ruil-eadh caill-each

ris a' bhal(a)g, Ruil-eadh caill-each sheat-adh caill-each,

Ruil-eadh caill-each ris a' bhal-(a)g, 'Ruil-eadh caill-each

sheat-adh caill-each, Ruil-eadh caill-each ris a' bhal-(a)g,

Dann-sadh caill-each ri caill-ich 's sheat-adh caill-each

ris a' bhal-(a)g, Ruil-eadh caill-each ri caill-ich,

Dann-sadh caill-each ri caill-ich Ruil-eadh caill-

each ri caill-ich 's sheat-adh caill-each ris a' bhal-(a)g.

Mixolydian or Ionian with variable 7th *

Scale

* Cf. note 1 on next page.

RUILEUDH CAILLEACH

Translation:

> An old woman would reel,
> An old woman would set,
> An old woman would reel to the bag,
> An old woman would dance to an old woman,
> And an old woman would set to the bag,
>
> An old woman would reel to an old woman,
> An old woman would dance to an old woman,
> An old woman would reel to an old woman,
> An old woman would set to the bag.

THE FAIRY SONGS (Orain Shìdhe)

This is not the place to discuss the existence or non-existence of the fairies. We must however set down the fact that Gaelic song includes quite a number of so-called fairy songs. Whether or not the modern Gael has any real belief in 'the little people' is also beside the point. What matters as far as this book is concerned is that, whatever its origin, this music does exist as part of the native tradition.

The 'fairy music' is in a curious way always looked upon by the Gael as a class of music apart from the rest. For this reason, even the adult-minded Gael will always be prepared to discuss in all seriousness whether or not a particular song is a 'fairy song' in the sense of whether or not it belongs to this tradition of fairy origin, a tradition which obviously stems from an age of greater superstition. It certainly does not necessarily mean that he himself 'believes in fairies', though it must be admitted that some credence in such ultra-normal phenomena does still exist[2] in the Highlands. So it comes about that, in the *Gesto Collection of Highland Music* for instance, we find a song '*Cailleach Beinne Bhric*' (The old woman of Ben Bhreac) labelled in the most matter of fact way and without inverted commas, as a fairy song (this in English and not in Gaelic).

The fairy tradition as far as the songs are concerned, ranges from such

---

[1] Here we meet for the first time in the book with a scale possessing a *variable note*. In the course of the tune we find both B flat and B natural, the flat and the natural seventh. We therefore have the choice of thinking of the scale of the tune either as a mixolydian scale (which has the flat seventh) with the addition of an alternative natural seventh; or as an Ionian (i.e. Major) scale (which has the natural seventh) with in addition an alternative flattened seventh. A variable note in a scale, not always the seventh, is a common feature in later Scots music of the late eighteenth and early nineteenth century, particularly the fiddle music.

[2] Cf. *The Fairy Faith in Celtic Countries*, W. Y. E. Wentz 1911. (Wentz visited Barra in search of fairy stories.)

supernatural creatures as the water-horse (*each-uisge*) which was said to inhabit the lochs and rivers, and which will be looked upon by most as pure fantasy, to a race of 'little people' resembling the human race but not of it, who were said to live in the *dùn sìdhean* or *sìodhbrugh*, the fairy hill or mound. Nineteenth-century writers, headed by Andrew Lang, have attempted to rationalize this last as a folk-memory of an earlier race of human beings who lived in the beehive dwellings and wheel-houses which were of an underground or semi-underground type, 'subterraneans' as Kirk called them in his *Secret Commonwealth*, possibly a conquered race who lived apart on the fringes of human habitation.[1] J. F. Campbell of Islay's exposition[2] is typical. He says:

Men do believe in fairies though they will not readily confess the fact. And although I do not myself believe that fairies *are*, in spite of the strong evidence offered, I believe there once was a small race of people in these islands, who are remembered as fairies, for the fairy belief is not confined to the Highlanders of Scotland.

'*They*' are always represented as living in green mounds. They pop up their heads when disturbed by people treading on their houses. They steal children. They seem to live on familiar terms with the people about them when they treat them well, to punish them when they ill-treat them.

. . . I lately saw a house in South Uist found in the sand hills close to the sea. It was built of loose boulders, it was circular, and had recesses in the sides; it was covered when found, and it was full of sand. . . .[3]

[1] Since writing this chapter the writer must frankly admit to finding that not all his Gaelic-speaking friends agree on the question of the fairies. One most responsible person claims that 'they *have been seen* in Barra and in the Isle of Muck in his time'; another 'that they seem to be definitely a psychic phenomenon'. For that matter the writer himself has met two people in different islands of the Western Isles who have claimed 'to know someone who has seen the fairies'—one who saw them being the father of the informant—but he has never met anyone *at first hand* who has claimed to have seen them himself.
Father Allan, priest on Eriskay, records in his notebooks the native tradition that the fairies are the angels who remained *neutral* when Lucifer rebelled. As a punishment they were cast out of heaven and condemned to live for a long space of time on earth; this time is now nearly up. (Information from J. L. Campbell.)
[2] J. F. Campbell, *Popular Tales of the West Highlands*, I, xvc, xcvi.
[3] This was doubtless a 'wheel-house' of which another such was found at Kilphedar in South Uist by a friend of the writer a few years ago. The writer has seen one of the smaller 'beehive' dwellings in one of the islands of the Inner Hebrides. On poking about among the sand with which it had become filled, he himself found in the stones of the doorway a piece of an ancient knife-blade, probably put there to keep the fairies away—which would suggest that the inhabitants of these dwellings themselves had a fear of the fairies, and took the acknowledged remedy of putting a piece of iron in the doorway as a charm to keep them out. Another piece of what was obviously the same knife-blade had been previously found and removed by the archaeologist friend of the writer, who had opened up the dwelling a month or so before.

Let us see what the people of the Hebrides say of the fairies [continues Campbell]. There was a woman benighted with a pair of calves, and as she went for shelter to a knoll, she began driving the peg of the tether into it. The hill opened, and she heard as though there was a pot hook 'glee-gashing' on the side of the pot. A woman put up her head, and as much as was above her waist, and said, 'What business hast thou to disturb this tulman, in which I make my dwelling?' This might be a description of one of my Lapp friends, and probably is a description of such a dwelling as I saw in South Uist. If the people slept as Lapps sleep, with their feet to the fire, a woman outside might have driven a peg very near one of the sleepers, and she might have stood on a seat and poked her head out of the chimney.

The magic about the beasts (*i.e.* the fairies) is but the mist of antiquity; and the fairy was probably a Pict. Who will say who the Pict may have been?

Perhaps it is worth adding a single sentence by Andrew Lang upon the subject, who says:

We cannot deny absolutely that some such memory of an earlier race, a shy and fugitive people who used weapons of stone, may conceivably play its part in the fairy legend.[1]

To all the above it must be added that informed archaeological and ethnological opinion puts the date at which these underground dwellings ceased to be used at between A.D. 200 and 230.[2] It is unthinkable that folk memory could extend so far back.[3]

To return to the songs: in addition to the two classes of fairy songs we have mentioned, i.e. the fantastic and the 'pseudo-rational', in which the songs themselves are attributed to fairy origin and composition, there is a third class of song which, though associated with the fairies, is of self-evident human origin, as for instance the lament of a human being for the loss of a fairy lover. Such songs, though of admittedly human composition, are nevertheless included, because of their association with the fairy world, in the category of fairy songs.

Of the first class of fairy song, the song of the water-horse or *each-uisge*, and such creatures of fantasy, several have been noted down. The

[1] Andrew Lang's edition of *The Secret Commonwealth of Elves, Fauns, and Fairies*, London, 1893.

[2] Cf. *The Souterrains of Southern Pictland*, p. 24, F. T. Wainwright (Routledge and Kegan Paul, London, 1963).
The 'Wheelhouse Dwellings' and related structures may be dated from about 100 B.C. to the first and second centuries A.D. (Information from Dr Anne Ross, author of *Pagan Celtic Britain*; Routledge and Kegan Paul—in preparation.)

[3] It has been somewhere asserted, though the writer is unable to supply the reference that the popular memory for local events runs for about 350 years.

water-horse had the power of assuming the likeness of a handsome man, and in this guise was wont to trick a maiden into marrying him. The most frequently recurring story in the songs is how the duped girl discovers by the sand in his hair and on his breast, while he is asleep, that he is the water-horse in disguise. She flees from him, leaving both him and the child she has borne him. The water-horse tries to tempt her to return to him by singing pathetic songs to the child, lamenting that it is 'without fire and shelter, forlorn and wailing for her without ceasing'. Francis Tolmie gives three of these lamentations or lullabies of the water-horse. (Tolmie Nos. 5, 6 and 7.) The melodies are striking and beautiful, and well worth looking up.

Concerning the creature further, it may be worth a quotation from the *Tour of the Hebrides and Western Islands* by the distinguished Border scholar Dr John Leyden. Writing from Callander on 16 July 1800, he says: 'Our guide informed us that the people of the vale had been a good deal alarmed by the appearance of that unaccountable being, the water-horse (*each-uisge*) during the spring, which had not been seen since the catastrophe of Corlevrann,[1] *the wood of woe*, when he carried into the loch fifteen children who had broken Pace Sunday.' The inference would appear to be that the children met their fate as a result of breaking the Sabbath, of the sanctity of which the water-horse, in that part of the country, would seem to have been the guardian!

Of the songs said to have been composed by the fairies of the 'little folk' type, most have for their theme the bewailing of a tragic love-affair between a fairy and a mortal. One of these, a song of Hebridean locale, is well known to Lowland Scots through the words set to it by James Hogg, the Ettrick Shepherd. This is, *Buain an Rainich*[2] (Pu'in' bracken). The story is of a maiden who had a fairy lover who used to help her in her tasks of cutting bracken and drying peats on the hillside. Her brothers, finding out her secret, hid her in a distant part of the country. The fairy was afterwards heard lamenting her absence in the song:

BUAIN A' FHROINICH

Tha mi sgìth 's mi leam fhìn   buain a' throin-ich,

---

[1] A Gaelic colleague says 'This must be *Coille a' Bhròin*, badly distorted.'
[2] Alternatively, *Buain a' fhroinich*, as in the music example.

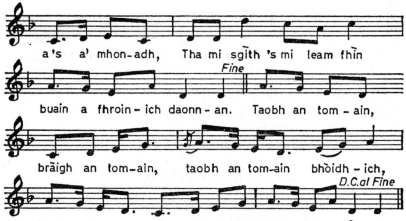

a 's a' mhon-adh, Tha mi sgìth 's mi leam fhìn
buain a fhroin-ich daonn-an. Taobh an tom-ain,
bràigh an tom-ain, taobh an tom-ain bhòidh-ich,
Taobh an tom-ain, bràigh an tom-ain, huil-e lath-a m'on-ar.

Translation:

I am weary and alone, pulling the bracken on the moor; I am weary and alone, always pulling the bracken.

Beside the knoll, on top of the knoll,
Beside the pretty knoll; beside the knoll,
On top of the knoll; every day alone.

In another song on the same theme, '*Sealgair a' Choilich Bhuidhe*' (The hunter of the yellow cock) it is a human youth and a fairy woman who are concerned. Here the young man's brothers follow him secretly to the fairy tryst and put him to death with an arrow from the bow. It is his fairy mistress who sings the lament:

SEALGAIR A' CHOILICH BHUIDHE

Singers: Calum and Annie Johnston, Isle of Barra

Transcribed E.C.

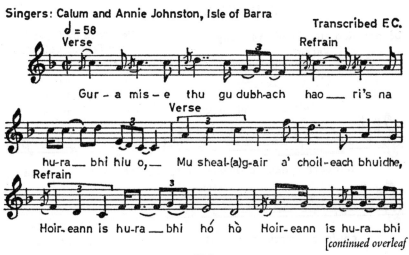

Gur-a mis-e thu gu dubh-ach hao ___ ri's na
hu-ra ___ bhi hiu o, ___ Mu sheal-(a)g-air a' choil-each bhuidhe,
Hoir-eann is hu-ra ___ bhi hó hò Hoir-eann is hu-ra ___ bhi

[continued overleaf

hó   hi   ro   o   Hoir-eann is hu-ra___ bhi hó hò.

Translation by James Ross:

(*The fairy sings*)	The Sorrow is mine
(*Refrain*)	Hao ri 's na hu ra bhi hiu o.
	For the hunter of the yellow cock,
(*Refrain*)	Hoireann is hu ra bhi ho ho,
	Hoireann is hu ra bhi ho hi ri o,
	Hoireann is hu ra bhi ho ho.

I heard your scream on the hillside,
But I did not heed it
Until I heard the voice of the raven.
A thousand curses on the brothers;
They have left before me a mirror,—
The blood of your chest, of your mouth
And of your throat,—
And you lying in the peat moss.

The following fairy song, collected in the isle of Vatersay by the writer and a colleague, has a double interest. The story of the song, as told by the singer, is of a woman who had a child by a fairy lover. 'Her people were hostile to her, and made her leave the child close to the fairy mound where his father would find him. In the morning, the fairy man arose and found the child beside the hillock. He made the song and this is it':

A MHOR A GHAOIL

Singer: Nan Mackinnon, Vatersay   Recorded by James Ross
and Francis Collinson

Dh'éir - ich mi moch, dh'éir-ich mi moch

b'theàrr nach d'dh'éir - ich, Mo chreach léir na

chuir a mach mi; Hill ó bhà hó, hill ó bha hó.

Scale

as major scale with gap at fourth.
(The melody however centres round F♯
as a secondary final)

A MHÓR A GHAOIL

Translation by James Ross:

> I rose early, I rose early,
> It were better that I had not;
> I deplore what sent me outside.
>
> My darling[1] was by the side of a hillock
> With no fire, no protection or shelter.
>
> Mór, my darling, return to your little son,
> And I will give you a beautiful speckled ribbon.
>
> I will give you wine, I will give you wine,
> And everything you desire, I will give you
> A bright speckled ribbon.

The song possesses a secondary interest also in that a number of the lines are identical with those of the lamentation of the *each-uisge* or water-horse already described, and the song may in fact be an example of this which has been given another story. For a complete text of this song, see *Carmina Gadelica*, Vol. V, p. 136.

Not all the fairy songs are on the theme of disappointed love however. Francis Tolmie gives us the traditional song of the fairy who appeared in the castle of Dunvegan, took the infant heir to the Macleods into her arms out of the cradle, and sang a fairy lullaby to him, leaving behind her the famous fairy flag of the Macleods. This lullaby was regarded afterwards as a charm to protect the infant heir of Macleod from harm, and no woman was said ever afterwards to be allowed to nurse the infant heir of Macleod who could not sing it to him.[2]

In another song, "*S olc an obair do theachdairean cadal*', a fairy sings to tell a man waiting for the tide to recede so that he may cross a ford on a journey, that his wife has died in his absence.

[1] 'My darling' here refers to the fairy's baby by Mór, whom Mór has left lying on the fairy mound. In the next verse, 'My darling' refers of course to Mór herself.
[2] The tune of the 'Fairy Flag' of Dunvegan is given by Francis Tolmie. *Tolmie Collection*, No. 20.

'S OLC AN OBAIR DO THEACHDAIREAN CADAL

Singer: Annie Johnston, Isle of Barra

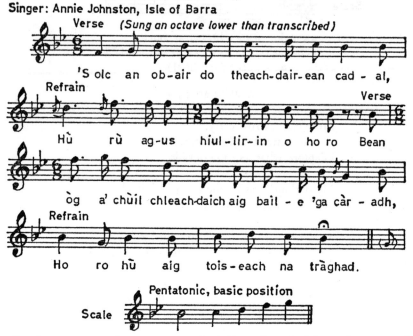

In subsequent verses the extra note on the B flat at the end of the 9/8 bar, required by the word *bean*, does not recur, and the bar becomes a straightforward 6/8.

Translation:

Sleep is bad work for messengers[1]

(*Refrain*)   Hu ru agus huillirinn o ho ro

The young woman of the curled ringlets—
    being laid out in the township;

(*Refrain*)   Ho ro hu, at the beginning of the ebb tide.

In yet another song, '*E o ho, a Raghnaill ud thall*', a fairy woman sings to entice a young man to cross a running stream to her. Fairies are traditionally said to be unable to cross running water.

E HO RO A RAGHNAILL UD THALL

Singer: Calum Johnston   Recorded by John L. Campbell

[1] i.e. Sleeping is a bad thing for messengers to be doing.

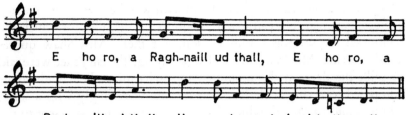

E ho ro, a Ragh-naill ud thall, E ho ro, a Ragh-naill ud thall, Hu o ho, nach im-ich thu nall.

Translation:

> E ho ro, Ranald yonder!
> E ho ro, Ranald yonder!
> E ho ro, Ranald yonder!
> Hu o ho, won't you come over?

Of the third class of fairy song, that of which, although included in the fairy category, the human origin is self evident, there are a number of examples. There is for instance the song of the young girl whose mother discovers that she is having clandestine meetings with a fairy. She plaits into the girl's hair the leaves of a plant which are a charm against fairies. The fairy, unable to reach her because of the charm she wears, leaves her for ever; and it is the girl herself who composes and sings the lament.

Another example, '*A ghaoil, lig dhachaidh gu m' mhàthair mi*' (My love, let me home to my mother) of which Margaret Fay Shaw gives words and tune in her book,[1] is of a young girl who, expecting to meet her sweetheart at the cattlefold, is met by the *each-uisge* or water-horse, who forcibly prevents her from returning home. Her song is an appeal to the *each-uisge* to let her go home to her mother as he found her. Miss Shaw also gives '*Mo chùbhrachan*', the lament of the woman whose infant has been stolen by the fairies, and who sings despairingly as she searches the hillside for it: 'I searched the hill from end to end to the edge of the streams; I did not find my *cùbhrachan*.' The word is a term of endearment. The song is widespread, and seems to be particularly well known in the Isle of Skye.

Finally there is the song of '*Crodh Chailein*', too well known to need quotation. Of this, one story is that Colin's beautiful young wife was spirited away, Mary Rose fashion, by the fairies on the day of her wedding. They allowed her to return each day to milk Colin's cows, but cast a spell over her so that she was invisible to him, although he could hear her voice as she sang her milking song. The spell lasted for a year and a day, after which she was restored to him. Another story, given to

[1] *Folksongs and Folklore of South Uist.*

Margaret Fay Shaw, was that Colin himself was the fairy, who married a mortal woman. His cattle were the deer on the hills, for which she composed the song as a milking song for them. Miss Shaw quotes another writer, Mrs Mary MacKellar, as saying, 'the fairy race were said to milk the deer on the mountain tops, charming them with songs composed to a fairy melody'. This ties up interestingly with a song, '*An robh thu 's a bheinn*', which the late Miss Annie Johnston sent to the writer, in which the words refer to this milking of the deer on the mountain tops.

Volume V of *Carmina Gadelica* by Alexander Carmichael gives the texts of some thirty fairy songs,[1] with copious notes by Carmichael and by the late Professor Angus Matheson, who edited the volume. These are however without music, as unfortunately are many other publications of traditional Gaelic poetry where the tunes would have been of great interest.

Of the extent to which fairy belief exists today in Scotland, Dr Anne Ross, Research Fellow in Custom and Belief, School of Scottish Studies, Edinburgh University, contributes the following note:

'Belief in fairies is one of the most difficult things to investigate, because if people really do believe in them, they are very chary indeed about mentioning them, and also often ashamed of their latent belief because it goes against their Church faith. In the islands, I have frequently met with the attitude that, like the mermaids, they *did* exist, but (like the herring shoals round the west coast) they have gone. They did dance round the fairy knolls and people were carried off by them, but it doesn't happen any more. In Breadalbane, I have met with more instances of actual continuing belief, and have met people who have had direct contact with people who have claimed all their lives to have fairy experiences. Some old people say, "I have never actually seen them myself, but I know people who have, and although *I* haven't seen them, they are there just the same." So I think we can by no means conclude that people in the Highlands today have stopped believing in the little people (some of them claim they are not so little, being two or three feet in height), but where a latent belief survives, it is not lucky or desirable to speak of it.

'I have never yet met the attitude that fairies are silly or never were, and always they are treated with respect as something that the old people actually believed in, and sometimes still do. They were very much associated with magic wells, Bronze Age burial mounds, glacial cairns, etc.'

[1] Airs of at least six of them have been preserved. Two of them are here. J. L. Campbell.

A SELECTION OF WORKS FOR THE STUDY OF GAELIC FOLK-SONG

The Francis Tolmie Collection of a hundred and five songs of Occupation from the Western Isles of Scotland. *Journal of the Folk Song Society*, Vol. **IV**. London, 1911.

Amy Murray, *Father Allan's Island*, New York, 1920. Reprinted The Moray Press, Edinburgh, 1936.

Margaret Fay Shaw; *Folksongs and Folklore of South Uist*, London, 1952. (The excellent bibliography in this book should also be consulted.)

J. L. Campbell; *Gaelic Folksongs from the Isle of Barra*, Booklet and set of field recordings; The Linguaphone Institute, London (undated, *c.* 1950).

Professor Otto Andersson; 'On Gaelic Folk Music from the Isle of Lewis', *The Budkavlen*, 1952, Abo, Finland. (Offprint in English.)

Keith Norman MacDonald, *The Gesto Collection of Highland Music*, Leipzig, 1895.

Mrs Kennedy Fraser, *Songs of the Hebrides*, London, 1909 *et seq. From the Hebrides*, Mrs Kennedy Fraser, Glasgow, 1925. The Introductions to the volumes are useful. (The actual arrangements are too freely adapted to provide material for scientific study—see article in the *Scots Magazine*, January 1958 by J. L. Campbell.)

Donald Campbell, *A Treatise on the Language, Poetry and Music of the Highland Clans* (with music) (which however is badly transcribed). Edinburgh, 1892.

Keith Norman Macdonald, *Puirt-a-Beul*, Glasgow, 1901 (tunes in Sol-fa notation).

Margaret Fay Shaw, contributions of six and seven Hebridean Folk Songs in *Journal of the English Folk Dance and Song Society* (London, 1943 and 1944).

Lucy Broadwood, Contributions of Gaelic Songs to *Journal of the Folk Song Society*, 1931 and to *Journal of the English Folk Dance and Song Society*, 1932.

Patrick MacDonald, *A Collection of Highland Vocal Airs*, Edinburgh, 1784.

Simon Fraser, *The Airs and Melodies Peculiar to the Highlands of Scotland and the Isles*, Edinburgh and London, 1816 (Revised Edition 1874).

J. L. Campbell and Francis Collinson *The MacCormick Collection of Waulking Songs* (The Clarendon Press, 1969).

THE TUNES USED BY THE LATER GAELIC SONG WRITERS AND BARDS:
MATERIAL FOR STUDY

It is the common practice of the Gael to select an existing tune and compose verses to fit it, rather than compose a new tune for the song, or still less, to write the verses for someone else to set to music. To this extent the Gael and the Lowlander follow the same practice in Scots song—which is the practice of Burns and Ramsay and Lady Nairne. The difference between the two is that the Gael seldom writes verse which is *not* intended for singing.

Sometimes the Gaelic bard will specify a Lowland tune for his song, as—'Thro' the Wood Laddie', 'Tweedside', etc., both set down by Alasdair Mac Mhaistir Alasdair; 'Sweet Molly' by Rob Donn Mackay. or 'Wat ye wha I met Yestreen'[1] by William Ross; though more often perhaps an indisputably Gaelic tune is used.

Such tunes may be found in the various printed collections of Gaelic tunes, though not always specifically as song airs, some of these being among the fiddle or bagpipe collections. *The Gesto Collection of Highland Music*, though a fine collection, is typical of this, containing song airs both with and without the words, many of the latter being indistinguishable from instrumental tunes. The collections of Patrick MacDonald and of Simon Fraser of Knockie contain song airs, though those of the Fraser Collection are set out for the violin or pianoforte, while many of the airs in the MacDonald collection require a Gaelic scholar to identify them in relation to the songs to which they belong.

The tunes used by Rob Donn Mackay for his songs may be found in the edition of his works by Adam Gunn and Malcolm MacFarlane (Glasgow, 1899). 'The Songs of John MacCodrum' published by the *Scottish Gaelic Texts Society* (Edinburgh, 1938) give a number of tunes at the end of the book which are well worth study. A number of out-of-the-way Gaelic song airs, (though these are mostly of the anonymously traditional class rather than of the songs by named bards), are to be found in *Albyn's Anthology,* the collection of airs gathered in the Highlands by Alexander Campbell and set to Lowland Scots words by Sir Walter Scott.

The annual collections of Gaelic songs published by An Comunn Gaidhealach for their competitions, *Orain a' Mhòid* and *Coisir a' Mhòid*, form a valuable vade-mecum of Gaelic song tunes for those who are familiar with the sol-fa notation. Other useful collections are *Songs of the Gael* by Lachlan MacBean; and *Binneas nam Bàrd* (Bardic Melody) which contains some interesting Heroic Ballad tunes and words, by Malcolm MacFarlane, both published by Aneas Mackay (Stirling); *Songs of the Highlands* (Logan and Co., Inverness); *A' Choisir-Chiuil* (The St Columba Collection of Gaelic Songs); and *Minstrelsy of the Scottish Highlands*, by Alfred Moffat, both published by Bayley and Ferguson. *Orain na'h-Albainn*, edited Finlay Dun (Edinburgh, non-dated); *The Killin Collection of Gaelic Songs*, Charles Stewart (Edinburgh, 1884). (The last three mentioned have both Gaelic and English words.)

---

[1] A Gaelic colleague of the writer claims however that these tunes were also in general circulation in the Highlands as *Gaelic tunes*, and that the use of their Lowland titles was merely a convenient means of identifying them.

Amy Murray, *Father Allan's Island*, 'Child Songs from the Island of Youth' (article in *Celtic Review*); many articles in the *Transactions of the Gaelic Society of Inverness* (many of these in English).

MOURNING AND FUNERAL MUSIC (Seisig-bhàis; Tuiream)[1]
THE CORONACH

On the occasion of a death in a Gaelic household, it was the custom, up to about a hundred to a hundred and fifty years ago (and in isolated cases, much more recently), to sing the virtues and mourn the loss of the person who had died, to a special kind of music. This was usually sung by a professional mourning-woman, the *bean-tuiream* (plural, *Mnathan-tuirim*). It was a ritual which was looked upon as the proper right and need of everyone high or low, to ensure their happy passage to the next world, the *bàs sona* or 'happy death'. The mourning-woman was therefore as much a necessity to the Highland community as the midwife, and it is not surprising to read, in Carmichael's *Carmina Gadelica* (V, page 345) from the account of an informant, that 'there was a mid-wife and a mourning-woman in each townland in Barra'. The highland townland or township is often no more than a few scattered houses—a clachan, and it follows both that the Mnathan-tuirim must have been a numerous body and that their special music was often heard and well known.

By Carmichael's account, there were two distinct kinds of mourning song, one which was sung in the house, the '*Seisig-bhàis*' (literally the death-tune or air) often shortened to *seisig*, or *seis*; and one sung during the procession of the coffin to the burial ground, the '*tuiream*'. 'Keening'[2] is the popular name for the mourning song in the house, though this seems to be derived from Irish usage in the word '*caoineadh*', and the use of it in Scotland is probably an invention of the 'Celtic Twilight' school of writers.[3] The proper Scottish Gaelic word for the act of

---

[1] Also spelt 'tuirim' (*Carmina Gadelica*, Vol. V, p. 339).

[2] William Matheson observes: 'The anglicized form "Keening" has doubtless been borrowed from Ireland, but this does not prove that *caoineadh* was not used in the Highlands when the custom existed.'

[3] *Caoineadh* is also used in Scottish Gaelic. It is the usual word for weeping, e.g. in the Uists. *Gul* is the common word in Lewis. (Information from a Gaelic colleague.) John MacInnes observes: *gal* is what I always heard as a boy in Uig.

J. L. Campbell observes that *caoin* is used as the word for 'tune' in some dialects, and that he has come across this in Nova Scotia.

(The singing of Gaelic folk-songs is actively kept up among the descendants of Scottish Gaelic immigrants, many of their forebears being victims of the Clearances.)

mourning, according to Carmichael, is *gul*, *gal* or *guil* meaning weeping or wailing.

The song sung out of doors during the progress of the cortege, the *tuiream*, the elegy or dirge, is the 'coronach' of popular usage. The *Oxford English Dictionary* gives an Irish derivation for the word also, in *coranach*, from *comh* together or in fellowship, and *rànaich*, a crying, an outcry. It gives 1530 as the earliest recorded date of the use of the word in the popular English form of 'coronach'. This disposes of the statement, which the writer has heard himself, that the word was coined by Sir Walter Scott![1]

The *tuiream* or coronach for the ordinary member of the community would naturally be on a more modest scale than for someone of public importance, and would doubtless be performed by a single *bean-tuirim* of the locality. Nevertheless it seems always to have been something of a spectacular performance. Carmichael says, 'the bean-tuirim followed the body, every now and then striking the coffin with her hands like a drum and making all the din possible, and keeping time with the movements of the men (i.e. the bearers). All the virtues of the dead, and a few more, were mentioned and extolled, and the genealogy for many generations praised and lauded.'

The clapping of the hands seems to have been a characteristic of Gaelic mourning, and we may read of it in the words of such songs of lament for the dead as '*Griogal Cridhe*':

'I . . . beside thy grave, smiting my two hands.'

Joseph MacDonald in his *Compleat Theory of the Highland Bagpipe* refers to this striking of hands as the 'bais bhualadh'.

The tuiream or coronach at the funeral of an important person, and particularly of a chief, seems to have been a spectacle beyond all imagining. In the hands of Sir Walter Scott, as he describes it in the *Fair Maid of Perth*, at the funeral obsequies of the chief of the Clan Quhele, while his body was borne by funeral barge across the waters of Loch Tay to the burial ground of the chiefs on an island in the loch, the coronach is 'quite something', and worth reading again in this context. Scott gives also an interesting note on the coronach in Canto III of *The Lady of the Lake*, and adds what he describes as a 'literal translation' of a Gaelic coronach, though this has the appearance of being literary rather than literal! The form may be best studied in

[1] Hugh Barron has suggested in the *Transactions of the Gaelic Society of Inverness* that 'coronach' is not an actual Gaelic word; but it occurs in the Argyll Synod Minutes (when the Argyll Synod tried to forbid it). (Note by J. L. Campbell.)

Carmichael, who gives a number of texts in Gaelic and in translation (*Carmina Gadelica*, V, page 338).

Perhaps the strangest performance of the coronach was at the arrest of Simon Fraser, Lord Lovat, following the Jacobite rising of 1745. Being unable, from his great age and infirmity to ride on horseback to Fort Augustus, he was carried there on a litter. Knowing well that he was going to eventual execution for his part in the rising, he is said to have made the womenfolk sing his coronach by the side of the litter as he was carried along.

Both the *seisig-bhàis* and the *tuiream* seem to have had their proper traditional tunes. The late Duncan MacDonald of South Uist, a great teller of folk-tales with a wide knowledge of Gaelic song, sang two of these to the writer in company with Father (now Canon) John Mac-Cormick, then priest of Benbecula, in 1953. Unfortunately there was neither the means nor the time at that moment to record these; and the sudden death of Duncan MacDonald shortly afterwards means that these are now irrecoverably lost. The writer can only say that the music to which he sang them was of an extensive compass, with some resemblance to pibroch tunes.

Calum Johnston of Barra told the writer that he had once heard, and could remember, a tune for the house-mourning (the seis). He wrote this out for the writer in musical notation. Later this was recorded from him for the School of Scottish Studies by Miss Elizabeth Sinclair, the School's archivist, and transcribed by Miss Gillian Johnstone. The text seems to be mostly of the type of vocables without meaning, of the typical Gaelic refrain.

Mourning Song - Keening - (Seisig - bhais)

Singer: Calum Johnston   Transcribed by Gillian Johnstone

Pill-il-il iù ___ pill-il-ill-il-il-il Eó-ghainn; Pill-il-il

iù ___ pill-il-ill-il-il-il Eó-ghainn; Pill-il-il iù pill-il-ill-il-il-il

Eó-ghainn; Pill-il-il Aodh-ainn, Pill-il-iò h-e-óin Pill-il-il

iù   pill-il-il-il-il-il Eó-ghainn, Pill-il-il   iù   pill-il-il-il-il-il-il

Eó _ ghainn,   Pill-il - il   iù ,   pill-il-il-il - il-il

Eó-ghainn_ Pill-il-il   Aodh-ainn, Pill-il - iò   h-e - óin.

↑ = sung slightly sharper than written
↓ = sung slightly flatter than written

Calum Johnston also uses this same piece, music and words, as the subject of a story of a piper who, after tuning his pipes (with descriptive sounds) would begin to play them, 'and then it would be—"*Pill-il-il-iu*",' etc.

Calum Johnston has since informed the writer that the vocables here given refer to the use of the tune in the folk-tale only. He claims on the authority of a reliable informant that the melody itself was one of the *keening tunes*.

The writer would add however that the vocables '*pill-il-il-iu Eoghainn*' sound remarkably like the '*hullulu*' and still more, the '*ulogohne*' of the Irish keening as described by Pennant, and it seems possible that the vocables and tune may well have both been taken over for the purpose of an amusing and slightly satirical tale about the sound of the bagpipes.

This mourning of the dead in song is described by Pennant in his *Tour in Scotland* as being akin to the '*Ululatus*' of the Romans and the '*Ululoo*' of the Irish. The prevalence of the sound 'l-iu' in this example may therefore not be without significance.

What is even more interesting however is the resemblance of the unusual scale, to a scale described as 'the minor mode in Gaelic music' by Necker de Saussure, in his *Voyage en Ecosse* (1820). He sets out the intervals of this as follows:

Between 1st and 2nd   —   1 tone.
   „   2nd and 3rd   — $\frac{1}{2}$ tone.
   „   3rd and 4th   —   2 tones.
   „   4th and 5th   — $\frac{1}{2}$ tone.
   „   5th and Octave —   2 tones.

In musical notation the scale is as follows:

and is in effect, a *minor* version of the pentatonic scale.

Reverting to the Calum Johnston example; with allowances for some ambiguity of intonation, and having heard the singer's actual performance, the writer would say that the scale may reasonably be interpreted as follows:

Transposed down a fourth, it will be seen that, with latitude for the variable fifth note A and the additional hexatonic note B flat, the five-note basis of the scale is in fact the third inversion (fourth position) of Necker's minor pentatonic, i.e.:

Necker de Saussure adds that he only knows very few airs entirely in this mode. The writer himself has never come across any other example of it, and it is possible that the scale was confined to these mourning songs and dirges. The scale may however throw a new light on the scale of the bagpipe, which contains two intervals which are for some hitherto unexplained reason, *flattened*, i.e.:

Could it be that the flattening of the two intervals may have originated in a concession and partial approach to this minor pentatonic, as in the following?

For clearness, the modified intervals are here shown as *sharpened minor*

intervals, though in the actual scale of the pipes they approximate more nearly to flattened major intervals.

In the same connection it is worth remarking that Gaelic traditional singers of the old school frequently flatten the major third and sixth, in a manner somewhat akin to these intervals of the bagpipe scale, though not enough to constitute a minor interval. This may suggest in its turn a vocal derivation of the bagpipe scale not inconsistent with the one-time existence of this 'Gaelic minor mode'.

Necker de Saussure also remarks that '*Les laments ou airs funèbres resemblent beaucoup aux pibrocks* (sic); *mais le motif en est plus lent encore et plus lugubre.*' The writer only came across the remark after forming the same opinion, on hearing Duncan MacDonald sing the two tuiream airs described above, of their resemblance to pibroch tunes.

It may be appropriate to quote what Angus Fraser, son of Simon Fraser of Knockie has to say about these keening tunes. In his manuscript he says: 'The high laments sung of old by the bards at funeral processions were composed to different pathetic airs consisting of one or more phrases in slow sextuple (i.e. six-eight) time, and in stanzas of three verses, conformable to the melodic designs of the music.'

Sir Walter Scott, in his note to the coronach referred to above (*Lady of the Lake*, Canto III) remarks that even in his day the sung coronach was gradually falling into disuse, and was giving place to the lament played on the pipes. Carmichael says that the tune generally used on the pipes was that of a sacred hymn, '*Tha mi dol dachaidh leat*' (I am going home with thee). The tune of this is not given, but he observes that there is a secular song to the same air, '*Boineid is it, agus breacan is féile*' (Bonnet and feather and tartan and plaid). The writer has been able to note the tune of this poem from two of his Gaelic colleagues, William Matheson, who learned it from his mother, and John MacInnes, both of whom have now recorded it. It is basically the same air as 'The Campbells are comin'' in slow tempo. This air has also been used for the Gaelic satirical song '*Banais am bail' Inbhir Aora*' (The Wedding at Inverary) and for the old song 'Why should I be sad on my wedding day.'[1]

It is still common practice for the piper to play a lament at the head of the funeral cortège and at the graveside in the Highlands, but nowadays it is usually one of the pibroch laments that is played, such as Patrick Mór Mac Crimmon's beautiful 'Lament for the Children'.

[1] This is the title of the tune said to have been played on the bells of St Giles Cathedral, Edinburgh (doubtless under official prompting), at the Union of the Parliaments of Scotland and England in March 1707.

CHAPTER IV

The Vocal Music of Lowland Scotland

IN a first approach to the traditional vocal music of Lowland Scotland
two main avenues of exploration present themselves, the song and
the ballad. By chronological sequence we should probably give
precedence to the ballad. We may perhaps discount the fanciful suggestion of William Motherwell in his *Notebook* that the ballad of Cospatrick
relates to the far-from-immaculate conception of the mother of
Macbeth (tenth to eleventh century) by the devil, in the guise of a fair
young man, when she was out for a ramble of an afternoon! We still
have however the ballad of Sir Patrick Spens, which is thought to have
for its historic background the embassy which carried the daughter of
King Alexander III of Scotland across the North Sea to her wedding
with King Eric of Norway in 1281. It is not perhaps the most felicitous
example to cite, for some doubt has been expressed at various times as
to its authenticity, notably by Chambers, by David Laing, and by
Rimbault. On the other hand it has been accepted by the greatest ballad
authority of all, Francis Edward Child, whose opinion common sense
tends to confirm. It cannot of course by any means be suggested that a
ballad is always as old as the event of which it sings. It could only be as
old as the ballad verse-form. It is impossible to say how old this may
have been in oral tradition. We can only say that the earliest written
example, 'Judas' was to be found in an English manuscript of the
thirteenth century,[1] and that that one was a particularly early example,
anticipating the general appearance of the ballad form by about two
centuries. In some cases of course, the story of a ballad may have existed
in an earlier metrical form, and before that as a prose tale.

The event forming the subject of the earliest known Scottish *song*,
on the other hand, runs the ballad of Sir Patrick Spens pretty close, for
it laments the death of the same Alexander III in 1286, which only
allows the ballad a bare five years precedence. Here the actual words of

[1] It was in the library of Trinity College Cambridge but has become lost. Cf. Child,
The English and Scottish Ballads, Vol. I, p. 242.

the song are preserved in *The Orygynale Cronykil of Scotland* by Andro of Wyntoun. Unfortunately the music has not come down to us.

While the ballads therefore win a shaky precedence in theory, in practice it will be found more convenient to deal with the songs first, for the good reason that the first few scattered ballads and ballad tunes to reach print appeared in the *song* collections, which must therefore first be described.

THE LOWLAND SCOTS SONGS

Whereas the Gael, as we have seen, has tended to keep his tunes in his head rather than on paper, the Lowland Scot early became interested in writing them down and putting them into print. So, while the earliest collection of Gaelic song airs to be committed either to manuscript or print was that of the Rev. Patrick Macdonald minister of Kilmore in Argyl, *A Collection of Highland Vocal Airs* printed about 1780, we find Lowland Scots tunes in manuscript a full century and a half earlier, and in print by 1725, i.e. the 'Orpheus Caledonius'.

At the present day we find a parting of the ways between the Lowland Scots songs of the song-books and the folk-songs; for the folk-songs have continued to grow and develop, while those of the song-books have set and become crystallized. It must be realized however that until the first printed song-books appeared in the eighteenth century, all the Lowland Scots songs were folk-songs, circulating entirely by oral transmission; and even when the first printed song-books did appear, they were so scarce and costly that the main means of circulation must have remained that of oral transmission for a surprisingly long time afterwards; for even when Robert Burns started to provide songs for the great printed collection of *The Scots Musical Museum* in 1787, though the words of many songs had been printed by Allan Ramsay, no more than two hundred songs had been printed with their tunes. It was still largely with folk-song that Burns found his work, and he was able to con-tribute both songs and tunes that had never reached print before.

But by the time Scots songs began to be printed, or even written down in manuscript, many had already become forgotten except for their titles, and must regrettably be accounted lost for ever. In this we find a marked difference between Lowland Scots and Gaelic song, where, if the title of a song exists, the probability is that it can still be found somewhere among the Gaelic speaking community. A remark-able exception in Lowland Scots song however exists in the 'Lament for Alexander III', mentioned above.

The words are of great beauty:

> Quhen Alysander oure kinge wes dede,
> That Scotland led in luve and le,
> Away was sons of ale and brede,   [sowans]
> Of wyne and wax, gamyn and gle;
> Owre gold wes changyd into lede;
> Cryst, borne into vergynyte,
> Succour Scotland and remede!
> Thay stayd is in perplexitie.[1]

Two fragments of song, one of which refers to Edward I 'with his lang shanks' at the seige of Berwick (1296) and the other, to the defeat of the English at Bannockburn (1314) are to be found in English manuscripts.

We find the titles of a number of these forgotten songs in early Scots poetry. In 'Peblis to the Play' one of the poems said to be written by James I of Scotland (1394–1437) the first stanza describes how a young man:

> cleikit up ane hie ruff sang,—
> 'Thair fure ane man to the holt.'[2]

The fifteenth-century comic vernacular poem 'Cockelby's Sow' gives the names of a few more songs of the time. These include:

> The Bass,
> Twysbank
> Cock craw thou quhile day.
> Be yone woodsyd,
> Maister Peir de Cougate, etc., etc.

Twysbank was thought by John Leyden to refer to the song 'When Tayis (Tay's) bank wes blumyt bricht'.

In the 'Complaynt' of Sir David Lyndsay of the Mount (1490–1555) he reminds his royal patron James V of when he played 'twenty *springs*' (lively dance tunes); but that he loved 'Gynkerton' best. This tune of Ginkertoun is also referred to in another manuscript:

> 'till hear him "Ginkertoune" play on a lute.'

It is in Wedderburn's *Complaynt of Scotland* (1549?) that we find the richest vein of these song names (some of which are recognizable as songs or ballads known today) such as the ballads:—

---

[1] Set by the writer for voice and harp to the old ballad tune of 'Jamie Douglas'.
[2] i.e. 'There went a man to the wood.'

> Brume, brume on hill,
> The Battle of Hayrlau,
> The huntis of Chevat,
> The Percy and the Montgomerie met,

and the songs:

> Cou thou me the rasches grene,
> The sang of 'Gilquisker',
> Richt sairly musing in my mynd, etc.

The Bannatyne manuscript, a collection of Scots poems compiled in 1568 by George Bannatyne, of Newtyle, Forfarshire, an Edinburgh merchant, gives us the words (complete) of 'The wowing of Jock and Jenny' (the tune of this is known), 'The ballat of Evil Wyffis' and 'The ballat of Guid Fallows'; while the official report concerning the meeting of witches at North Berwick in 1591 gives us the names of two songs or tunes, 'Cummer goe ye on before' and 'The silly bit chicken'.

The collection known as 'The Gude and Godlie Ballatis' of 1567 or possibly earlier, consisting of crude religious adaptations of popular songs, furnishes us with a few song-names, some of which are known today, such as:

> Johne cum kiss me now,
> Quho is at my windo?
> Till our Gude-man,
> With huntis up,
> All my lufe leif me not.
> All my hart this is my sang,
> Musing greitlie in my mynde (mentioned above)
> My lufe murnis for me.

Various musical manuscripts which have come to light or have been made available to the student in the libraries (some as recently as the present century) bring us the first actual Scots tunes known. Some of these are collections of tunes for obsolete or little-used musical instruments such as the *viola da braccio*, the *viola da gamba*, the *lyra-viol*; some for lute in various forms of tablature, and some, of eighteenth-century date, for violin or flute. The most important, as far as native Scots airs are concerned, are the Skene, Straloch and Blaikie manuscripts.

These Scottish musical manuscripts cannot all be regarded as having been source books for the early printed collections, as some of them were long in private hands, and unavailable to the compilers of these. The Skene manuscript for instance, which contains a greater number of Scots airs than any, was privately owned by the family of Skene of

Hallyards in Midlothian until about 1820, when it was bequeathed to the Advocates Library in Edinburgh (since incorporated in the National Library of Scotland). It was not likely to have been seen by many of the early compilers or restorers of songs in print, and certainly never by Robert Burns, the greatest compiler, restorer, and editor of all. The Margaret Sinkler manuscript, full of Scots airs, only became publicly available a few years ago, as did the Panmure manuscripts, now on loan to the National Library.

The Blaikie and Straloch manuscripts have both been lost, but fortunately were largely transcribed; the Blaikie manuscript by James Davie of Aberdeen, and the other by Farquhar Graham. On the other hand, an important manuscript containing Scots airs which provided William Stenhouse with much material for his notes on Scots songs, the Crockatt manuscript, is lost without ever having been transcribed; so also is the first of three volumes of the Mcfarlan manuscript belonging to the Society of Antiquaries, Edinburgh.[1]

Edinburgh University Library is the repository of the Rowallan manuscript. This was long thought to be the oldest Scottish musical manuscript in existence, until the recent researches of Kenneth Elliott and Helena Mennie Shire[2] on the Panmure Collection of musical manuscripts (National Library) and other sources showed that as far as *composed* music was concerned such a statement could not be upheld, though it still seems true of *traditional* Scots airs. The Rowallan manuscript is a lute book in tablature on a stave of six lines, written sometime between the years 1612 and 1628 by Sir William Mure of Rowallan in Ayrshire, who describes its contents as 'for kissing, for clapping, for loving, for proving', and adds, 'set to the lute by me, W. Mure'. It contains some Scots airs such as 'Mary Beaton's Row', 'Cornyards', 'Cummer Tried' (i.e. true or faithful) and 'Ouir the Deck (dyke?) Davy', a tune with a distinct resemblance to 'Tullochgorum'. Most of the airs however are either English or from further afield.

In Edinburgh University Library also is to be found the Guthrie manuscript. This has always been something of a puzzle and a challenge to musical antiquarians, for it has never been satisfactorily deciphered, though numerous attempts have been made to do so. It contains the titles of some forty Scots airs, some of which are not otherwise known. The tablature, for *viola da braccio*, is now thought to consist of *accompaniments* to the airs named, of which the airs themselves do not appear, a

---

[1] The remaining two volumes are now in the National Library of Scotland.
[2] Cf. 'Music of Scotland 1500–1700', *Musica Britannica*, Vol. XV, Stainer and Bell, London, 1957.

tantalizing state of things, for some of the titles, like 'Ow'r late among the broom', 'Bonny Maidlen Wedderburn', 'The Windie Writer', and 'The Gee Wife', are not a little intriguing.[1] The manuscript was discovered, believe it or not, neatly sewn into a book of *written notes of sermons* preached by the great Covenanting minister James Guthrie, who suffered death for his beliefs at the gallows at Edinburgh Cross in 1661.

These musical manuscripts, though they may not have been available as source books for the printed collections, are interesting as showing the songs which were sung at their period. Of different category is the Herd manuscript, now in the British Museum, which definitely was a source book. This is a collection of words of songs and ballads which were still current at the time (though many of the songs were in fragmentary form), made by David Herd, an Edinburgh accountant, in the mid to late eighteenth century. Besides being the basis for Herd's own printed collection, *Ancient and Modern Scottish Songs, Heroic Ballads, etc.* the manuscripts are known to have provided Robert Burns with much of his material for song restorations,[2] as well as Sir Walter Scott for his Minstrelsy of the Scottish Border.

THE PRINTED COLLECTIONS

The first printed collections to contain Scots *tunes*, in our meaning of the term, were English publications, and this at the time when the two countries were separate countries politically, though their thrones were united under James the Sixth. The earliest of these was *The English Dancing Master*, published in 1651 by John Playford. In this may be found the tunes of 'Cold and Raw' (under the title of 'Stingo or Oyle of Barley'); 'Broome Broome, the bonny bonny Broome'; 'The Scotch Cap' which sounds Scottish in tune as well as in title; and 'Woodicock', which from the sound of the music might be either Scots or Irish, though William Chappell in his *Popular Music of the Olden Time* insists that it is an English air. Another of John Playford's printed collections, *Musick's Delight on the Cithern*, 1666, is said to contain a few Scots tunes, including 'General Lesley's March',[3] 'Highlanders'

[1] Since publication, the writer has learned from Cedric Thorpe Davie that the Guthrie MS was deciphered by H. M. Willsher in 1935. Cf. Willsher's thesis 'Music in Scotland during three centuries', in St. Andrews University Library.

[2] Hamish Henderson observes however: 'Alexander Keith challenges Henley and Henderson (editors of the *Centenary Edition of the Poetry of Robert Burns*, London, 1896) on this point.' See A. Keith, *Burns and Folksong*, pp. 40 and 41.

[3] This is the song and air on which Sir Walter Scott based his well-known song

March' and 'Montroses March'. *Apollo's Banquet, for the Treble Violin* by the same publishers, advertises among its contents, 'Scotch Tunes'.

The Playfords, father and son, evidently found that 'Scotch' tunes were taking the fancy of the English people, for soon they issued a whole collection devoted exclusively to the tunes from north of the Border. This was *A Collection of Original Scotch Tunes (Full of the Highland Humours) for the Violin*, issued under the name of Henry Playford, the son of John of *The English Dancing Master*. These are mostly dance tunes, including many examples of the 'Scots Measure' a dance somewhat resembling in its rhythm and cadences the hornpipe (one of them in fact has quite a distinct resemblance to the well-known College Hornpipe). It also contains a number of airs which we recognize as song airs, including 'The Birks of Abergeldie' which Burns was later to rewrite as 'The Birks of Aberfeldy', 'Goodnight and God be with you',[1] the predecessor of Burns's 'Auld Lang Syne' for the termination of a social gathering, 'The Collier's Lass', 'Allan Water', 'For Auld Lang Gine my Joe', 'The Lass of Leving-Stone', etc. of all of which Robert Burns was later to make use.

Next came the prolific English song-writer, compiler and editor, Thomas D'Urfey, with his famous *Wit and Mirth* and its somewhat shocking sub-title of *Pills to Purge Melancholy* (by which sub-title, generally shortened to 'D'Urfey's Pills', the work came to be known). The first edition to be printed with the airs was in two volumes, issued in 1698. Further editions up to 1720 increased the numbers of volumes to six. It is important in the story as being the first publication to give both *words* and *music* of Scots songs, of which a few appear in its pages—along with a large number of the synthetic 'Scotch Songs' of English manufacture of the kind which were now becoming popular in England, and which were shortly to develop into a flood. Among the real Scots songs are 'Daintie Davie', 'The Lea Rig', 'My Mother's aye Glowering ower me', 'Over the Hills and far away', and 'Bonnie Dundee'.

For a fuller description of both the early Scottish musical manuscripts and the printed collections of English issue the reader is recommended to read *Ancient Scotish Melodies* by William Dauney (Edinburgh, 1838). This gives a particularly good account of the Skene manuscript, perhaps the most interesting and certainly the most important of them all.

And now at last, seventy-five years after the appearance of the first

---

[1] Later changed to 'Goodnight and joy be wi' you a'.'

'March! March! Ettrick and Teviotdale!' (Blue Bonnets over the Border—but there is also another older tune of this title.)

Scots tunes in *The English Dancing Master*, it began to filter through to Scotland itself that there could be some value, cultural and commercial, in its native songs and tunes. The first man to realize it was Allan Ramsay, a wigmaker who turned poet, playwright, publisher and bookseller. In 1718 he brought out a small collection of the words only of Scots songs. It was successful, and in 1724 he followed it up with his famous *Tea-table Miscellany* again containing only the words, without music, of the favourite songs of the day. It was a collection which ran into edition after edition—eighteen in all—and finally included the words of nearly five hundred songs. These consisted as he said in his preface, of 'old' (i.e. traditional) songs with or without additions; songs by authors unknown, and new songs to be sung to old tunes' The new songs, he announced, were by himself and 'some ingenious young gentlemen'. 'The rest' he continues, 'are such old verses as have been done time out of mind, and only wanted to be cleared from the dross of blundering transcribers and printers.'

It is to be presumed that the tunes were widely known, for except for the few existing in the English publications, which may have found their way north, they were not to be found in print anywhere in Scotland. One can imagine that not to know the tune for one of the favourites in the *Tea-table Miscellany* was to be out of the swim, and doubtless there must have been quite a keen learning and brushing up in private of tune repertoires among all classes in Scotland in the 1720s and 30s. The success of Ramsay's new venture showed how ripe was the time for the collecting and printing of all the songs that had hitherto existed only by word of mouth, or in ones and twos in older collections of poetry such as those of the printer James Watson which had appeared in the earlier years of the century.[1]

Nevertheless though Ramsay may have kept the folk on their toes as regards knowing or learning the tunes, he missed an obvious trick in publishing the songs without music, an omission of which a rival publisher was not slow to take advantage. This was William Thomson, a professional singer, who in 1725[2] published a song-book containing the words and music of fifty Scots songs, including a number from Ramsay's *Miscellany* (for there was no law of copyright in those days). He gave it the title of *Orpheus Caledonius*, and it was the first song-book to be printed in Scotland containing both the words and airs of the popular traditional songs of the country.

[1] Watson's *Choice Collection of Comic and Serious Scots Poems 1706-1711*.
[2] The book is undated, but the date seems to be generally agreed in standard bibliographies.

Ramsay was of course understandably annoyed at Thomson for stealing a march on him, and gave expression to it in his next edition of *The Tea-table Miscellany* with the words, 'From this and the following volume, Mr Thomson . . . cull'd his *Orpheus Caledonius*. This by the by I thought proper to intimate and do myself that justice which the publisher (i.e. Thomson) neglected.'

Ramsay hastened to recover the position by publishing in the year following, *Musick for the Scots Songs in the Tea-table Miscellany*, a small-sized, beautifully though somewhat inaccurately engraved collection of tunes only—a book of about four by five inches. The publication was however a failure, whereas the *Orpheus Caledonius* went on to its second edition, with the addition of another fifty songs to the original fifty—an edition of incidental interest in that it contains among its subscribers the name of General Wade, the man who was sent by the Hanoverian government in London to open up the Highlands with roads and bridges, following the unsuccessful Jacobite rising of 1715.[1]

In spite of the failure of Allan Ramsay's *Musick-book*, the appetite of the public for Scots tunes had obviously been whetted, for another collection of importance was compiled in 1730 by Adam Craig, a professional violinist in Edinburgh. This was *A Collection of the Choicest Scots Tunes*, since become a source book. The tunes, which are arranged for the harpsichord, are mostly song airs, and the collection must have been a sort of vade-mecum of airs for those who could play the harpsichord, and even for those who merely wanted to keep in the musical swim. It was the first of a long line of such publications that culminated in the enormous collections of the Gow family which were to come towards the end of the century and to spill over into the next. It would be tedious to list them all, and they may be conveniently scanned in the bibliographies of J. C. Dick's *Songs of Burns* and Glen's *Early Scottish Melodies*. They are of importance in that they formed the source-books of many of the song-writers and adaptors who were to follow. Of particular interest because they were used by Robert Burns for this purpose, are the collections of Scots tunes by Bremner, Aird, Dow, McGlashan, Cumming, Gow, Bowie, Riddell, and above all, the *Caledonian Companion* of James Oswald, which Burns studied continuously, and annotated profusely for the purpose of his song-writing.

[1] General Wade touches our story at another point in that, in driving the road through from Crieff to Aberfeldy, he had, in the 'Sma' Glen, to disturb a huge boulder which was reputed to cover the grave of Ossian. John Francis Campbell of Islay describes in his *Popular Tales of the West Highlands* how the Highlanders came from a wide distance to re-inter the bones of Ossian in a new grave on a neighbouring hilltop, an act which was performed with great and solemn ceremony.

James Oswald, compiler of *The Caledonian Companion* above mentioned, gave cause for a great deal of argument and speculation by saying that some of the tunes in his collection had been composed by David Rizzio, the musician-secretary of Mary Queen of Scots who was stabbed to death in her presence about a hundred and fifty years before. Oswald was uniformly branded as an impostor by all the musical commentators then and since for his statement, which, it was hinted, was an impudent forgery perpetrated merely to sell his books. Yet there does seem to have been a tradition, which cannot by any means be laid wholly at Oswald's door that Rizzio did indeed compose 'Scots' airs. Thomson of the *Orpheus Caledonius* had already put Rizzio's name to seven of the tunes in the first edition of the *Orpheus Caledonius*, though he omitted to do so in the second. Watt's *Musical Miscellany* (London, 1729) gave three tunes, different to those in the *Orpheus*, as Rizzio's. The whole story and argument may be read in lucid detail in Glen's *Early Scottish Melodies*, where Glen, without actually committing himself on the question of Rizzio's authorship of the tunes, ably shakes the arguments of those who would charge Oswald with deliberate imposture.[1] Modern experience, as most people will know, has shown again and again the danger of the dogmatic scorning of tradition, however logical may appear the arguments by which it may be demolished.

With all these printed sources to draw upon, and with the great manuscript collection of song fragments by David Herd already mentioned; with the first appearance in print of Gaelic tunes in the *Highland Vocal Airs* of Patrick Macdonald, and with the enormous amount of Scots song still existing uncollected in folk-song form, the scene was set for the work of Robert Burns, who changed the whole face of Scottish song.

Robert Burns provided the texts for over three hundred songs, and is credited by the musical antiquary William Stenhouse with collecting or contributing the tunes of forty-five of these to one publication alone out of the two he chiefly wrote for. Many or his song-lyrics were based upon fragments of old songs of which no more than a verse or two, or a refrain, indeed sometimes only the title survived by the time he came on the scene. Many of the songs which did survive at this period were too bawdy for general use, for Scots song was notoriously broad in its humour, and these Burns rewrote. Some of the originals he reserved in all their stark Scots frankness for his private collection printed for the use of the roistering eighteenth-century Edinburgh club, The Crochallan

---

[1] Two of the 'Rizzio' tunes, 'The Lass of Paties Mill' and 'Tweedside', were known and used by the early Gaelic song-writers.

Fencibles, *The Merry Muses of Caledonia*, of which an edition was recently reprinted[1] for private circulation only.

Burns wrote words for many tunes which had hitherto only existed as instrumental airs, and which he took from the printed collections already mentioned. He was the first man also to make extensive use of Gaelic tunes for Lowland Scots songs. Some of these he took from the *Highland Vocal Airs* of Patrick Macdonald; but he also collected many Gaelic airs himself on his tour of the Highlands[2] and made use of them in his songs. Sometimes he used these Gaelic airs for existing Lowland songs which wanted a tune, as with 'When I am frae my dearie'; and sometimes he wrote new lyrics especially for them, as for instance 'How Pleasant the Banks of the Clear Winding Devon'. Burns was an avid collector of both tunes and words of old Scots songs. There are no exact figures for any of his work however, for he quixotically chose to do his song-writing anonymously and without financial reward. Stenhouse is the sole authority for the statement regarding his authorship and collection of those lyrics and tunes respectively which he contributed to the Museum; but the evidence which could have proved it, the musical manuscripts which Burns is said in many cases to have written out in his own hand for the publishers, have all disappeared except for two airs.[3] William Stenhouse, who was an Edinburgh accountant, was notoriously careless in his statements; but he was not wilfully dishonest as have been certain other commentators on Burns, and there is no reason to disbelieve him when he says, as he does so often, that both the words and tune of a song were contributed by Burns, and that he, Stenhouse, had had the manuscript through his hands.

It cannot be too strongly emphasized that Robert Burns was a knowledgeable and talented folk-musician and folk-musicologist as well as a

[1] This edition was printed for the Auk Society, Edinburgh in 1956. Though it is certainly not for the drawing room, it is of great interest to the student of Scots song.

[2] Robert Burns commenced his Highland Tour on 25 August 1787 and returned to Edinburgh on 16 September of that year.

The unnamed 'Gaelic Tune' to which he set his song 'How Long and Dreary is the Night' is a version of the tune used by Iain Lom for his 'The Day of Inverlochy'. See J. C. Dick, *The Songs of Robert Burns*, No. 20.

[3] These two musical manuscripts in the handwriting of Robert Burns are: (*a*) *Altho' my back be at the Wa'* of which the manuscript is in the British Museum. It was reproduced in *The Scotsman* in the spring of 1959 at the instance of the writer; (*b*) The other is *What merriment has ta'en the Whigs* to the tune of 'The German Lairdie'. According to James C. Dick, the manuscript was, at the time of his writing, i.e. 1903, in the private possession of John Adamson of Brooklands, Dumfries. Unfortunately this cannot now be traced, and it looks as if it has become lost also, during the present century.

great poet, for the most grotesque mistakes have been made on this score. His first and official biographer, Dr Currie, described him in the words of his schoolmaster Murdoch as being musically dull as a boy and hardly able to distinguish one tune from another; and the statement was seized upon, embroidered and exaggerated until it reached its full height of absurdity in a standard book of reference on English literature in 1943, with the statement that 'Burns was *entirely destitute* of an ear for music'; a statement which then proceeds to its own condemnation with the words, 'Yet, by some *inexplicable instinct* he could fit new words to old tunes without a failure. (the writer's italics). The statement fails to add that he was able to, and did advise his publishers on musical points in a hundred different ways, including which was the best version of a melody to use, and where it was to be found, hardly a task within the capabilities of a person of such musical disability! What could this 'inexplicable instinct' be, one wonders, but musicality.

The two great publications for which Burns wrote, restored, or amplified songs were *The Scots Musical Museum* published by James Johnson, and *Scottish Melodies* and its kindred succeeding publications by George Thomson. *The Scots Musical Museum* was, and still is, in many ways the standard and definitive collection of Scots songs. James Johnson the publisher of it, who was a printer of music in Edinburgh probably born in Ettrick, was said on all sides, and particularly by Robert Burns himself, to have been a 'worthy and honest enthusiast'; but he seems to have been fitted neither by education nor cultural status for the editing of such a work, being in fact, as can be proved, unable even to spell properly. The artistic editorship of it was in consequence soon taken over, though informally, by Burns himself, with the aid of Stephen Clarke, an Edinburgh organist, who harmonized the melodies, and supervised the musical side of the production at the technical level.

The other publisher for whom Burns provided songs, George Thomson, was a government clerk who had a keen amateur interest in music. Thomson set out to publish the songs of Scotland, and later those of Ireland and Wales also, with accompaniments by such famous continental musicians as Haydn, Beethoven, Pleyel, Kozeluch and others. It was for Thomson that Burns wrote many of his most famous songs, including 'Scots wha hae' and 'Auld Lang Syne'. The whole subject is well written up by J. C. Dick in his *The Songs of Robert Burns*, a book which also contains invaluable documentation and information about Scots song airs. Dick also published Burns' notes on Scots songs in his own interleaved copy of the *Musical Museum*, a mine of information which Dick brought to light in his researches, and the existence of which was hardly known.

Ramsay and Burns were the chief figures in a long line of song-writers and patchers of old songs. Among the others, the best known were Sir Walter Scott, with his 'Blue Bonnets over the Border', 'Bonny Dundee' and 'Jock o' Hazeldean', all adapted from old songs; Lady Nairne, whose nostalgic Jacobite songs such as 'Will ye no' come back again' and her 'The Auld House' are treasures of Scots song for all time; James Hogg, 'The Ettrick Shepherd', and Tannahill (though he wrote many of his songs to new composed melodies). Other writers of Scots songs, some of whom were contemporary or even before Burns, include Robert Crawford who wrote 'Tweedside'; the Rev. John Skinner, author of 'Tullochgorum'; Lady Ann Lindsay who wrote 'Auld Robin Gray'; Miss Jane Elliot and Mrs Alison Cockburn, both restorers independently of the song fragment of 'The Flowers of the Forest';[1] and a host of others. A good account of the Lowland Scots song-writers up to the date of the *Musical Museum* may be read in the notes of William Stenhouse (corrected by the much more accurate David Laing) in the reprint by Blackwood of the *Scots Musical Museum* in 1839 (recently reprinted anew). John Glen in his *Early Scottish Melodies* (Edinburgh, 1900) gives a later summing up of the information given in the 'Museum' with added researches of his own, and with an informative chapter on the eighteenth-century musicians, publishers and engravers.

Since the epoch-making publication by James Johnson of the *Scots Musical Museum*, with the first bold attempt at systematic documentation of the songs in the reprint, collections of Scots songs have poured out in a steady never-ending stream. Out of these one may be mentioned for the excellence of its notes on the songs. This is *The Songs of Scotland* published by Wood and Co., with notes by Farquhar Graham. Farquhar Graham was the best editor and commentator on Scots song of the nineteenth century, as Robert Burns was of the eighteenth. Farquhar Graham takes the story up to just beyond the middle of the nineteenth century, and his notes may be classed as essential reading.

Other collections of Scots songs which give useful information are *Scots Minstrelsie* with notes by John Greig (Edinburgh, 1892) and *Minstrelsy of Scotland* by Alfred Moffat (with notes by Frank Kidson). For brief notes on the chief figures of Scots music and song,

---

[1] The version of the air of 'The Flowers of the Forest' to which Miss Jane Elliot wrote her words is in the Skene Manuscript. That which Mrs Cackburn set may be found with variations added in James Oswald's *Caledonian Pocket Companion*.

traditional and otherwise, up to the end of the nineteenth century, David Baptie's *Musical Scotland Past and Present* (Paisley, 1894) may be consulted, though Dr H. G. Farmer declares the existence of inaccuracies in it.[1]

THE BALLADS

The history of ballad collecting in Scotland, as far as the tunes are concerned, has been one long tale of neglected and lost opportunity; of the texts of ballads being divorced from their tunes and put into print without them as if the tune were a sort of banana-skin to be discarded and thrown away; and this in spite of the fact that most of the ballads must have been written down initially from informants who knew and sang the tunes (and who, indeed, as we can say assuredly from our knowledge of the ways of folk-singers, would have been incapable of giving a ballad in any other way than by singing it!).

The word ballad is difficult to define. One can say it is a folk-song of a particular type which tells a story by a mixture of strongly condensed narrative and dialogue. It has a characteristic directness that is shorn to the bone of all superfluous descriptive matter and explanation; one has to be alive and on the *qui vive* as to what it is about from its opening line onwards. It has a mobility of scene that resembles more the sequences of a film than the telling of a story. It has conventions of expression and language and pictorial image that belong to the ballad and to nothing else, such as:

> He hadna gone a mile a mile,
> *A mile but barely three.*

> Gae saddle to me the black, the black,
> Gae saddle to me the brown.

> He has written a *braid letter*.

> Ye lie
> *Sae loud's I hear ye lie!*

> And she has built a *bonny ship*.

> To kiss her cheek and chin.

> He's ta'en her by the middle sma'.

[1] H. G. Farmer, *A History of Music in Scotland*, p. 433.

a little pen-knife (or a wee pen-knife)

A gay gowd ring.

These of course are textual characteristics which do not affect our particular study, which is the music.

But while it is difficult to say in one sentence what a ballad is, it is easy to say what it is *not*. Let Professor B. H. Bronson say it from the introduction to his gigantic work, *The Traditional Tunes of the Child Ballads*:

Question: When is a ballad not a ballad?
Answer: When it has no tune.

It is, as they say, 'as simple as that!'

The earliest appearance of a ballad in Scottish manuscript collections seems to have been in the Bannatyne Manuscript, made we may remember, about 1568, where there appears 'The Wife of Auchtermuchty', an early ballad version of the John Grumlie story of the farmer and his wife who struck a bargain that each would do the other's work of the farm and of the house, with disastrous results to the farmer. There also appears in the same collection the ballad of John Barleycorn, under the name of 'Why should not Allane honorit be?' Allan being Allan o' maut, or the seed of the barley. The Bannatyne Manuscript did not however reach print in its entirety until 1896, when it was published by the Hunterian Club, though selections of it were published by Allan Ramsay[1] in 1724 and by David Dalrymple, Lord Hailes, in 1770.

Wedderburn's *Complaynt of Scotland*, published in 1548 or 1549, gives in the list of song titles already described, 'The Battle of Harlaw', 'The Hunt of Cheviot', both well-known ballads, and what is thought to be a historical ballad now completely lost, 'The sang of Gilquhisker'.

In a number of Scots musical manuscripts of the seventeenth century we find a few more of the ballads, but this time, for a change, with the *music* and *not* the words. The Rowallan Manuscript, of date about 1625, now in Edinburgh University Library, gives the tune of 'The Battle of Harlaw'. The Guthrie Manuscript, in the same library, has among its tunes, that of the ballads of 'Long a-growing', 'The Bonny Broom', and 'Sweet Willie' (thought to be 'Sweet Willie and Fair Annie', or Annet). The tunes of the Guthrie Manuscript, however, are said never to have been successfully deciphered from its lute tablature which is

[1] Cf. *The Evergreene: A Collection of Scots Poems wrote by the Ingenious before 1600*, published by Alan Ramsay, 1724.

thought by some to be only an accompaniment to the airs. The Blaikie Manuscript 1692, now lost, but of which a transcript exists in the Wighton Collection at Dundee, has the tune of 'Where Helen Lies'. The Skene Manuscript, of date about 1615–30, gives a tune for 'The Fire of Frendraught' (Lady Rothemay's Lilt) and 'Johnny Faa' (Lady Cassilles Lilt).

Helena M. Shire gives in *Scottish Studies* (Vol. V part I, 1961) the information of her discovery in the Panmure Manuscripts (on loan to the National Library of Scotland) of important texts of 'The Sheath and the Knife' (Child 16), of 'Leesome Brand' (Child 15), and Little Musgrave (Child 81).

The earliest printed collection in which Scots ballad tunes appear is D'Urfey's *Pills to Purge Melancholy*, in which appear 'Chevy Chase' and a very incorrect version of the air of 'Gilderoy'.

Allan Ramsay's *Tea-Table Miscellany*, first published in 1724, contains the words of a few ballads, namely, 'Waly, Waly', 'Sweet William's Ghost', 'Willie Drowned in Yarrow', 'Johnny Faa', 'The Broom of the Cowdenknowes', 'Barbara Allan', 'The Gaberlunzie Man' and 'The Bonny Earl of Murray'.

Allan Ramsay may thus be said to have been the first man in Scotland to indulge in the pernicious malpractice of printing the texts of ballads without their tunes, which was to grow into a standard convention that has persisted almost to the present day—a practice which has left Scots native music very much the poorer.

In the same year as the *Tea-table Miscellany* appeared (1724) Ramsay brought out *The Evergreene*. This was a selection of poems, grossly touched up by Ramsay himself from the Bannatyne Manuscript, to which he had been given access by its owner Lord Hyndford or his brother William Carmichael. As well as the poems from the Bannatyne Manuscript, Ramsay included in *The Evergreene* the words of a few ballads, namely 'The Battle of Harlaw', 'Johnny Armstrong', 'The Wife of Auchtermuchty' (Bannatyne Manuscript) and the spurious ballad of 'Hardyknute' by Lady Wardlaw, which she had reprehensibly attempted to pass off as 'an old fragment'. Ramsay says of 'Johnny Armstrong' that he had copied it 'from a Gentleman's Mouth of the Name of Armstrong, who is the sixth generation from that John'. If this gentleman (or 'his mouth') knew the tune of the ballad, Ramsay ignored it, for *The Evergreene* appeared without any music.

It was in the *Orpheus Caledonius* that Thomson gave both the words and tunes of the ballads for the first time in a Scottish collection. Unfortunately there is only the merest handful of these, consisting of

'The Broom of the Cowdenknowes', 'The Bonny Earl of Murray', 'Gilderoy' and 'Rare Willie drowned in Yarrow'.

In Allan Ramsay's 'reply' to Thomson's *Orpheus*, his '*musick for the Scots Songs in the Tea-table Miscellany*' he gives only the tune of one ballad, 'The Broom of the Cowdenknowes', and he has in any case rewritten that as a lyric song instead of a ballad in the *Miscellany*.

We can see that in all those early collections, the inclusion of either texts or tunes of *ballads* was more or less incidental, their main contents being the lyric *songs*. With the appearance of Percy's *Reliques of Ancient English* (*sic*) *Poetry* in 1765, we see the first considerable collection of Scottish ballads, not indeed *per se*, but as part of the so-called 'English' poetry of its title. Thomas Percy, who was vicar of Easton Maudit in Northamptonshire when he published the *Reliques*, became domestic chaplain to the Duke of Northumberland, then became Dean of Carlisle, and finally Bishop of Dromore in Ireland. He took the English poems in his collection from an old manuscript which he is said to have rescued in the house of a friend just as the housemaid was about to light the fire with it! This became known as the Percy Folio Manuscript.[1] The Scottish ballads in the *Reliques*, which number roughly about twenty (with border-line cases) were sent to Percy, as he himself tells us, by David Dalrymple, Lord Hailes[2] whom he thanks in his Introduction for his 'most beautiful Scottish poems'[3] (sic). There were no tunes given for any of these however, and the *Reliques* appeared without music.

The next important collection to contain ballads, which Sir Walter Scott was later to characterize in his *Introductory Remarks on Popular Poetry*, as 'the first classical collection of Scottish Songs and Ballads', was by David Herd. Herd, born about 1732, was by profession a clerk to an Edinburgh accountant. He was an enthusiastic collector of the words of Scots songs and ballads, and his manuscript collection, known as 'the Herd Manuscript' became famous. He gave liberal use of it to Burns, Scott, and Robert Jamieson.[4] Scott used nine ballads from it and passed on three more to Robert Jamieson for his collection.

It is not known from whom Herd collected his material, except that he copied a few songs from Ramsay's publications. It seems probable

---

[1] Published in 1867-8 by Hales and Furnivall. The manuscript is now in the British Museum.

[2] Lord Hailes published *A Collection of Ancient Scottish Poems from the Bannatyne Manuscript* in 1770.

[3] Hamish Henderson observes: 'Hailes' "Edward" does, in fact, look like a "poetic" re-write of a ballad.' Mr Henderson has recorded two tunes for the ballad in the field —a notable contribution to Scottish balladry.

[4] Cf. Robert Jamieson, *Popular Ballads and Songs from Tradition*, Edinburgh, 1806.

that he amassed his collection more from written records and correspondence than from the singing of informants. This idea of song-collecting seems to have occurred to him from the example of Thomas Percy and the success of his *Reliques*. He collected no tunes for his songs. or at least made no effort to write them down, and so helped to perpetuate the bad example of his predecessors in this. He published, in 1769 and later editions, *Ancient and Modern Scottish Songs, Heroic Ballads, etc.*, the collection which Scott praised in the words given above.

The next ballad-collector, and in some ways one of the best of his period, was Robert Burns—a fact which is apt to be overlooked. According to such authority as is available, which is mostly either William Stenhouse or William Tytler of Woodhouselee reprinted by Cromek, he collected and contributed to the *Scots Musical Museum* both the words *and the tunes* of versions of 'As I cam' down by yon Castle Wa', (The Laird of Drum); 'Lord Ronald my Son', 'Geordie', 'Tam Lane', 'Lord Aboyne', 'The Lochmaben Harper', 'The Cruel Mother', and 'Sheath and Knife'. Of ballad texts without music, he is said by Stenhouse to have contributed to the *Musical Museum* 'Long a-growing', 'Hughie Graham', 'Gude Wallace' and 'Where Helen Lies'; while to his friend and musical antiquary William Tytler of Woodhouselee, he sent the words of 'Willie's Rare and Willie's Fair', and of 'Young Hyndhorn'. He also noted down in his *Commonplace Book* 'The Ballad of John Barleycorn', which was published in the Edinburgh edition of his poems in 1787.[1]

It is unfortunate for Scots music that ballads, as distinct from songs, seemed to evoke only a half-hearted interest in the mind of Robert Burns. Of the ballad of Hughie Graham for instance, he tells us in one of his notes to the *Musical Museum* that he had forgotten the tune of the ballad, and tantalizes us by going on to say 'it originally had a simple old tune'. He confesses indeed to this lukewarm interest in a letter to William Tytler, when he sent him a small group of ballads which he described as 'a sample of old pieces', and added—'I once had a great many of these fragments and some of them here entire; but as I had no idea that anybody cared for them, I have forgotten them.'[2] This is the greater pity as Burns was one of the few collectors who had the musical knowledge and skill to write down the tunes himself, which indeed he appears to have done in most of the examples quoted above.

---

[1] This is the ballad which, as mentioned before, appears in the Bannatyne Manuscript (1568) under the title of *Why Should not Allane honorit be?* (Cf. James C. Dick, *The Songs of Robert Burns*, Note 332.)

[2] Op. cit., Note 347.

Following close upon Burns, and indeed anticipating by a year some of the posthumous publications of the works of that poet, came the greatest ballad collector of the period (who now takes us into the nineteenth century), Sir Walter Scott, with his *Minstrelsy of the Scottish Border*. Strange to say it is with Sir Walter that we see the sad tale of neglected opportunities in the collecting of our ballad tunes fully unfold itself; for Scott printed no tunes at all in the first edition of his *Minstrelsy*, and such tunes as did eventually appear in editions of some thirty years later were inserted posthumously by his son-in-law, J. G. Lockhart.

This is the more remarkable in that Scott was a great enthusiast for Scottish songs and their tunes, and he once wrote to the composer Clarke Whitfield, 'I believe no man in Britain had more songs of all kinds by heart than I could have mustered'. His letter books are cram-med with references to Scots songs of all kinds, and their tunes. To his Highland friends the Clephanes for instance, he writes asking them to send him *any Gaelic airs they knew* or could get hold of: to Alexander Macdonald of Glengarry—'can you tell me any person in Edinburgh who is likely to give me the [air of the] 'Glangarry Gathering' in genuine purity?' and to his own son Walter, 'I wish you could pick up the Irish lilt of a tune to "Patrick Fleming".' These are only a few of the hundreds of instances almost that could be given of Sir Walter Scott's enthusiasm for his native tunes.

Scott almost certainly did not possess the technical musical skill to write down the tunes himself as Burns did, but there were many people available among his helpers who could have done it for him. There was John Leyden, who helped him to collect the ballads and who not only knew many of the tunes (for he was a Borderer himself) but was able to collect and memorize the tunes from others, as Scott describes in a scene when Leyden burst into an assembled company at dinner 'chant-ing a desired ballad with all the energy of what he used to call the *saw-tones* of his voice.[1] It turned out,' Scott continues, 'that he had walked between forty and fifty miles and back again, for the sole purpose of visiting an old person who possessed this precious remnant of antiquity.'

James Hogg, the 'Ettrick Shepherd', was another who could have given him the tunes of the ballads which his mother knew and sang. Hogg, who played the fiddle with great assiduity and enthusiasm, must have had a fair amount of musical knowledge, for even with the help of William Stenhouse, which he acknowledges, he could hardly have edited his two well-known volumes of both words and tunes of Jacobite

---

[1] Quoted by Lockhart in his *Life of Sir Walter Scott*, Vol. I, p. 326 from Scott's *Essay on the Life of Leyden*.

songs[1] without it. It was Hogg's mother, Margaret Laidlaw, who exclaimed to Scott, in words since become famous (for they have been quoted by almost every writer on the subject of ballads since):—

'There war never ane o' my sangs prentit till ye prentit them yoursel', and ye hae spoilt them awthegither. They were made for singin' an' no for readin'; but ye hae broken the charm noo, and they'll never (be) sung mair. An' the worst thing of a' they're nouther richt spell'd nor richt setten down.' (Hogg, *Domestic Manners of Sir Walter Scott.*)

'They were made for singing and not for reading.' What a truth is in these words—truth that would have made a world of difference to our balladry if there had been ears to hear the wisdom of this homely but talented woman. Time and again Scott recounts in his introductions to the various ballads in his *Minstrelsy* that he got them from informants who *sang* the ballad to him, as he did from this same Margaret Laidlaw of whom he recounts that 'she sings or rather chants' (a particular ballad) 'with great animation'. Often Scott, it is true, refers to collecting a ballad from the *recitation* of an informant; but everyone with any experience of folk-song knows that recitation of a ballad means singing it; and indeed, as William Montgomerie has pointed out,[2] there is direct confirmation of this as far as the ballads of the *Minstrelsy* are concerned in the notebook of Thomas Wilkie, one of Sir Walter's sources, in such entries as:

'I took this down from the recitation of Janet Scott Bowden, who sung it to a beautiful plaintive air', and, 'I took this down from the recitation of a friend . . . the air she sung to it was lively (and) simple.'

Often Scott himself refers to the tune of a ballad though he does not give it; as, of the ballad of 'Lord Randall': 'There is a beautiful air to this old ballad.'

Perhaps the most provoking example of this is that of 'The Fray of Suport', of which Scott says, 'It is usually chanted in a sort of wild recitative, except the burden, which swells into a long and varied howl, not unlike to a view hollo.' So the tune of this wonderful wild ballad of the 'Debatable Land', with its exciting refrain of:

'*Fy lads! shout a'a'a'a', My gear's a' gane!*'

is lost to us for ever, unless a miracle brings it yet to light. The writer has searched endlessly for it in the Borders himself.

The loss, too, of the old ballad of *My name is Little Jock Elliot and*

---

[1] *Jacobite Relics* (Edinburgh, 1819).
[2] 'Sir Walter Scott as Ballad Editor', by William Montgomerie (*The Review of English Studies*, New Series, Vol. 7, No. 26, April 1956.)

wha daur meddle wi' me? is so unaccountable as to be almost ludicrous, for in Scott's and Leyden's day it seems to have been as well known in the Border as '*Teribus ye Terioden*' is in Hawick still. Yet, probably because no one thought of writing it down, the tune has been lost, and the words survive only in a dubious version.[1] Leyden relates how once when he was ill in bed, Sir John Malcolm his physician found him, as he thought delirious, singing at the pitch of his voice; but it was no delirium—he was just singing the ballad of 'Little Jock Elliot' for his own enjoyment! A version of the ballad is sung in Jedburgh today which, though it is good in its own way, is a frank reconstruction by a Jedburgh man, Matthew Gotterson, written and published about the beginning of the present century,[2] and set to a version of the air of 'Woo'd and married an a' ' (which incidentally has the merit according to Stenhouse, of being a tune current in the Border in Allan Ramsay's day and before). This version has become mistaken locally for the real ballad, and was sung to the writer as such a few years ago.

Nine of the tunes to the ballads of Scott's *Minstrelsy* were given at last in the edition of 1833 (the year after Scott's death) edited by Scott's son-in-law, J. G. Lockhart; that is, thirty-one years after the original edition, of which the first two volumes were issued by James Ballantyne from Kelso in 1802, and a third volume from Edinburgh a year later. The tunes given in this 1833 edition are—'The Battle of Otterburn', 'Johnny Armstrong', 'Dick o' the Cow', 'The Lord Maxwell's Goodnight', 'The Battle of Bothwell Bridge', 'The Douglas Tragedy', 'The Dowie Dens of Yarrow', 'The Wife of Usher's Well' and 'Thomas the Rhymer'.

Lockhart says that the selection of airs includes those which Sir Walter Scott himself liked the best; but it does not say where, when, or how he got them. Some, we know, were collected by Alexander Campbell, an old friend and former music master of Scott's who made a tour of the Borders in 1816. Campbell states in his collection, *Albyn's Anthology*, that he got the air of 'Lord Ronald' from Sir Walter Scott's daughter Sophia, which shows that the tunes were known at Abbotsford itself. The airs of 'Jock of the Side' and 'Dick of the Cow' were sent to him by 'Auld Thomas o' Twizlehope' via Robert Shortreed.[3] The air of 'Lord Ronald' mentioned by Alexander Campbell in his *Albyn's Anthology* is the 'beautiful air' referred to by Scott in the *Minstrelsy*, but not given by him. It is as beautiful as he has said, and so may be given here:

[1] Cf. *The trustworthiness of the Border Ballads* by The Hon. Fitz-William Elliot, 1906.
[2] The writer is indebted to Mr John Hewie of Jedburgh for this information.
[3] Cf. *The Centenary Edition of Scott's Letters for 1815*, p. 26.

LORD RONALD

O where hae ye been, Lord Ron-ald my son? O where hae ye been, my hand-some young man? I hae been to the wild wood, moth-er, make my bed soon, For I'm wear-y with hunt-ing and fain wad lie down.

Scale — Hexatonic

as Dorian or Mixolydian with gap at 3rd.

(From *Albyn's Anthology*, Alexander Campbell.)

Scott divides the ballads into two classes, *Historical* and *Romantic*. Both kinds are to be found throughout Lowland Scotland. There is also a sub-class of the Historical Ballads which belongs especially to the Border itself, and which has become known as the 'riding ballads'. They recount the minor Border raids, always of course made on horseback, hence their name, which the notorious freebooters of the Borders made upon the cattle and goods of their neighbours, particularly upon those living on the English side, as it then became a matter of patriotism as well as booty! Among the best known of these are 'Jamie Telfer of the Fair Dodhead', 'Kinmont Willie', 'Jock o' the Side', 'Dick o' the Cow', 'Hobie Noble' and 'Archie o'Cawfield', of all of which only three of the tunes have been preserved. It may be of interest to give one of them here, for though they possess the basic characteristics of Scottish melody they seem also to have acquired something of their style from the southern side of the Border as well—as if the raiders has lifted tunes as well as cattle! Perhaps the best to quote is that of 'Jock o' the Side', as the collection in which it appears, Campbell's *Albyn's Anthology*, **is** not easy to come by:

JOCK O' THE SIDE

As it happens, the writer is able to contribute one of the riding ballad tunes himself, which he collected as far afield as East Anglia! This is 'Archie o' Cawfield' of which the title has become 'Bold Archer'; but it is plainly identifiable, and it supplies one of the missing airs, though possibly in a form as much altered in its travels as is the title:

BOLD ARCHER
(Archie o' Cawfield)

Collected by Francis Collinson from a singer in East Anglia

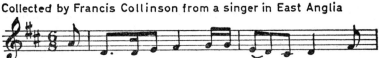

[continued overleaf

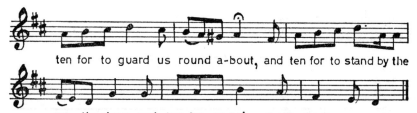

ten for to guard us round a-bout, and ten for to stand by the

cas-tle door, and ten for to bring bold Arch-er out.

An arrangement of the song by the writer for voice and pianoforte is published in *Songs of the Countryside* by Paxton and Co., by whose kind permission it is here quoted.

Some of Scott's informants were themselves ballad collectors. C. K. Sharpe, a continuous correspondent of Scott, published in 1823 a printed collection of ballads (without tunes) for private circulation, limited to thirty copies, which was later reprinted by Blackwood. Robert Riddell of Glenriddell, the friend of Burns, was another who provided Scott with material. The Riddell Manuscripts are now in the National Library. A minor collector was Dr Elliot of Reidheugh in Liddesdale, who gave ballad texts to Scott, and earlier to Caw's *Poetical Museum*, a Hawick publication of 1784 in which some of the Riding Ballads appear in print for the first time.

Joseph Ritson, the celebrated musical antiquary, was also a correspondent of Scott and supplied him with ballads in manuscript. Two more of Scott's correspondents for *The Border Minstrelsy* should be particularly noted; Richard Surtees, the historian of Northumberland, because he sent a ballad to Scott, 'The Death of Featherstonhaugh' which he represented as having been taken down from the recitation of an old woman, and which he later confessed to be a forgery concocted by himself. By reason of this, another which he also sent to Scott, 'Barthram's Dirge', must be also regarded as suspect.

Another collector correspondent was the famous Mrs Brown of Falkland, whom it is worth identifying further. Born Anna Gordon 1747, she was the daughter of the professor of philosophy at King's College, Aberdeen, Thomas Gordon. She married the Rev. Andrew Brown of Falkland. She sent a number of ballads to Scott and Jamieson, to William Tytler (which are now lost) and to Alexander Fraser Tytler (Lord Woodhouselee) both musical antiquaries, and to others. Her ballad collecting was done in Aberdeenshire, a county which has always been a fruitful field. A number of her tunes were taken down by a nephew from her singing, but not very skilfully, and these can only betentatively interpreted.[1] The Brown Manuscripts are now in the library at Harvard.

[1] Cf. B. H. Bronson: *The Traditional Tunes of the Child Ballads*, Vol. I, p. 101. Princeton University Press, 1959.

Skene of Rubislaw was another correspondent of Scott. He made a manuscript collection of thirty-two ballads which he took down from an unnamed lady also in Aberdeenshire. Scott called these 'The Old Lady's Collection' and it is now always referred to by that name.

Robert Jamieson published in 1806 his *Popular Ballads and Songs from Tradition*. Jamieson made a notable contribution to the subject in discovering that the stories of a number of the romantic ballads were also to be found in the ballads of Denmark, a discovery which laid the foundations for modern comparative research in balladry. Jamieson published no tunes.

Peter Buchan of Aberdeenshire, also a correspondent of Scott, was a collector so assiduous that he must be regarded as one of the major ballad collectors in his own right. He was the cruel victim of a hoax in the form of a 'ballad fragment' sent to him by a practical joker. Unfortunately Buchan is said to have 'blotted his copybook' by 'finding' some missing stanzas of the said fragment. He has been not unconvincingly defended however by modern research, notably by Alexander Keith in his introduction to the ballad collection of Gavin Greig published by the Buchan Club; and his reputation must be considered to be restored to a considerable extent thereby. His two great collections are *Gleanings of Scotch, English, and Irish Scarce Old Ballads* (1825) and *Ancient Ballads and Songs of the North of Scotland* (1828).

There is no need to list all the ballad collections which have appeared from this period onward, many of which were obviously inspired by the work of Sir Walter Scott. Three major collections may however be mentioned: George R. Kinloch's *Ancient Scottish Ballads* (1827) with tunes; William Motherwell's *Minstrelsy Ancient and Modern* (Glasgow, 1827) also with tunes. The collection of Robert Chambers *The Scottish Ballads* (Edinburgh, 1829), though important for its texts, gives no tunes; but in 1844 Chambers brought out *Twelve Romantic Scottish Ballads with the original airs*. By far the most important of the three is the Motherwell Collection, which gives no less than thirty-three tunes, many of them exceedingly beautiful—the greatest number of tunes in any collection up to that date. The fine tune of 'Jamie Douglas' may be quoted as an example.

JAMIE DOUGLAS

O   come down stairs Jam - ie Doug-las,   O

[continued overleaf

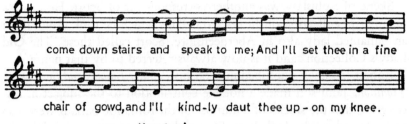

come down stairs and speak to me; And I'll set thee in a fine

chair of gowd, and I'll kind-ly daut thee up-on my knee.

Hexatonic

Scale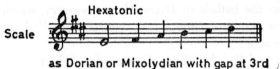

as Dorian or Mixolydian with gap at 3rd

The first really extensive publication of Scottish ballads *with their tunes* was the work of William Christie and his son, W. Christie, Dean of Moray. This was *Traditional Ballad Airs* published in 1876. Unfortunately the editor, Dean Christie, took rather a wide view of what was editorially permissible in 'improving' his material, and many of the texts, as Alexander Keith observes, were subjected to 'pretty severe editorial usage'. He is also thought to have himself added second strains to the melodies where such did not exist in the original. Nevertheless it is a valuable collection in providing the *only known tunes* for a great number of ballads; and it showed the way for future ballad collecting, even if it did not at once bear fruit in respect of his including of the tunes. The editor found it necessary by the taste of the times, to quote his words, to 'expunge from the unpublished ballads all that was unpresentable, and where any of them have been altogether unsuitable, he has adapted the beautiful airs to modern songs to which no airs have been hitherto given,' a process which of course does not recommend itself to the serious student.

This brings us to the period of modern ballad scholarship, and presents us with an ever widening sea of ballad collections and of books about ballads. The greatest of these as far as the texts are concerned is the vast work of scholarship of Francis James Child, *The English and Scottish Popular Ballads*, in five folio volumes (1893–8). This may be described as the bible of balladry, and is, as it certainly almost certainly will be for all time, the standard authority on Scottish and English ballad texts. Child's numbering of the ballads from 1 to 305 has been accepted as the recognized means of identifying any particular ballad; so much so that it has even become unnecessary to mention the name of Child; the number in brackets after a ballad title is sufficient to indicate that this is the number as the ballad appears in Child's volumes. Most unfortunately

Child died before he could provide an introduction to the work, and so what would undoubtedly have been the greatest exposition of the subject to date has been denied to us. Unfortunately he follows the example of his predecessors in almost ignoring the music of the ballads; for while he prints all the known versions of the three hundred and five ballads which he accepts as genuine, the airs which he has assembled for them, numbering a meagre fifty-five, are relegated to an appendix. What can be said in mitigation is that if he had set himself to collect all the known tunes as well as the texts, he could not have finished the work.

Child may be said to have been an editor rather than a collector. He may have made desultory efforts to collect new ballad material from oral sources, but if so it was without any conspicuous success, and he came to believe that all the material he needed for his great work was best sought either in manuscript or print.[1]

A man was to follow however whose achievements in the field were equal to those of Child in the library. This was Gavin Greig, born at Parkhill, Newmachar, Aberdeenshire in 1856—thirty-one years after Child. A schoolmaster by profession, he became intensely interested in the ballads and folk-songs of his native county of Aberdeenshire. He was an accomplished musician and became organist of his parish church, which meant that he was competent to take down the tunes as well as the words of the ballads. He became a most ardent and enthusiastic collector, and by the end of his life, he and his collaborator the Rev. J. B. Duncan had amassed the amazing number of 3,050 ballad texts and 3,100 ballad tunes.[2] (This is apparently not counting *folk-songs* and their tunes, of which he also collected an enormous number.[3])

His methods of collection and ordering of his material were systematic and accurate, and his manuscripts, extending to over ninety volumes, now in the Library of Kings College, Aberdeen, forms one of the greatest and most valuable archives of folk-song and ballad in existence. The best of his ballad texts with their tunes have been published by the Buchan Club, Aberdeen, as *Last Leaves of Traditional Ballads and Ballad Airs* with a valuable introduction and notes by Alexander Keith. The book is essential reading for all who are interested in the subject.

One more work on the ballads must be mentioned, for it particularly

[1] Hamish Henderson adds: 'William McMath supplied quite a number of ballads to Child from oral tradition.'

[2] The figures are taken from Gavin Greig; a memoir, by Alexander Keith in *Last Leaves of Traditional Ballads and Ballad Airs*, Aberdeen; The Buchan Club, 1925.

[3] Hamish Henderson says however that this number covers folk-songs as well as ballads.

concerns our subject, which is the music. This is the assembling from all sources, printed, and manuscript, of all the known tunes of the Child Ballads, by Professor Bertrand Bronson of the University of California, in *The Traditional Tunes of the Child Ballads*. This work, of which two massive volumes have already appeared, is still in course of completion at the time of writing. It is a noteworthy, scholarly and commendable attempt to rectify the omissions of the past and to gather together all the ballads with their tunes where these can be found. It will ultimately be the standard authority on the tunes as Child's work is on the texts. This collection will make a massive contribution to the material of our present study, the native music of Scotland, in which the ballad airs play so considerable a part.

Since 1951, the collection of ballads and their tunes has become part of the work of the School of Scottish Studies. Field work has shown that the ballads are still sung in Scotland in considerable numbers, and many have been recorded by the School by means of tape recorder. These include the tunes of rare ballads such as 'Tam Lane', 'Childe Maurice', 'The Baron of Brackley' and 'Glenkindie'. The The last named appears to be the only tune ever recorded for this ballad, and may be set down here for the record.

GLENKINDIE

Singer: Miss M. Douglas Gordon

Collected and transcribed
by Francis Collinson

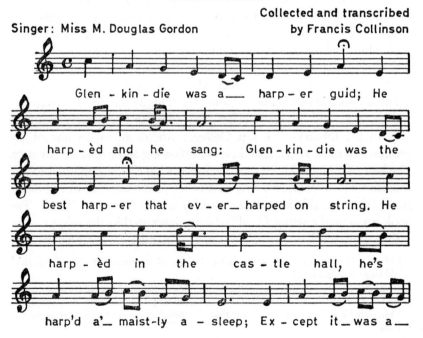

Glen - kin - die was a___ harp - er guid; He
harp - èd and he sang: Glen - kin - die was the
best harp - er that ev - er___ harped on string. He
harp - èd in the cas - tle hall, he's
harp'd a'___ maist-ly a - sleep; Ex - cept it___ was a___

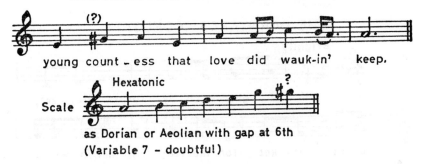

young count-ess that love did wauk-in' keep.

Hexatonic

Scale

as Dorian or Aeolian with gap at 6th
(Variable 7 - doubtful)

Field-work by the School of Scottish Studies has brought to light a number of talented singers of the great Scottish ballads—singers who have preserved a style of singing them which is obviously authentic and of age-old tradition. These include Jeannie Robertson, John Strachan, 'Princie' and 'Lordie' Hay,[1] and a number of others, some of whose performances may be heard on discs issued by the School and on commercial recordings.[2]

THE BOTHY BALLADS: THE FOLK-SONGS

The term Bothy Ballad is capable of two definitions; firstly it may be defined as the kind of song which was sung in the farm bothy when bothy life—that circumscribed almost monastic existence of the male farm-worker which continued until well into the present century—was the rule.

Regarded in that light of course, it is practically synonymous with Scots folk-song itself; and it possesses a repertoire so enormous as almost to defy classification. Certainly with all the ramifications of theme of such songs, it would be impossible to attempt the task in a single chapter of a book such as this.

In its second and more manageable sense, the bothy ballad may be narrowed to mean that kind of song which sang about farm life. Such ballads are interesting in a documentary sense for the glimpses they give of the whole picture of farm life of their period. They usually commence with the feeing market, where the farm-workers congregated for the purpose of hiring themselves out to the farmer for a prescribed period of time. One of the best, and certainly possessing one of the best tunes, is the now well-known 'Barnyards o' Delgaty'.

[1] Hamish Henderson adds: 'Alas, no. "Princie" died before he could be recorded.' 'Princie' and 'Lordie' Hay, as they were always known, were two Aberdeenshire farm-workers born in the Edwardian era.

[2] See also article in 'Scottish Studies' Vol. 9. I by Hamish Henderson and the writer.

THE BARNYARDS O' DELGATY

Brightly

It's I gaed doon by Tur-ra Mar-ket,

Tur-ra Mar-ket for tae fee; I met in wi' a

fair-mer chiel by the barn-yards o' Del-gat-y.

Refrain

Lin-ten ad-ie, toor-in ad-ie, Lin-ten ad-ie toor-in ee,

Lin-ten lour-in lour-in lour-in, Lin-ten lour-in lour-in lee.

Often the bargain is sealed with the payment of a shilling or more and a drink of ale, as in the bothy ballad of 'Ellon Market':

> And to a tent he then set sail,
> And bid me follow at his tail;
> He calléd for a glass of ale
> Therein to keep us sober.

'Drumdelgie', 'The Weary Farmers', 'Swaggers', 'The Guise o' Tough', 'Sleepytown' and 'South Ythsie' are other good examples of this class. In these songs, which again commence with the singer's engagement at the feeing market, may be found descriptions of the enclosed hierarchy of the farm of those days, a hierarchy with a strict order of precedence to be observed on all occasions, and particularly at the table at meal times, scanty though some of those meals sometimes were if the farmer was the mean type, and generally consisting mainly of oatmeal brose. 'Castles o' Auchry' is one of the most comprehensive in this respect, and mentions in succession the foreman (who in this song is the singer himself) the second, third and fourth 'chiel' (child or fellow) each with his 'pair' (i.e. of horses) under his charge; the 'orra man' who does the odd jobs, the 'baillie' who looks after the cattle—and perhaps a second cattleman if the farm is a big one. There is often mention of the farmer's wife, housekeeper or 'kitchie (kitchen) maid' who prepares the food for them all—and sometimes comes in for censure if it does not come up to standard.

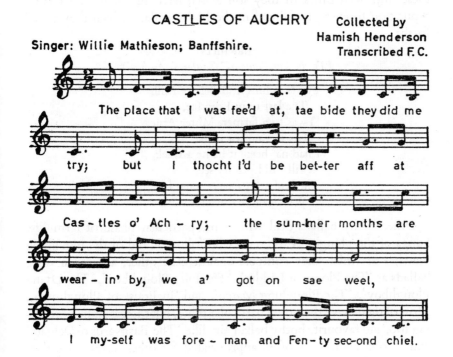

CASTLES OF AUCHRY

Collected by Hamish Henderson
Transcribed F. C.

Singer: Willie Mathieson; Banffshire.

The place that I was fee'd at, tae bide they did me try; but I thocht I'd be better aff at Castles o' Achry; the summer months are wearin' by, we a' got on sae weel, I myself was foreman and Fenty second chiel.

Ironside ca'ed the third pair
　And Black he ca'ed the fourth,
And Connon second cattleman,
　Some stirks he had to sort,
Noo that is a' the single lads,
　As you may understand,
William Ross he is head cattleman
　And he is a married man

We have a gay young kitchenmaid,
　Miss Wilson is her name
Her and the cook they canna' 'gree
　But the lassie's nae tae blame
And when Miss Wilson goes from home,
　She's always companie,
Her and the second cattleman
　I doot they've cast an ee.

etc.

Some of the songs sing particularly of the bad conditions of work and life, and of the meanness of the farmer or his wife. The farms of Newhills, Bogieside and Little Benton, whatever their condition may be in these improved times (if they still exist), have an unenviable former reputation forever proclaimed in the bothy ballads which they called forth:

NEWHILLS

(To the same tune as 'Castles o' Auchry')

> I to Newhills near Sclatty Mills
> The last term I did fee,
> 'Twas to a farmer, Mister Arne,
> His servant for to be;
> I had na' been at hame a week
> Till I did plainly see,
> The tables they were unco bare,
> Which did na' well suit me

Other bothy ballads deal with some particular phase of farm life. Songs of the plough, of the men who follow it and of the ploughing matches in which they compete against each other, abound in such ballads as 'The Plooman Laddie', 'The Jolly Ploughboy', 'The Dying Ploughboy', 'The Ploughing Match', and 'In Praise of Ploughmen'. Most of them have their own particular tunes, but there is some borrowing too, and favourite bothy ballad airs like 'The Barnyards o' Delgaty' and 'Drumdelgie'[1] are often appropriated for other songs when they happen to fit.

There is a large body of songs about the busy but pleasant time of harvest in the old style, with its shearers and bandsters and its undertones of courting in the sunshine. Among the best known of these are 'The Hairst o' Rettie', 'The Lothian Hairst', 'The Gallant Band o' Shearers' and 'Johnnie Sangster'. Harrowing, haymaking, gleaning, herding and milking all have their songs also.

THE HAIRST O' RETTIE

Singer: George Hay ("Lordie")   Collected by Hamish Henderson
Transcribed F.C.

I hae seen the hairst o' Ret-tie, aye an'

[1] Hamish Henderson comments: 'Drumdelgie is the air of "The Irish Jaunting Car".'

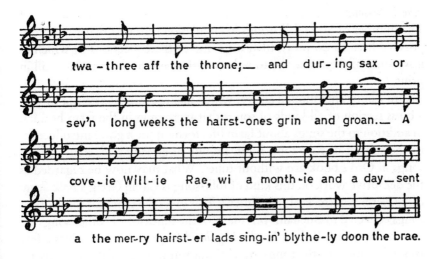

twa-three aff the throne;— and dur-ing sax or sev'n long weeks the hairst-ones grin and groan.— A cove-ie Will-ie Rae, wi a month-ie and a day—sent a the mer-ry hairst-er lads sing-in' blythe-ly doon the brae.

The tunes of the bothy ballads are simple but always catchy and rhythmic, though they have not always the beauty of the older Scots airs. Some of them like 'Nicky-Tams' have an interesting modal flavour:

NICKY TAMS

When I was scarce-ly ten year auld I left the parish school; my par-ents fee'd me at the Mains to hae my milk and meal; I— first put on my nar-row breeks to hap my spin-dle trams; an' busk-it roon' my knap-pin' knees a pair o' Nick-y Tams.

The standard work on the bothy ballads is *Bothy Songs and Ballads* by John Ord.[1] Unfortunately Ord does not publish as many of the tunes as one would have liked.

[1] Published by Alex Gardener, Paisley, 1930.

The Folk-songs

The number of Scots folk-songs in circulation is so vast that it is hardly possible here to do more than list some of the collections in which at least some of them may be found, though many of these are not still in print.

Ord's book, mentioned above, which makes a valiant attempt to give a cross section of all kinds of songs that were sung in the farm bothies, in addition to the songs about farm life, forms quite a good introduction to the subject of folk-song itself, though as already said, many of the songs in Ord's book are without tunes. What may now be regarded as the definitive work on this kind of folk-song is Gavin Greig's *Folk Songs of the North East* (recently reprinted). This gives the tunes for some of the songs collected in Buchan,[1] but many of the tunes for the other songs are here lacking also. Robert Ford's *Vagabond Songs and Ballads* gives a few tunes, but most of the songs are without music. One of the most useful collections of Scots folk-songs *with tunes* is Ewan MacColl's *Scotland Sings*.

In addition to all the usual facets of human life which we find reflected in the folk-songs of Scotland, a word may be said about that curious and characteristically Scottish class of songs dealing with beggars and begging, of which we find a whole cluster. It should be said that in the former life and customs of Scotland, the beggar, far from being an outcast, had his own acknowledged niche—sometimes not entirely an unimportant one. Sir Walter Scott, in his introduction to *The Antiquary* may be here quoted apropos of the beggar Edie Ochiltree, who was a 'Blue-Gown' the highest degree of the begging fraternity, with a licence to beg and a badge.

'Many of the old Scottish mendicants', he writes, 'were by no means to be confounded with the utterly degraded class of beings who now practise that wandering trade. Such of them as were in the habit of travelling through a particular district, were usually well received both in the farmer's ha' and in the kitchens of the country gentlemen. . . . If the mendicant chanced to be a King's Bedesman, or Blue-Gown, he belonged, in virtue thereof, to the aristocracy of his order, and was esteemed a person of great importance.' Scott's introduction to the novel is worth reading in the light of the surprising number of songs that are to be found of this type. The old Scots word for the beggar or

[1] Hamish Henderson adds: 'Greig's *Folk-song in Buchan*, reprinted from the *Transactions of the Buchan Field Club*, and included in the reprint, does include ten of the tunes, but the articles which originally appeared in the *Buchan Observer* contain texts only.'

the gangrel was the Gaberlunzie, from the gaberlunzie or wallet which he carried hung low upon the body.

We find a number of these 'gaberlunzie' songs in the Scots song-books, of which the best known is 'The Gaberlunzie Man'. This song is associated in legend with King James V, who was said to have been fond of roving about the countryside disguised as a beggar; indeed it has been thought by some that the song was written by him, though this is now somewhat discounted. *The Child Ballads* also include two of the begging songs, 'The Jolly Beggar' (279) and 'The Beggar Laddie' (280). Still current in folk-song we have 'The Beggar Man', 'The Beggin' Trade' and 'To the Beggin' we will go'.[1]

THE BEGGAR MAN

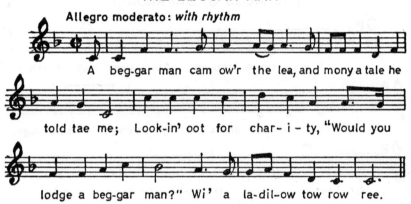

A beg-gar man cam ow'r the lea, and mony a tale he told tae me; Look-in' oot for char-i-ty, "Would you lodge a beg-gar man?" Wi' a la-dil-ow tow row ree.

Besides the actual begging songs there are the songs concerned with the various other gangrel or 'ga'in'-aboot bodies' such as the tramps, the hawkers, the pedlars, and, of a different type and stratum, the tinkers. Examples that come to mind are: 'The Pedlar 'or 'The Hoose o' Glenneuk', 'The Tinker Loon', 'To Pad the Road wi' me', 'Come all ye Tramps and Hawkers' and 'The Moss o' Barradale'.

COME ALL YE TRAMPS AND HAWKERS

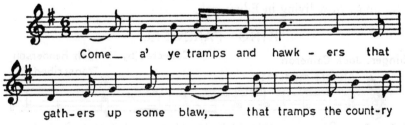

Come— a' ye tramps and hawk - ers that gath-ers up some blaw,— that tramps the count-ry

[1] 'These last two are really the same song.' Hamish Henderson. [*continued overleaf*

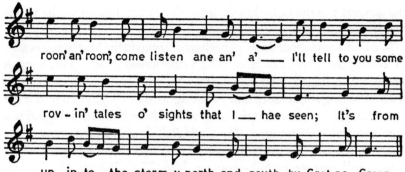

roon' an' roon', come listen ane an' a' ___ I'll tell to you some
rov - in' tales o' sights that I ___ hae seen; It's from
up in-to ___ the storm-y north and south by Gret-na Green.

Sung by Jimmie MacBeath. Collected by Hamish Henderson.

THE MOSS O' BARRADALE

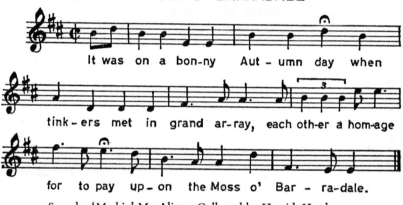

It was on a bon-ny Aut - umn day when
tink - ers met in grand ar-ray, each oth-er a hom-age
for to pay up - on the Moss o' Bar - ra-dale.

Sung by 'Markie' MacAlister. Collected by Hamish Henderson.

One would hardly expect still to find in folk-currency a Jacobite song of the Rising of 1745 which had not reached the printed song-books. It may be fitting therefore as an example of the tenacity and widely ranging themes of Lowland Scottish folk-songs that are still being sung, to conclude the chapter with the following song of the Battle of Prestonpans in the '45, collected recently from oral tradition by Hamish Henderson, from the singing of Jock Cameron, a retired Fife miner now living in Edinburgh.

KING FAREWEEL

Singer: Jock Cameron

Collected by Hamish Henderson

Transcribed F. C.

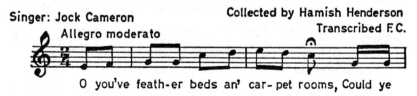

Allegro moderato

O you've feath-er beds an' car-pet rooms, Could ye

no' put doon a wee Ger-man laird-ie? For a bet-ter man sure than

ev-er he was lay a-mongst the hea-ther wi' the kilt and plaid-ie!

Refrain

King fare-weel! King fare-weel! It's a' to guard our king; Fare-weel!

THE CHILDREN'S SONGS

A survey of Lowland Scots song would not be complete without reference to the children's songs and nursery rhymes (or 'Nursery Songs' as they were earlier called) which have always formed a considerable and not unimportant part of it.

A fair number of nursery rhymes are common to both Scotland and England, as for instance 'The Wedding of the Frog and the Mouse' ('Kitty alone and I'), 'Old King Cole', 'The Fox and the Goose', and such rhymes as 'Old Mother Hubbard', 'Little Tom Thumb', 'Ding dong bell', 'Little Miss Muffet', 'Humpty Dumpty', and all those others which form the common currency of childhood in the two countries. To admit discussion of these would be to involve the whole subject of nursery rhymes in general, which is far beyond our scope. For the interested reader a good introduction to the subject will be found in Lina Eckenstein's *Comparative Studies in Nursery Rhymes* (London, 1906).

Scottish nursery rhymes and their tunes are to be found scattered through the whole literature of Scottish song. The well-known 'There was an old woman (wee wifie) wrapped up in a blanket' goes to a tune based on 'the rock and the wee pickle tow' which first appears in John Playford's *Musick's Handmaid* of 1663. The tune of 'Katie Bairdie', a nursery song pure and simple, appears in the Rowallan Manuscript circa 1620, and also in the Skene Manuscript (though it is not there recognizable as the same tune). 'Tom the Piper's Son' with its tune is to be found in D'Urfey's *Pills to Purge Melancholy* (1698–1720).

A number of the great Scottish ballads exist also in the form of children's versions. 'Willie Doo', or 'The Croodlin Doo' is a nursery version of Lord Randal (Child 12). 'The Fause Knight upon the Road' (Child 3) may be looked upon either a as ballad proper or as a nursery song, according to its use or circumstances. The children's song of 'Sandy Seaton's wooing' is a derivative of 'Kempy Kay' (Child 23). There is a children's version of the ballad of 'Glasgow Peggy' (Child 228) and a number of children's versions of the riddle ballads such as 'The Elfin Knight' ('My plaid awa') (Child 2). All these are to be found as major ballads in Child's work, and he gives several times as one of his sources for his own work Halliwell-Phillipps' *The Nursery Rhymes of England* (London, 1842).

There seems to be no very early collection of Scottish nursery songs as such. Perhaps it is because the transmission and circulation of the nursery song is more dependent upon oral transmission than upon the printed page. It is a poor mother or nurse who has to go to a book for a song to sing to her child! There are but six songs in the Herd Manuscript which have been brought together under the heading of 'Nursery Songs' by Hans Hecht in his *Songs from Herd's Manuscripts*. These are:

King Coull (Old King Cole).
When I was a wee thing (tune, 'John Anderson my Joe') (sic)[1]
The Dreg Song.[2]
The Nurse's song.
The Wren.
Robin Redbreast's Testament.

There is also a small group of material from the Herd Manuscript which Hecht has classified under the heading of 'Popular Rhymes', of which one or two may well have been recited or sung in the nursery, such as 'The Hunting of the Wren' ('Will ye go to the wood?' quo' Fozie Mozie) and 'Some say the devil's dead and buried in Kirkaldy'.

The first actual collection of Scots nursery rhymes was that made in 1826 by Robert Chambers in his *Popular Rhymes of Scotland*. Unfortunately, though it is a good collection, and worth study, there are only five tunes given for the Nursery Songs section of it, and but one other complete tune, with two small musical scraps, in the whole of the rest of the book. Obviously the songs of the nursery have suffered the same neglect of their tunes as the ballads did, and were collected by Chambers not for their value as songs, but for the much more doubtful one, as poetry. Even Chambers's declared purpose in his preface, 'to supply a presumed desideratum in popular antiquities' should have shown the desirability of publishing all the tunes possible.

---

[1] Properly spelt 'my Jo' = my dear, or my sweetheart.
[2] This is almost certainly one of the traditional rowing songs of the oyster fishermen of the Firth of Forth, and the writer would doubt the validity of its inclusion by Hecht as a nursery song. See article by the writer in 'Scottish Studies' Vol. 5. I. 1961.

In connection with this collection by Chambers, which may be regarded as the classic of the subject, a collection published in 1933 by Alfred Moffat, *Fifty Traditional Scottish Nursery Rhymes* (Augener Ltd) contains an interesting statement by Moffat in his introduction. He says:

> Many years ago I had the good fortune to be allowed access to a manuscript collection of traditional Scottish airs. This manuscript was in the possession of a well-known firm of booksellers in Edinburgh. It was undated and unsigned, but must have been written between the years 1845 and 1850. It contained a number of tunes which the compiler had evidently known to be the original airs to many of the songs collected by Dr Robert Chambers in his *Popular Rhymes of Scotland*. . . . It has enabled me to furnish a number of old rhymes with their traditional melodies, many of which have been forgotten, or, at the most, now linger in the memories of only a few elderly people.

Moffat's collection does indeed supply a number of the tunes which are missing in Chambers. The *Transactions of the Rymour Club* also give a useful number of nursery rhymes with their tunes.

Of later collections, three by Norah and William Montgomerie are useful and comprehensive. The first, *Scottish Nursery Rhymes*, gives a number of tunes; the second, *Sandy Candy* (Hogarth Press, 1948), gives two tunes only. *The Hogarth Book of Scottish Nursery Rhymes* gives texts only.

Children's game songs are of course a separate class and almost a separate study. The standard work is *The Traditional Games of England, Scotland and Ireland* by A. B. Gomme (1894) but this gives no tunes. A number of singing games both in Scottish and English versions with their tunes may however be found scattered throughout the journals of *The Folk Song Society*, with useful annotations by such experts on Scottish folk-song as the late Annie Gilchrist.

More recently an Edinburgh-made film of a few years ago, *The Singing Street*, shows a number of children's games as still sung in the Scottish capital. The words of a number of the rhymes and games have been published in booklet form.[1]

The traditional songs of childhood have been maintained in their proper forms from one generation of children to the next with a correctness of musical and textual constancy that is comparable to

[1] *The Singing Street: A Merry-Ma-Tanzie.* The Albyn Press, Edinburgh, 1951.
Since this book was begun there has appeared a full-length book under the same title of *The Singing Street*, by James T. R. Ritchie (Oliver & Boyd, 1964). This is a magnificent collection as far as the words of the songs are concerned and likely to be the definitive work on the subject for a long time to come. Unfortunately however it includes no tunes.

Gaelic tradition. One can well imagine of course that in the age groups in which they are sung, to get a word-sequence wrong would be to incur the scorn of one's contemporaries!

At the same time, and running concurrently with the 'classics' there has always been, as with the adult songs, a separate stream of *folk-song*, adding new material to the repertoire, though a good deal of it is evanescent. Some of this has been a commentary on current events, a parallel to the 'Stone of Destiny' songs in the adult corpus. Some rather frightful examples of this were to be seen in the children's songs to which the Burke and Hare murders of the early nineteenth century gave rise, of which the following, taken from *Sandy Candy* quoted above, is a fair sample:

> Burke and Hare,
> They were a pair;
> Killed a wife
> And didna care.
>
> Then they pit her
> In a box,
> And sent her aff
> Tae Dr Knox.

A less blood-curdling specimen of children's folk-song is that which concerns itself with the Peeblesshire 'sweetie' that was cried in the streets of the Border towns in the late years of the last century, and which has more recently become popular on the radio.

COULTER'S CANDY

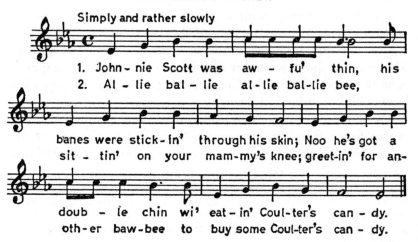

Simply and rather slowly

1. John-nie Scott was aw - fu' thin, his banes were stick-in' through his skin; Noo he's got a doub - le chin wi' eat-in' Coul-ter's can - dy.

2. Al - lie bal - lie al-lie bal-lie bee, sit - tin' on your mam-my's knee; greet-in' for an-oth-er baw-bee to buy some Coul-ter's can - dy.

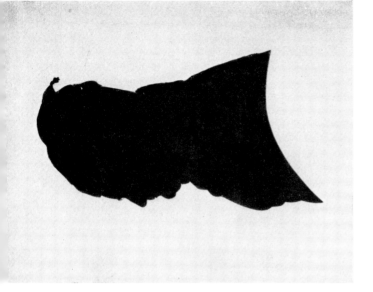

1 LEFT Frances Tolmie, born Skye 1840, died 1926. Collector and notator of Gaelic songs

2 ABOVE Patrick MacDonald, Minister of Kilmore, Argyll. Collector of 'Highland Vocal Airs'. Artist unknown

I will not goe to my bed till I sald die

The flowres of the forrest.

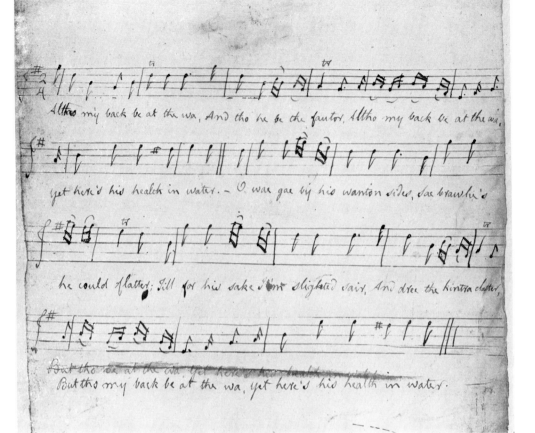

Altho my back be at the wa, And tho he be the fautor, Altho my back be at the wa,

yet here's his health in water. — O. wae gae by his wanton sides, sae brawlie's

he could flatter; Till for his sake I'm slighted sair, And dree the kintra clatter,

But tho my back be at the wa, yet here's his health in water.

6 James Hogg, the Ettrick Shepherd. Portrait by
Wm. Nicholson

7 RIGHT Double (drone?) pipe
player at the purification sacrifice
inaugurating the Roman Wall in
Scotland, *c.* 140 A.D., found at
Bridgeness East Lothian about 1870

8 BELOW Angel playing bagpipes.
Detail from the capital of a pillar in
Roslin Chapel, Midlothian. (15th
century)

This represents old Geordy Sime
a Famous Piper in his time

9 Geordy Sime, Lowland Scots bagpiper. Kay's Edinburgh
portraits, c. 1835. The wording reads—

> *This represents old Geordy Sime*
> *a Famous Piper in his time*

10 McArthur, Piper to Ranald Macdonald Esq. of Staffa

24 Called McGrigors Gathering
1st Hiharin hiodroveho cherede cheodrog, hiharin hiodroveho cherede cheodrodin, hihorodo hintroem barie herore hechedroo

2 Hiharin hiodroveho cherede cheodrodin hihorodo hintroembarie herere hiche dare chevehoe hio droembarie herere hechedroo

3 Hiharin hiodroveho cherede chedare the treho cheve ches hee hoe hiotrohoo hiharin four times

1 Hiharin hiodrod ho cherede cheodroo, hiharin hiotralho cherede cheodrodin hihorodo hintro dile herere hechedroo

2 Hiharin hiodrod ho cherede cheodrodin hihoro do hintrodile herere hede dare cheve hoe hiodrodile herere hechedroo

11 ABOVE A page from the Colin Campbell (Netherlorn) Canntaireachd

12 OPPOSITE LEFT Thought to be a self-portrait of Joseph MacDonald, author of *A Compleat Theory of the Scots Highland Bagpipe*

13 OPPOSITE RIGHT Rebec player. Stone carving on outside wall of south transept, Melrose Abbey. (12th century)

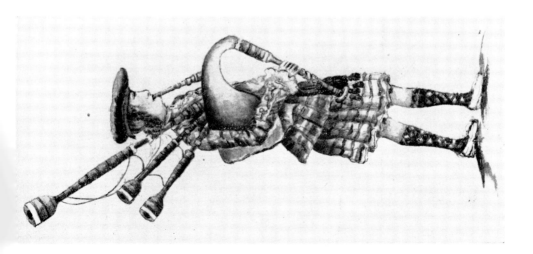

The Effigie of PATIE BIRNIE.
The Famous Fidler of Kinghorn;
Who gart the Lieges gawff and girn ay.
Ay till the Cock proclaim'd the Morn:

Tho baith his Weeds and Mirth were pirn.
He roos'd those Things were langest worn.
The brown Ale Barrel was his Kirn ay.
And faithfully he toom'd his Horn.

14 Patie Birnie, born c. 1635. Reputed composer of *The Auld Man's Meer's Dead*. Portrait by Wm. Aikman

15 Niel Gow, 1727-1807. Portrait by Sir Henry Raeburn

16 OPPOSITE *The Highland Dance* by David Allan (1744-96). The fiddler and 'cello player in the picture are Niel Gow and his brother Donald

17 ABOVE William Marshall, 'the first composer of strathspeys of the age' (Robert Burns). Portrait by John Main

18 ABOVE James Macpherson's fiddle, on view at the Clan Macpherson Museum, Newtonmore, Inverness-shire

19 LEFT Stone carving; seated harper on a cross-shaft from Monifeith, Angus. (10th century A.D.)

20 RIGHT The Queen Mary Harp
(c. 1500 A.D.)

21 BELOW Seventeenth century
carved oak panels from Greenlaw,
Kirkcudbrightshire with figures of a
fiddler and a piper with a single
drone bagpipe. These and similar
carvings in Dumfriesshire are thought
to be the work of a local Galloway
craftsman

22 ABOVE Harper's Gallery at Towie-Barclay, Aberdeenshire

23 RIGHT Hilda M. Campbell of Airds, Honorary Life
President of *Comunn na Clarsaich*. (The Clarsach Society)

CHAPTER V

The Bagpipes

SPECULATION on the origin of the bagpipe in Scotland must be largely futile, as the instrument is everywhere so ancient as to be beyond the means of establishing whether it was indigenous, or where otherwise it came from. W. H. Grattan Flood in *The Story of the Bagpipe* cites possible reference to Jubal and the bagpipe in the book of Genesis, and to the instrument in Nebuchadnezzar's private band in the third book of Daniel, referring to a Chaldean sculpture illustrating the first of these. He also writes of other sculptures depicting the instrument in Nineveh and Assyria. Pipes have been found at Panopolis in Egypt dating from 1500 B.C. (op. cit.). A Hittite slab on which is sculptured a bagpipe player, is dated by its discoverer, Professor Garstang at 1000 B.C. (op. cit.).

Gratton Flood continues with the chronicling of the finding of a bas-relief of the bagpipe on an arch at Kermanshap in Persia; of a terracotta of a piper playing the bagpipe, of date 250 B.C. at Tarsus, the birthplace of St Paul; of reed pipes of the drone type on an ancient fresco in a tomb near Thebes; of Chinese tradition of the discovery of the principle of the pipe in 2585 B.C.; of forms of the bagpipe in Ancient India; of references to the instrument by St Jerome; of the tradition of the playing of the bagpipes by the shepherds at the Nativity. There is an old English carol in a manuscript at Balliol College, Oxford, 'Ut Hoy! Jolly Wat's Song', which contains the lines as sung by the shepherd Jolly Wat:[1]

> O Jesu I offer to thee my scrip,
> My cloak and my tar-box and eke my pipe.
> (*Refrain*)   For he was a good herdes boy, Ut Hoy!
> For in his pipe he made so much joy.

Further references to the instrument exist, notably by the Greek writer Dion Chrystomos about A.D. 100; by the poet Martialis Valerius of the Epigrams about A.D. 105; by Seneca; and by Virgil.

---

[1] Set for voices by the writer and published by Stainer and Bell Ltd.

W. L. Manson in *The Highland Bagpipe* mentions a vow of the Roman Emperor Nero (A.D. 37–68) as recounted by Suetonius, that if he should be granted escape from his enemies he would play the bagpipe at the public games—a form of penance that suggests that the piper in Rome was one of the lower forms of life!

We know that the bagpipe was used in England by the Romans, from the finding of a sculptured bronze at Richmond Castle, Kent (Manson, op. cit.); and from the evidence of a sculpture at Stanwix near Carlisle, one of the stations of Hadrian's Wall, which shows a piper playing his pipes, that it was brought by the Romans to the North of England. That it was used by the Romans in Scotland itself we find from a similar sculptured stone found at Bridgeness near Bo'ness about 1870, depicting a party of Roman soldiers on the march[1] to the music of a piper (Manson). According to Manson also, the bagpipe is mentioned by Procopius, a Greek historian, as the instrument of the Roman Infantry, the trumpet being that of the cavalry.

In later times the bagpipes have existed or still exist all over Europe— in Russia as the *Volynka*; in Finland as the *Pilia*; in Germany as the *sackfpeife*, *chalemie* and *dudelsack* or *duday*; in France as the *cornemuse*[2] and the *musette*; in Naples as the *surdelina*, etc., etc.

In the face of all such evidence that the bagpipe has obviously been invented independently in many countries of the world, there is no need to suppose that the bagpipe must necessarily have been introduced into Scotland from outside. Certainly the Celts could have brought it with them, but it is just as possible that they found some form of musical pipe already in existence in the country when they got here.[3]

Iconography in Scotland itself shows the bagpipe in use at an early date. Two sculptures, according to Dalyell in his *Musical Memoirs*, were at one time to be seen at Melrose Abbey. The Abbey was built in 1136, but there seems to be some doubt as to whether both were contemporary with the building of the Abbey itself. The first is not now to be found and may have been removed or have perished with the weather. It stood above the apex of a window or doorway and showed an apparently aged musician playing the bagpipes. The other is a gargoyle in the form

---

[1] The National Museum of Antiquities of Scotland, where the stone is on view, describes the soldiers not as on the march but as taking part in a purification sacrifice. See plate 7.

[2] Necker de Saussure in his *Voyage en Ecosse* (Geneva, 1821) refers to the Scottish Highland Bagpipe as 'The Cornemuse'.

[3] R. L. C. Lorimer observes: 'Then why use a Latin name for it? (plob < pipa).' Nevertheless the writer feels justified in sticking to his point. It can only of course be a matter of opinion.

of a pig playing or holding a bagpipe. Manson mentions a tradition that this figure of the pig was placed there in the reign of James IV as a royal satire on the Highlanders, with whom it is said he did not always agree! Sculptures of animals—and, for some strange reason, of pigs particularly are a commonplace however, and if the tradition as regards James IV depends upon the pig for its authenticity it may well be disregarded, and the gargoyle accredited to a period possibly coeval with the rest of the Abbey.

Two other Scottish carvings of the pipes and pipers are to be seen in Roslyn Chapel, built in 1440. One, in the Lady Chapel, is of an angel playing the pipes. The other is of two human figures, one apparently lying asleep, the other playing the pipes. Illustrations of all four carvings may be seen in both Dalyell and Manson.

That the pipes were early in use in Scotland is borne out also by Highland Clan tradition, which states of both the Clan Menzies and Clan MacDonald that they had their pipes playing before them at the battle of Bannockburn (1314); and both Clans claim that the actual pipes or relics of them used at the battle are still in existence (Manson, pages 38–9). It should be said however that the bagpipes are not mentioned by Barbour, who only writes of horns and trumpets; and there seems to be no actual historical evidence of the bagpipes being played at the battle. It was however probably not till about 1375 that Barbour wrote (he is thought not to have been born until about two years after the battle) and it was perhaps too long after it to be trustworthy about such musical details, important as they may be to the student of Scots music.

Another early tradition of the use of the pipes was of their being played at the celebrated Battle of the North Insch of Perth, between the Clan Quhele and Clan Chattan, when the clans are said to have 'stalked in to the sound of their own great war pipes'. (James Mac-Kenzie, *History of Scotland*.) The earliest literary reference to the bagpipes in Scotland seems to be that in the poem of 'Peblis to the Play' said to have been written by James I of Scotland (1406–37) and he is said to have been a performer upon the instrument himself as well as upon the harp, trumpet, 'Shepherd's reed' and other instruments. As the scene of the poem is the town of Peebles however it is probable that the instrument intended in the allusion was the Border Bagpipe.

An ancient 'pibroch', '*Ceann na Drochaid Mhoridh*' (sic) (The End of the Great Bridge) said to have been 'composed in the midst of the Battle of Inverlochy' in 1427 is to be found in Donald MacDonald's *Ancient Martial Music of Caledonia*. The well-known pibroch of '*Donald*

Dubh' (Black Donald of the Isles' march to that battle) is said also to be a contemporary composition, though with what truth it is impossible to say.[1] This battle of course is not to be confused with the second battle of Inverlochy fought by Montrose in 1645, on which a pibroch, '*Ceann na Drochaid Beag* (sic) (Head of the Little Bridge) also known as 'The Clans' Gathering' was also composed. This is to be found in the same collection.

From Manson it may be quoted, again from the statement of the historian James Mackenzie, that at the battle of Harlaw the Highland host came down 'with pibrochs deafening to hear'. Manson observes however that the earliest known copy of the music of the Battle of Harlaw (which was also the title of a ballad) was not in bagpipe form.

George Buchanan (1506–82) mentions the bagpipe as the military instrument among the Gaelic-speaking people of Scotland, having supplanted the horn and trumpet on the battlefield. Alexander Hume, in the Bannatyne Manuscript, writes of 'Heiland pipes, Scottis and Hybernicke'. *The Complaynt of Scotland*, written about 1548 mentions the following instruments as then in use:

> The drone bagpipe.
> The pipe made of ane bleddir and of ane reid.[2]
> The trump (Jews' Harp)
> The Cornpipe.
> The pipe made of ane gait (goat) horne.
> The recorder.
> The fiddil.
> The quhissil.

The first pipes had probably only one drone, and according to Manson the second drone was added about 1500. The two-drone bagpipe was for long the standard instrument of the Highlands. Duncan Fraser, in his *The Bagpipe* (Edinburgh, undated), has a photograph of what he calls 'The Great Two-Drone War Pipe of the Highlands' of which the actual set of pipes is to be seen in the National Museum of Antiquities of Scotland.[3]

The Bass Drone or Great Drone, which, to quote Joseph MacDonald

[1] See however note on this tune by R. L. C. Lorimer on the sleeve of Waverley Records ZLP 2034, 'PIBROCH Volume 1'.
[2] According to Leyden this is the Cornemuse. (Introduction p. 152).
[3] The household accounts of Dunvegan show that a two-pipe (i.e. two-drone) set of bagpipes was bought for one of the MacCrimmons in 1711. Cf. *The Macleods*, I. F. Grant, Faber & Faber, London, 1959.

in his treatise on the Highland bagpipes, 'adds vastly to its grandeur' both in sound and show' was added some time after 1700. Manson is vague about this. Under the date A.D. 1700[1] he says: 'about the beginning of the nineteenth century the big drone was added to the bagpipe' (page 52). Later (page 72) he says 'the bagpipe had originally but one drone. A second drone was added about 1500 and a third *about 1800.*' Dalyell however gives an illustration of a set of bagpipes with the great drone, which he dates as 1745, though he does not substantiate the date.

Apparently the addition of the bass drone did not find immediate favour throughout the Highlands, for Joseph MacDonald writing in 1760–3 goes on to say: 'The reason given by the Pipers of the West Highlands for *laying aside the use of the Great Drone* was frivolous and unfounded, namely that the loudness of it drowned the sound of the Chanter music. But this is a mistake, and should it happen so, it is easily rectified by weakening the reed of the Great Drone.' Duncan Fraser observes that the three-drone Highland Pipe of today was not much used in the Highlands until the nineteenth century, and continues, 'In my young days, the Inverary Gipsies, who were—many of them— great pipers, never used any but a one-drone or two-drone Bagpipe'. Manson says, writing in 1901, 'Bagpipes with one drone are still used occasionally, and so late as the winter of 1899 an itinerant player might sometimes be seen, late at night, playing for coppers at Jamaica Street corner, Glasgow, on such an instrument.' He adds the interesting information that 'the *two-drone* pipes were barred at competitions owing to some supposed advantage they gave the player, and they appeared last in 1821'.

THE BAGPIPE SCALE

The scale of the Scottish Highland bagpipe is a highly individual one. It is approximately that of the Mixolydian scale on A, with an extra G natural below the keynote (bottom A), i.e.:

The intervals differ noticeably from those of either the natural or the tempered scale, which we are used to hearing in other music.

It is this deviation from the natural scale which makes the instrument difficult of acceptance to many ordinary musicians, who will probably

---

[1] This looks like a misprint for 1800.

bluntly declare that to them the bagpipes sound out of tune—an observation which was once made to the writer in these very words when lecturing to a body of musicians—*in Scotland*!

It must be remembered however that the notes of the bagpipes are never intended to be *sounded together in harmony*, as are wind instruments in an orchestra. The bagpipe is a *solo*, or at least a *unison, melodic* instrument which is only required to harmonize to the sound of its own drones. It is therefore not fundamentally necessary that the intervals should be of the standard sizes of tone and semitone which match and combine with each other in concert; and it is obvious that a scale must necessarily have greater variety and characteristic quality in which the successive steps do not so conform to each other like houses in a row or peas in a pod. It may be said indeed, that in the individual scale of the bagpipes each note of it, because of this very difference of interval, has its own particular flavour; and it is largely a question of becoming familiar with it to be able to appreciate and eventually to savour its sound.

Many attempts have been made to measure the scale of the pipe, by such means as comparison with tuning forks or with the aid of the monochord, in which latter the length and therefore the pitch of a vibrating string can be varied by means of a movable bridge, and so made to correspond exactly with the pitch of each note of the pipe in turn. The pitch can then be calculated from the length of the vibrating string.

The first investigation was made by the celebrated writer on accoustics, A. J. Ellis, who published his results in the additions to his translation of Helmholtz's *Sensations of Tone* in 1885. Ellis's results, which have since been shown to be inaccurate, purported to show that the scale from low A upwards (for some reason he ignored the low G) was composed approximately of two intervals, the full tone and an interval mid-way between a semitone and a full tone—i.e. a semitone and a half, or three-quarters of a tone, as shown on next page.

A number of further attempts to measure the scale have been made since, both by accoustical scientists and by pipers, but all with widely varying results as between one instrument, or one player, and another; and the results cannot be said to be very conclusive.

Between 1954 and 1961 however, J. M. A. Lenihan[1] and Seumas McNeill[2] of Glasgow University made a series of measurements by

[1] J. M. A. Lenihan is Physicist to The Western Regional Hospital Board (Scotland).
[2] Seumas McNeill is Senior Lecturer in Natural Philosophy, Glasgow University, and Principal of the College of Piping (Glasgow).

ELLIS'S SCALE

High

A

— a full tone.

G

— ¾ of a full tone (or a semitone and a half).

F

— ¾ of a full tone (or a semitone and a half).

E

— A full tone.

D

— ¾ of a full tone (or a semitone and a half).

C

— ¾ of a full tone (or a semitone and a half).

B

— A full tone.

A

Low

means of a double-beam oscillograph in conjunction with a valve-maintained tuning fork.[1] This is probably the most accurate system yet used; but it must be said that in readings taken from 18 different pipers, the results are disappointingly lacking in unanimity, and for two of the readings there is actually an admitted deviation of as much as 22 cents. It may be accepted however from the work of these two investigators that the pitch of the low A of the chanter—the 'keynote' of the scale—is 459 vibrations or 'frequencies' per second. This is nearer the present orchestral A sharp (467) than to orchestral A (440).

From the average of the readings observed by them, the following general comparison between the natural scale and the pipe-scale may be observed:

Natural Scale	Pipe Scale Compared
High	
A —	In tune.
G (G♮)	Sharp.
F (F♯)	Slightly flat.
E —	In tune.
D —	Sharp.
C (C♯)	Flat.
B —	In tune.
A —	Starting point.
G (G♮)	Slightly flat.
Low	

[1] Cf. Seumas MacNeill, *Piobaireachd*, 1968, pp. 26-9.

165

It must be emphasized of course that the above table is merely the comparison of one scale with another. It is quite incorrect to say that because the pipe interval varies from the natural scale it is out of tune. It is in tune in its own right.

From the above comparison the following deductions may be made:

1. As the C ♯ of the pipe scale is flat compared with the natural scale, and the B is in tune, the interval between B and C ♯ must be less than a full tone.

2. As the D of the pipe scale is sharper than that of the natural scale, the interval between C and D must be greater than a semitone.

3. As the note E is in tune, and the D is sharp, the interval between D and E must be less than a full tone.

4. As the F ♯ of the pipe scale is flat, the interval between E and F ♯ must be less than a full tone.

5. As the high G of the pipe-scale is sharp, the interval between F ♯ and G must be greater than a semitone.

6. As the high A is in tune and the G is sharp, the interval between the high G and high A must be less than a full tone.

If now for the sake of distinction we call the interval which is less than a full tone a *minor full tone* and the interval which is greater than a semitone a *great semitone* we may express the intervals of the pipe scale in tabular form as follows:[1]

```
High
A
     — A minor full tone.
G
     — A great semitone.
F
     — A minor full tone.
E
     — A minor full tone.
D
     — A great semitone.
C
     — A minor full tone.
B
     — An ordinary full tone.
A
     — Slightly more than a full tone.
G.
Low
```

[1] The writer's own theory is that the origin of these pitch inflections of the bagpipe may have been a vocal one, arising from the instinctive tendency which the writer has long observed in the untutored traditional singer to divide the gap of a minor third in the pentatonic scale by an approximation towards a mid-way point. This has the

The pitch of the drones of the bagpipe must next be considered. To the ear of most people, the tenor drone appears to be in unison with the low A of the chanter, and the bass drone an octave below; and in fact this is stated by Manson to be the case. The investigations of McNeill and Lenihan however, who give the frequencies of the tenor and bass drone as 227 and 114 respectively, show that the fundamental note of the tenor drone is actually the A on the top line of the bass clef (i.e. an octave below the low A of the chanter) and the fundamental note of the bass drone, the A on the bottom space of the bass clef (i.e. two octaves below the low A of the chanter). The tenor drone has however a first (octave) harmonic so strong as to appear to the ordinary ear to be the actual fundamental note of the drone, and so to make the pitch of this drone seem to be an octave higher than it really is. The bass drone on the other hand is shown by these investigators to have a strong *second* harmonic giving the effect of a fifth.

The scale and pitch of the chanter and drones of the Scottish Highland bagpipe may therefore be set down as follows:

The bagpipe has existed in the Highlands of Scotland in different sizes. Joseph MacDonald, writing about 1760 says in his treatise:

> Though the Reels and Jigs peculiar to the Pipe are in large companies as at Weddings, etc. played to good effect on the greater Pipe, yet they have besides, thro' the Highlands in general, a smaller Bagpipe, Compleat, the same in form and apparatus with the greater, differing only in size, and used for Dancing Music alone, altho' all other Music peculiar to the instrument may be played on it as truly, though not so grandly, as on the large Pipe.

In a catalogue of prices in the early editions of J. and R. Glen's *Collection for the Great Highland Bagpipe* (first published in 1870) three different sizes or types of bagpipes are listed, viz.:

---

effect of increasing or sharpening the upward step of a *semitone* within the Pentatonic gap, and of flattening the upward step of a *whole tone*, as in the pipescale itself. It would however take more space than is warranted here to develop the theory. Cf. the writer's article on the subject in the *Piping Times*, Vol. 16, No. 8; May 1964.

1. The Great Highland or Military Bagpipes.
2. Half-size or Reel Bagpipes, blown with mouth or bellows.
3. Miniature or Chamber Bagpipes, blown with mouth or bellows.

In a still earlier price-list by Alexander Glen in 1860, in addition to the three types mentioned above, there appears also the Lovat Reel Pipe, also blown either by mouth or bellows, which seems to have been an intermediate size between types 2 and 3, i.e. between the half-size or reel pipe and the miniature or chamber bagpipes. A specimen of the miniature or chamber bagpipes, mouth-blown, may be seen in the Royal Scottish Museum in Chambers Street, Edinburgh. Half-size pipes, or rather half-*scale* pipes (for the pipes are the standard length) of the same pitch as the full-sized Great Highland Bagpipe, but of smaller diameter and softer reeds, are still occasionally manufactured, and the writer has seen a newly manufactured set in the shop of a bag-pipe maker in Edinburgh. Pipes smaller than the Great or Battle Pipe are frequently mentioned in Gaelic song, and must have been in common use at one time.

THE LOWLAND OR BORDER BAGPIPE

The Lowland or Border bagpipe seems to have gone out of use about the middle of last century. It was a flourishing instrument in the Borders in the days of Sir Walter Scott, whose uncle Thomas Scott of Monklaw, Roxburghshire, was a skilful performer. Alexander Campbell, the organist of the Episcopal Chapel in the Cowgate, Edinburgh, who taught music to Sir Walter Scott as a boy, made a tour of the Borders in 1816, in the course of which he interviewed this Thomas Scott at Monklaw and elicited much information from him about the pipers of the Scottish Borders past and present. These included the famous Hastie family, who were reputed to have held the post of town-pipers of Jedburgh since the time of Flodden—three hundred years. (Leyden, in his introduction to *The Complaynt of Scotland*, tells us that the then living representative of the family showed him a set of Border bagpipes which he averred were the very pipes which his ancestor had played at the battle of Flodden!) Alexander Campbell's notes on the border pipers may be conveniently read in the notes to Johnson's *Scots Musical Museum* (Laing's additional notes).

The chief characteristic of the Scottish Border bagpipe was that, like the later forms of the Northumbrian types, the bag was blown with a bellows instead of by the mouth through a blowpipe. The bellows was worked by the right arm and it filled the bag held under the left arm by a wind-pipe which lay across the chest.

The Border or Lowland pipes seem to have been made in several different forms, and as the present expert on them and on the Northumbrian pipes, Mr William A. Cocks, informs the writer, each maker appears to have been a law unto himself.

Manson says (page 66) that 'the real Lowland bagpipe never got further than two drones; but this is not borne out either by the specimens surviving of them or by contemporary illustrations, all of which show three drones. It is possible that like the Highland bagpipe it started with two—perhaps even one, and acquired a third drone later. Mr William Cocks lists the several types as follows:

1. The commonest ordinary form, with two 12-inch tenor and one 24-inch bass drone all in one stock and all sounding tonic harmony. Bores varying in diameter.

2. Similar to above, but with one treble, one tenor one bass drone. These all sound tonic harmony. The treble drone is a unison with the lowest finger hole of the chanter.

3. Similar to (1) but with one tenor, one bass, one dominant between. When playing D tunes, the dominant must be silenced. It is this form which was played often in Northumberland, but the others are also found there.

4. A form of hybrid Irish Union Pipe, generally having two tonic drones in octaves, and a 'regulator' all in one stock. The chanter is like that found on the Irish pipe, but it has an added foot joint and is played as the ordinary Scots form. This type appears to have been in use in the later half of the eighteenth and the early nineteenth centuries, but has completely died out. Neither Ireland nor Scotland will own to it.

5. The small-pipes, both Lowland and Highland, the Lowland being bellows-blown and the Highland being mouth-blown. They are alike in other respects, and all have drones in one stock. Chanters $6\frac{1}{2}$–7, drones 5–6, $6\frac{1}{2}$–7, 10–$10\frac{1}{2}$ inches, sounding keynote, octave lower, and fifth between. Chanters usually tapered outside but with parallel bore, open ended.

It will be noticed that number 3 among the full-sized pipes and number 5 (the small-pipes) differ from the Highland pipes in that the drones sound the dominant fifth as well as the tonic, the fifth being between the octave tonic drones. Contrary to a good deal of popular supposition there is no fifth in the drones of the Highland bagpipe, though the third harmonic of the bass drone, which sounds the fifth, is so strong as to be easily mistaken, even by a trained musical ear, for a drone note.

It will be seen from Mr Cocks's account that as far as the chanter scale is concerned, and irrespective of the arrangement of the drones, there were two main sizes of the Border bagpipe; (a) the larger, whose chanter scale was the same as the Great Highland bagpipe, namely running upwards from G natural, the second bottom line of the treble stave, to A, nine notes higher, the scale being the mixolydian scale on A (that is, the scale of A with a G natural); and (b) the smaller size, the 'small-pipes'—perhaps the more interesting because of their differences from the Highland pipes.

Accounts of the scale and pitch of the Scottish Border small-pipes are unfortunately conflicting. Probably the only way to make certain of it would be to try to have a scale played on one of them, which indeed would be an interesting thing to do. From the evidence at present available, the writer's guess would be as follows:

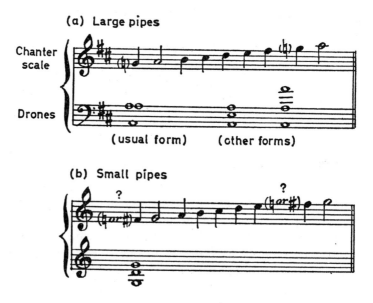

It must be added that the Border or Lowland piper had a method of extending the upward compass by a note or two by the technique known as 'pinching' which was a special way of covering the back hole of the chanter with the thumb-nail; and one of the best known of the Border pipe-tunes, 'Soor Plooms of Galashields' was of a compass which required this particular art to reach the top notes of the melody. The Selkirk version of 'The Flowers of the Forest', that known as

'The Lilting', is another Border pipe melody which would have required the same technique for a similar reason.

The chief difference between the Scottish and the Northumbrian small-pipes is that the chanter of the Northumbrian instrument is stopped up at the end, so that when all the holes are covered by the fingers, the sound ceases. By this means it is possible to repeat a note and even to articulate the notes of the scale *staccato*, a feat impossible with the open-ended chanter, where, the wind-stream being unbroken, the sound is continuous and the repetition of a note can only be *suggested* by means of intervening grace-notes or 'cuttings' between the note and its repetition. The Scottish Border small-pipes have the usual open-ended chanter. In the Highland pipe technique these 'cuttings' referred to are highly conventionalized and the piper conforms to them very strictly: but according to Joseph MacDonald there were no such standardized patterns of grace-notes in the Lowland techniques. (MacDonald, page 28, 1927 edition.)

The Lowland and Border pipes seem to have gone out of general use by the time the nineteenth century was half-way through, though a few individual pipers seem to have continued to play them here and there until nearer the end of the century. Grattan Flood mentions their particular popularity in the Falkirk district. Manson, writing in 1901, even goes as far as to say (page 60) that the Lowland pipe was not then completely extinct, and 'a few years ago there were at least two performers on it'.

The Border piper was a popular figure at all the fairs and weddings and similar public gatherings, of which there is a passing allusion in 'Peblis to the Play'. He was particularly welcomed in the harvest field. Leyden tells of how 'the intervals of labour during harvest were often occupied in dancing the Ring-dance to the music of the piper attending the reapers'. This ring-dance, in which 'every aged shepherd leads his wife by the hand and every young shepherd the maid whom he loves best, was the common dance at the Kirn or the feast of cutting down the grain'. (Leyden, page 130.)

Leyden adds also the extremely interesting information that:

Besides the characteristic melodies of the Lowlands of Scotland, the Borders, particularly the middle and west Marches, possessed a peculiar style of music, well adapted to the bagpipe, the wild and ferocious expression of which corresponded to the fierce and energetic character of the Border clans. The original airs of the *Gathering songs* and Historical ballads have no inconsiderable resemblance to the martial tunes of the Welsh, Irish, and the Scottish Highlanders, and formed the favourite music of the Border pipers, among whom the perfection of the art was supposed to consist in being able to sing, dance and play on the bagpipe at the same time.

With the town pipers, there is the utmost reason to believe that many ancient airs have perished. The last piper at Jedburgh, whom I have often heard play on the bagpipe in infancy, always affirmed that he was acquainted with some ancient airs unknown to every other person. I can only recollect 'The Hunting of the Fox', which from its uncommon expression and the irregularity of its modulation seemed to have a strong resemblance to a Highland Pibroch.

If such music really existed, it seems only too certainly lost to us for ever—a loss at which the mind of every Borderer must positively reel with exasperation and regret. It is, one fears, too much to hope that one day a fragment of it may turn up in some old manuscript music book, as the old volumes of Highland pibrochs turned up at a piping competition in the nineteenth century to open up a new vista of Highland music, an incident to be described in its proper place. There is no harm in hoping!

But whether the old lost pipe-music of the Borders, seemingly equivalent in some measure to the Highlander's *Ceòl-Mór*, ever turns up or not, plenty of the smaller Border pipe-tunes survive, if the instrument were there to play them. It seems strange, and a pity, that the Borderer's own musical instrument should have succumbed to the benevolent tyranny of the Highland bagpipe and its music. When we think of how popular and flourishing the Northumberland pipes are, not many miles across the Border, it might not seem out of place to suggest that a revival of the Scottish Border Bagpipe is long overdue.

THE NOTATION OF BAGPIPE MUSIC

There is an ancient system for the notation of *pibroch* called *canntaireachd*, in which both the note and grace-note figurations of that music is represented by vocable syllables. This will be discussed later and it is convenient to deal first with the conventional usage of staff notation in which bagpipe music is now printed. Briefly this consists of omitting all accidentals from the key signature, and writing everything as in the 'open key'. This is in accordance with the piper's own naming of the notes of his instrument, in which he customarily omits all reference to accidentals in the notes of the pipe scale. Thus C sharp is called simply C or 'the C, and F sharp similarly is referred to as F or "the F".' The earliest publications of bagpipe music, by the brothers Joseph and

Patrick MacDonald, are inconsistent in their use of key signature, and they use two sharps, one sharp and no sharps in arbitrary fashion in their examples. Joseph MacDonald's rather cryptic remark in his *Compleat Theory of the Scots Highland Bagpipe* may however not be without significance in the context, namely, that 'There is no natural C or F in the Bagpipe Scale, nor has it any Flats or Sharps, as neither the compass of this instrument, nor the Nature of its compositions can well admit of any.' Angus MacArthur whose manuscript collection of pibroch in staff notation is the oldest in existence by a professional piper, uses a system of his own, in which he writes the bottom note of the pipes (G) as middle C. The system is unique to himself.

Donald MacDonald, bagpipe maker in Edinburgh, who was the next in date with his *Collection of the Ancient Martial Music of Caledonia as performed on the Great Highland Bagpipe*, published in 1822, uses the key signatures of one sharp, three sharps, and open key apparently indiscriminately. He describes the collection however, which is mostly of pibroch, as 'Now also adapted to the Pianoforte, Violin and Violoncello'; and perhaps the use of key signatures is a concession to this, though the use of a key signature of *three* sharps is puzzling, for of course the third sharp, G sharp, does not exist on the instrument, the G being natural.

Angus Mackay, Raasay, was the first to publish a collection of pibroch *mainly* for the pipes alone, *A Collection of Ancient Piobaireachd or Highland Pipe Music* (Edinburgh, 1838). Even he cannot refrain however from adding a 'left hand part' to five of the more romantically titled pibrochs out of his total of seventy-one, including 'MacCrimmon will never return' and 'The MacIntosh's Lament. He gives the 'pianoforte versions' the key signature of three sharps (except, curiously, 'MacCrimmon will never return', which is printed without sharps); but all those which are printed for the pipes alone are in open key signature. As Angus Mackay's book was the 'piper's bible' of its day and long afterwards, the practice of writing bagpipe music without key signature may therefore fairly be said to stem from him.

It is a convenient system, and as the notes of the chanter are fixed, and not capable of being raised or lowered chromatically, is not without justification in use. It has to be admitted however that it can be a little confusing to the ordinary musician with the instinct of a lifetime in reading music according to its key signature. For the purpose of easier reading, the key signature of two sharps is therefore inserted in parenthesis in the examples following in this book.

CHAPTER VI

The Music of the Pipes

THE music of the bagpipe may be divided into two main types, *Ceòl-Mór* (Great Music) and *Ceòl-Beag* (Small or Little Music). The term *Ceòl-Mór* is confined solely to the musical form known as *pìobaireachd* (pibroch) and has no other meaning; while *Ceòl-Beag* includes a variety of the lighter types of music such as marches and quicksteps, and the common types of Highland dance music—the reel, strathspey and jig.

There is also another type sometimes mentioned, *Ceòl-Meadhonach* or 'middle music', i.e. neither great nor small. This is used to denote the music of song tunes, lullabies and sung laments such as for instance the well-known '*Crò Chinn t-Sàile*' (The Croe of Kintail)—though this probably has a piobaireachd basis—and also of the military Ceremonial Slow March, etc. Except for this last, the term is not solely confined to the music of the pipes like the other two, but is also usable in the wider musical sense of vocal music. It is however of much less common usage than either *ceòl mór* or *ceòl beag*. The Croe of Kintail is the tract of land between the head of Loch Duich and Beinn Fhada in S.W. Ross.

CEÒL MÓR ('*The Great Music*') OR PÌOBAIREACHD

The above is the correct spelling of the word popularly known as 'pibroch', a popularization of spelling and pronunciation which is attributed by Manson to Sir Walter Scott[1] (Manson, page 79). Something like the correct pronunciation can be approximated in the phonetic spelling *piparachk*, the *ì* having the sound of *ee*, the *b* having nearly the sound of *p*, and the final *d* having the sound of *k*. The word 'pibroch' is frequently taken by the uninformed to mean the bagpipes themselves. It is to be hoped that no one who has read this book thus

---

[1] The *Shorter Oxford English Dictionary* however records the word 'pibroch' as being in use in 1719, i.e. before the time of Scott.

174

far will make this **mistake,** but it is surprising how widespread the mis-apprehension is, even in Scotland itself.

Piobaireachd is a highly esoteric music, hardly known, even to the very meaning of the name, outside the circle of the pipers themselves (though radio has perhaps lifted a small corner of the curtain surrounding it in recent years). Yet it is in many ways the greatest, and certainly the most highly organized and extended form of Scottish traditional music. It is obviously music composed by gifted and trained composers, of whom tradition names a number, with their individual piobaireachd ascribed to them, notably the MacCrimmons. Nevertheless we must class it as *traditional,* firstly because, though the names of the composers are accepted by popular tradition, the authorship of very few pieces can be verified, and few modern collections of piobaireachd assembled by modern methods of research venture to give the names of any composers (even of the MacCrimmons) to individual pieces, except in the case of one or two later compositions where evidence is definite enough to be acceptable; secondly, because all of it, in a very special way, has been handed on by oral transmission from master to pupil, and not from the printed page. There was, as we have said, a special and most unique form of notation known as *canntaireachd,* but as far as can be ascertained, it was never used to play from as a musical score is used by the ordinary present-day musician. It seems to have been chiefly used as a means of vocal demonstration by the master of how each phrase should be played and phrased (we have incontrovertable descriptions from the older pipers that this was the method of teaching) and it seems only in a secondary sense to have been used as an aid to memory. It was expected of the player of *ceòl-mór* to store the music in his memory, and the great players are known to have had a repertoire by this means of as many as two hundred piobaireachd (compositions extending from about seven to as much as twenty minutes in length) as one such piper claimed to the writer.

The three main type-names of piobaireachd may be set down as 'The Salute', 'The Gathering' and 'The Lament'. It would not be possible however to docket every piobaireachd under these headings, and there are a number which it would be hard to classify under any of the three. They are all of the same form, with only minor modifications where any exist at all.[1]

[1] R. L. C. Lorimer adds: 'There are also a good many "Battle-tunes"—e.g. *Blar Bhatairnis* (The Battle of Waternish), *Blar Sliabh an t-Siorra* (The Battle of Sheriffmuir), *Ceann Drochaid Pheairt* (The Battle of the Bridge of Perth), etc. While most pibrochs in some sense are clan-music (e.g. "Lament for *Ruairidh Mór*", "Macleod's Rousing Tune", etc.) others express purely personal feelings, e.g. "Lament for the Children".'

It may be appropriate here to add that Thomas Newte, in his *Tour in England and Scotland* (1791) quotes one of the MacCrimmons (he does not say which) as declaring that 'Music in general was divided into four kinds; music for love, music for sorrow, music for war and music for *meat*' (i.e. feasting and celebration).

In form, piobaireachd may be described as an air with variations; but while some of the variations may be of a free melodic character of a simple order, others are of complicated *stereotyped* form, consisting of the application of certain extended grace-note patterns or formulae to the notes of the ground, or rather to selected notes of it. Each of these stereotyped patterns is progressively more intricate and of greater technical display that the one before it, but the whole piece ends with a dramatic return to the simple air itself.

The ramifications of the piobaireachd form within this prescribed formula are so great that it is hardly possible to make any statement about its form and construction without having to admit at once of exceptions to it. Nevertheless we may set down the basic standard form as consisting of four main sections:

1. The Urlar (Ground).
2. The Siubhal; or Dithis.
3. The Taorluath.
4. The Crunluath.

Each of these sections may have its own set of variations of a melodic type, some of which are called *doublings* (a term which bears much the same meaning as the French '*double*' in the classical dance-suites for keyboard by Handel, Bach and Couperin); and each of these may appear in one of several special forms, each of which has its own appropriate name, while the last two have an *additional* form called the Taorluath *a mach* or Crunluath *a mach*. So many exceptions exist in which one or more of the above movements may not appear however, that one must add that the only movement which one does expect to find in *almost* every piobaireachd is the Ground. Even this, paradoxical as it may seem of a Ground with variations, is dispensed with in one or two of the older 'gathering' piobaireachd where the piece begins with a movement in the form of the stereotyped variation known as the Taorluath Fosgailte.[1] Some piobaireachd have no *siubhal* or *dithis* movement and proceed straight from the ground and/or its own melodic variations or doublings to the Taorluath; some have no Taorluath; some no Crunluath; and

[1] See the three piobaireachd composed on the two battles of Inverlochy, in Donald MacDonald's collection.

some neither of these two movements. Some may have melodic variations or doublings of each section, while some may have no such variations at all.

The whole schedule of possible movements of a piobaireachd may be set out as follows:

1. The Urlar or Ground, with its variations and/or doublings, including (first) the high A or 'thumb' variation.
2. The Siubhal (or Dithis), with its doubling and, sometimes, trebling.
3. The Leumluath, with its doubling and, sometimes, trebling.
4. The Taorluath, with its doubling and, sometimes, trebling.
4a. (alternative) Taorluath Fosgailte, with its doubling and, sometimes, trebling.
4b. (alternative) Taorluath Breabach, with its doubling and, sometimes, trebling.
5. Taorluath a mach, with its doubling and, sometimes, trebling.
6. Crunluath, with its doubling and, sometimes, trebling.
6a. (alternative) Crunluath Fosgailte, with its doubling and, sometimes, trebling.
6b. (alternative) Crunluath Breabach, with its doubling and, sometimes, trebling.
7. The Crunluath a mach.
8. The return of the Ground.[1]

The Ground or *Urlar* (a Gaelic word of which *ground* or *floor* is the literal translation) often known to pipers as 'the tune', is a slow melody, usually of sixteen bars in length. In tempo it is an adagio, of the speed of about quaver = 60 to the minute. Joseph MacDonald, the first writer on the subject, tells us that the old pipers reckoned their rhythm not by bars but by 'fingers', and he says that the Ground or Adagio (as he calls it) was usually sixteen bars or fingers in length, divided into four quarters, each of four bars or fingers; that is to say in modern parlance that the sixteen bar Ground consisted of four phrases of four bars each. Strangely enough this does not conform to modern opinion regarding the scansion of a piobaireachd ground, which regards the Urlar in its most regularly recurring form as being divided into three phrases or sections of 6, 6, and 4 bars respectively, totalling 16 bars in this way. It is one of the puzzles of piobaireachd that the observations of Joseph MacDonald, a highly intelligent observer with a wide knowledge of music contemporary with the piping MacCrimmons when great piobaireachd were still being composed, should be so at variance in this

[1] The above table is based on Manson, p. 81.

respect with the opinions of later writers.[1] This is not the place to discuss the subject in greater detail however and the interested reader may be referred to the Introduction of *Ceòl Mór* by General C. S. Thomason, a devoted life-long student of the subject; and to recent researches by R. L. C. Lorimer published in *Scottish Studies* (vol. 6, pt. 1; and vol. 8, pt. 1. *contd.*).

The Urlar is commonly much ornamented by grace-notes conventional to this music and to the technique of the instrument. Most of these are too quick to be perceivable in their component notes by the ear of the non-piper, and the ordinary reader is recommended to disregard them in order to get the proper feel of the tune—at least to begin with. Here are the first eight bars (i.e. four bars repeated) of a typical Urlar, from the piobaireachd 'The MacLeod's Salute', traditionally attributed to Donald Mór MacCrimmon (*c.* 1570–1640) as it is noted by Angus MacKay of Raasay:

THE MACLEOD'S SALUTE

The reader is recommended to count two beats to a crotchet, and until he has got the feel of the time, to ignore all grace-notes, i.e. in reading it over to himself without a musical instrument.

The chief function of the *Siubhal* or *Dithis*[2] variation is to transform the melody of the Urlar into a regular rhythmic figure upon which the patterns of the Taorluath and Crunluath may be imposed. *Siubhal* is given in the Gaelic dictionary as meaning *moving*, and as the tempo usually quickens in the Siubhal or Dithis from the Adagio of the Urlar to something like crotchet = 76, the term will be seen to be apt. The figure of the siubhal is a rising one of two notes, of which the second, i.e. the higher of the two, is the theme note. A piobaireachd may con-

---

[1] Lorimer observes: 'The wonder is rather that modern "authorities" are so at variance with him!'

[2] Pronounced Gee-eesh (with soft G).

tain either a siubhal or a dithis but not both. The following example of
the first four bars of a siubhal is extracted from the piobaireachd '*An
Daorach Mhór*' (The Big Spree), ('The MacLeod's Salute' given above
contains the dithis type of variation instead of a Siubhal). The theme
notes are ringed round for clearness in this and the following examples.

In the Dithis form of variation the rhythmic two-note figure is in
general terms a falling one, in which the theme note is the first of the
pair, the second usually falling to A. The word Dithis means in Gaelic
simply *a pair, two*.[1] Here are the first few bars of the Dithis from 'The
MacLeod's Salute'. This should be compared with the ground given
above.

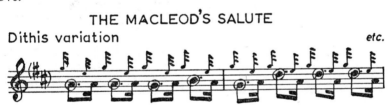

[*continued overleaf*

[1] There appears to be a certain amount of disagreement and vagueness as to the
precise use of the terms *siubhal* and *dithis*. In some of the earlier treatises, siubhal seems
to be used as a generic term to denote the transformation of selected notes of the Urlar
into a faster two-note rhythmic movement whether of rising or falling form, and a
certain amount of confusion and contradiction arises from this. Angus Mackay (1838)
nowhere uses the term *dithis*, and *siubhal* often appears in his collection above a dithis
figure. Donald MacDonald (1822) uses neither term, and the corresponding transformation of the Urlar appears simply under the heading of 'Variation', numbered.
The nomenclature set down by the writer appears to be the more modern one and is
deduced by him from the more recent collections. It is to be observed however that
both terms disappear from use half-way through the volumes of the Piobaireachd
Society; and that in the *Kilberry Book of Ceòl Mor* the term *siubhal* does not appear
anywhere in the musical text, but only in the introduction. The word *dithis* appears
only in one piobaireachd in the *Kilberry Book*, 'The Lament for the Union'; but this is
a piobaireachd remarkable for containing three different dithis variations in succession
and is a special case. Elsewhere in the *Kilberry Book* these movements are simply headed
'*variation*' with a numeral.

It may be noticed that not all the ringed notes in the dithis appear in the Urlar—the low G's for example, but they become the theme notes for the variations which follow, e.g. the Taorluath and Crunluath.

In the piobaireachd we are examining, 'The MacLeod's Salute', the *dithis* variation is followed by a *'doubling' of the variation*. The corresponding four bars of the *doubling* are shown for comparison. It will be seen that, as in many piobaireachd, the difference between the variation and its doubling, which is purely melodic, is small. Often there is even less difference, this being sometimes confined to a mere alteration of the phrase ending, generally by an additional two-note figure in place of a straight cadence (using the term *cadence* in the usual musical sense).

THE MACLEOD'S SALUTE

"Doubling" of dithis variation – 1st 8 bars

The *Taorluath*,[1] which is the third of the main sections of piobair-

---

[1] *Taorluath*, etymologically, is an unsatisfactory term untranslatable in Gaelic. *Luath* in Gaelic means swift, which is, however, exactly opposite in character, generally speaking, to this piobaireachd movement; for although it is the first of that series of movements of piobaireachd having quick chains of grace-notes following the theme-note, pipers of the old school actually often *steadied up* the tempo at that point, possibly for clarity of articulation. (Cf. *The Kilberry Book of Ceòl Mor*, p. 19, 'Method of Playing'.)

William Matheson says: '*Luath* in the nomenclature is a mistake. MacMhaighstir Alasdair gives it as *lùth*, and renders it "spring" which of course is a musical term in English. This must be correct, for *lùth* also has the other meanings in Gaelic that it has in English.' Nevertheless the word is now spelt *luath* in the piobaireachd collections.

Miss Mairi A. MacDonald of Inverness, daughter of Alexander MacDonald who published the 1927 reprint of Joseph MacDonald's *Compleat Theory of the Scots Highland Bagpipe*, sets down in *Transactions of the Gaelic Society of Inverness*, Vol. xxxix/xl (1942–1950), an interesting theory of her father's that the word *Taorluath* is a misspelling of *Taobhluadh*—a word of *harpist* derivation meaning 'side-falling' (i.e.

eachd, in its usual standard form consists of a chain of grace-notes coming *after* the theme note and finishing on the note A, as follows:

The Taorluath figuration

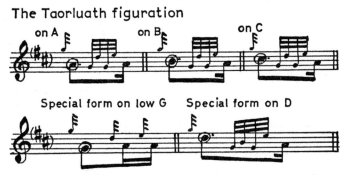

The special forms on theme notes low G and D are necessary for technical reasons of fingering.

The preliminary high G grace note is an essential feature, except when the theme note itself is on high G when the grace-note has perforce to be high A; or when the theme-note is high A, when the grace-note is omitted. Let us now see how the Taorluath figure is applied to the theme-notes of the previous variation, the *dithis*, in 'The MacLeod's Salute':

THE MACLEOD'S SALUTE

Taorluath – 1st 8 bars

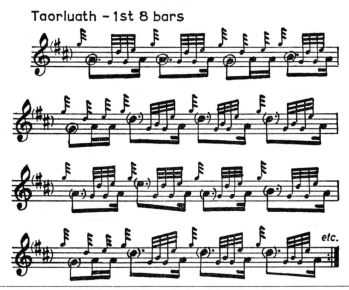

---

downward arpeggios?). The Taorluath of piobaireachd is of course, overall, a falling figure from the comencing theme-note to the last note of the grace-note chain (low A).

The Crunluath, the fourth main section of the Piobaireachd, is a term which is, strictly speaking, untranslatable. The Gaelic dictionary simply defines it as '*a quick measure in Highland music*'. Angus Mackay gives it as '*a finishing quick movement*', The word is often popularly translated as the 'crowning movement' of the piobaireachd, from *crùn* meaning a crown, and although it is a mistranslation, it is one not without merit in the picture it conveys.[1]

The formula of the Crunluath is the same as that of the Taorluath, with three additional notes, the whole figure now ending on E instead of A as the taorluath does. Again the figure comes *after* the theme-note:

The Crunluath figuration

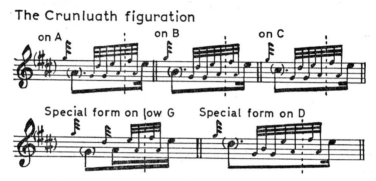

The perpendicular dotted line indicates the three extra notes which differentiates the crunluath from the taorluath. As applied to the theme notes of the *dithis* and *taorluath* variations of 'The MacLeod's Salute', the crunluath appears as follows:

THE MACLEOD'S SALUTE

Crunluath – 1st 8 bars

[1] In the earlier days of piobaireachd however (i.e. at the time Joseph MacDonald wrote his *Compleat Theory*) the 'crunluath' could not have been accorded even the (mis-)translation of 'crowning movement', for there were then several further varieties of grace-note-chain figures which exceeded the crunluath in complexity; whereas the crunluath consists of a theme note followed by a chain of eight grace-notes, other figures now obsolete contained, according to Joseph MacDonald, chains of nine, ten, eleven, thirteen and *nineteen* grace-notes following the theme-note.

The piobaireachd concludes with the customary return or recapitulation of the Urlar, exactly as in the opening.

The above demonstrates the movements and figuration of a piobaireachd of the simplest and most concise form. Few piobaireachd are as short as this however, and the schedule of movements of one of the longer piobaireachd, 'The Blue Ribbon' may be set down for comparison:

THE BLUE RIBBON
(Piobaireachd Society's version)

1. Urlar or Ground.
2. 'Thumb' Variation (i.e. melodic variation of the urlar of special type).
3. Doubling of the thumb variation.
4. Second variation of the Urlar (by use of a rhythmic figure).
5. Doubling of the second variation of the Urlar.
6. Third Variation (Dithis).
7. Doubling of the Dithis.
8. Fourth variation of the Urlar (a kind of anticipatory taorluath followed by a long B or D alternately in each bar).
9. Doubling of this Fourth variation.
10. The Taorluath proper.
11. Doubling of the Taorluath.
12. Crunluath.
13. Doubling of the Crunluath.
14. Crunluath a mach.
15. Return of the Urlar.

The 'thumb variation' (nos. 2 and 3) is a melodic variation of a special kind of which the name arises from the finger technique of the chanter. It simply means that the top A, obtained by uncovering the thumb-hole at the top of the chanter, is substituted for selected lower notes of the melody of the Urlar. The 'Crunluath a mach' (no. 14) is a further floriation of the crunluath figure.

In some piobaireachd there is to be found an extra stereotyped figuration called the *Leumluath*. This resembles a taorluath figure shorn of its final A, and therefore ending on E, e.g.:

Leumluath figuration

The *Leumluath* comes before the *Taorluath*. An example may be seen in 'Clanranald's Salute' (Kilberry and Piobaireachd Society collections).

There are a number of different kinds of Taorluath and Crunluath besides the ordinary form shown above. This is not the place to demonstrate these in detail, and they may be merely named as the Taorluath and Crunluath *Fosgailte*; the Taorluath and Crunluath *Breabach*; and the Taorluath and Crunluath *a mach*. The first two are *alternative* forms to the ordinary version; the Taorluath and Crunluath *a mach* are *additional* to the ordinary version.

One more feature remains to be explained. This is the so-called 'cadence' figure, which consists of the three notes:

The two semiquavers on G and D are so short as to be nearly imperceptible, while the E is so long as to be almost a pause note. (Sometimes the D is omitted.) The effect is simply that of a tenuto on E. This 'cadence' has nothing whatever in common with the word as understood by the ordinary musician. It is here in the nature of an anacrusis to the melodic phase which follows it, and bears much the same sort of function as the invocatory 'O' at the beginning of a line of poetry or song, as in 'O Waly, Waly up the bank', etc. Here is an example from the piobaireachd 'The Finger Lock'. The 'cadences' are marked with an asterisk.

A' Ghlas Mheur (The Finger Lock) Urlar

Now that the 'cadence' figure has been explained, the reader, while disregarding all grace-notes in reading the tune over to himself as recommended, should now read the cadence figure as a tenuto–like anacrusis-note to the phrase which follows it.

Extended piobaireachd such as 'The Lament for the Union' can take up to as much as twenty minutes in performance. The shorter ones may vary from about five to twelve minutes in duration. In earlier times the player used to make a return to the Urlar after the doubling of the Taorluath as well as at the end, which would extend the time duration of the piobaireachd considerably, at its slow tempo.

The composition of piobaireachd has for long been considered a lost art; not more than perhaps at most a dozen have been composed during the past hundred years,[1] including one by the writer himself.[2] This seemed however to start the ball rolling again, and several have been composed since, including particularly one by Pipe Major John Maclellan of the Army School of Piping at Edinburgh Castle.

It is hardly to be expected that the foregoing chapter will escape criticism greater or less, from the professional piper; for though the writer is the composer of a piobaireachd he is not a piper; and the subject of piobaireachd in all its aspects is a life-study. It must be emphasized therefore that these pages aim at no more than to lift the curtain on a difficult and little understood subject for the reader who may not know anything about it.

The various combinations of phrase-structure in which the ground may be composed are an important aspect of the study of piobaireachd. These have been classified as Primary, Secondary, and Tertiary piobaireachd and 'irregular tunes'. This is however too advanced a study

[1] Of these, notable mention must be made of 'The Cairn at Boreraig' composed by Angus Macpherson of Invershin (now living at Lairg).

[2] This is 'Lament for Calum MacLean' a colleague of the writer's at the School of Scottish Studies who died at the untimely age of 45. The piobaireachd was performed by the B.B.C. in 1961.

to be dealt with in this book. For a clearly written elucidation of these various forms for the novice, the reader is recommended to read *Music for the Highland Bagpipe* by Pipe Major John A. MacLellan (Instructor of Piping at Edinburgh Castle). For a more advanced study of piobaireachd form, see the articles by R. L. C. Lorimer in *Scottish Studies* referred to above, and the leaflet, 'Pibroch: Classical Music of the Scots Highland Bagpipe', issued by Waverley Records (Edinburgh).

THE GREAT PIPERS

The office of piper to a highland chief was a hereditary one, and piping schools and traditions of playing therefore tended to run in families. The earliest and most famous of the families of pipers and composers for the bagpipe was of course that of the MacCrimmons, who were hereditary pipers to the MacLeods of Skye. The first MacCrimmon of

A MacCrimmon Piper

whom we find mention was Iain Odhar (John of the dun hue). We have no record of any bagpipe compositions by him, but if Angus Mackay is to be believed he must have been a piper, for Mackay states, though on what authority is not known, that it was Iain Odhar who imparted to his more famous son Donald Mor MacCrimmon the art of piobaireachd playing. Donald Mór, who is said to have lived between *c.* 1570 and 1640, is the reputed composer of a number of piobaireachd. These include 'Donald Dughal Mackay's Lament', 'MacLeod's Controversy', 'The Earl of Ross's March', 'The MacDonald's Salute', and 'The MacLeod's Salute'. We are indebted for most of our information on the early piobaireachd composers to Angus Mackay, Raasay. He however wrote as late as 1838 and many of his statements must have come to him in the form of oral tradition. It is significant that none of the modern authorities on piobaireachd appear willing to commit themselves on the authorship of any but a few of the early compositions, though they do name the composers of a number of the later ones. Campbell of Kilberry, who says nothing about Angus Mackay's traditions as to the composers, gives the authorship of only twenty piobaireachd out of a hundred and eighteen, while the Piobaireachd Society, though passing on Angus Mackay's ascriptions of authorship to the reader, gives categoric authorship to only six piobaireachd out of a hundred and thirty two.

From the various printed sources available, the following tree of the piping MacCrimmons may be drawn:

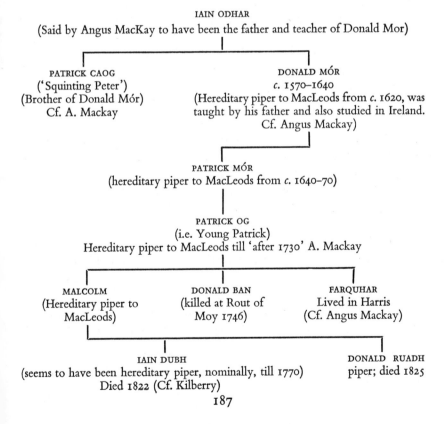

IAIN ODHAR
(Said by Angus MacKay to have been the father and teacher of Donald Mor)

PATRICK CAOG
('Squinting Peter')
(Brother of Donald Mór)
Cf. A. Mackay

DONALD MÓR
c. 1570–1640
(Hereditary piper to MacLeods from *c.* 1620, was taught by his father and also studied in Ireland. Cf. Angus Mackay)

PATRICK MÓR
(hereditary piper to MacLeods from *c.* 1640–70)

PATRICK OG
(i.e. Young Patrick)
Hereditary piper to MacLeods till 'after 1730' A. Mackay

MALCOLM
(Hereditary piper to MacLeods)

DONALD BAN
(killed at Rout of Moy 1746)

FARQUHAR
Lived in Harris
(Cf. Angus Mackay)

IAIN DUBH
(seems to have been hereditary piper, nominally, till 1770)
Died 1822 (Cf. Kilberry)

DONALD RUADH
piper; died 1825

187

The MacCrimmons had their famous College of Piping at Boreraig in Skye. This is thought by some authorities to have been started by Patrick Og, possibly when he became official piper to the MacLeods in *circa* 1730.[1] His reputation as a teacher was as great as his fame as a player and composer, and there are scarcely any of the famed piping schools that followed of which the founder did not study with Patrick Og.

Among the more notable of these pupils of Patrick Og was Charles MacArthur, founder of the MacArthur School and tradition of piping, a school that came almost to rival the MacCrimmons. The MacArthurs became hereditary pipers to the MacDonalds of Sleat. They are traditionally said to have come from Ulva off the West Coast of Mull,[2] and to have had a school of instruction there. From Pennant's account it seems that they must also have had a school at Peingown in Skye (Pennant visited Lord MacDonald's piper in 1774). Among the compositions of the MacArthurs, Mackay gives *Abercairney's Salute'* (Charles MacArthur); *Lady MacDonald's Lament* (Angus MacArthur); *The Highland Society of Scotland's Salute* (John 'Professor' MacArthur).

Of the famous piping Mackays of Raasay, John MacKay, born about 1767, also studied with Patrick Og. His son Angus (1813–58) was the compiler of the well-known collection of piobaireachd with traditional notes and stories about the piobaireachd players and composers from which we have quoted so freely. He also left a valuable collection of piobaireachd in manuscript.

Another piper who studied with the MacCrimmons was Donald Campbell of Corwhin, who with his sons became hereditary pipers to the Campbells of Mochaster in Argyll. Donald Campbell was a pupil of Patrick Og. His son, evidently a greater piper than he, became known as Caillan (sic) Mór. (Cf. A. Mackay.)

The Rankins, pipers to MacLean of Duart and later Coll were also, according to Angus Mackay, pupils of the MacCrimmons, though he does not specifically mention Patrick Og as their teacher.

The MacIntyres, whose teachers are not mentioned, were hereditary pipers to Menzies of Menzies. John Mackintyre, the son of Donald Mór MacIntyre, was the composer of the well-known piobaireachd of *The Battle of Sheriffmuir*.

Two main styles of playing developed among the schools, the MacCrimmon style and the MacArthur style; and though there has

[1] *Kilberry Book of Ceòl Mor* by Archibald Campbell (John Smith, Glasgow, 1953).
[2] William Matheson says however that they came from Islay, and that it was the Rankins who had the school at Ulva.

been a good deal of overlapping of teaching of the two schools in present-day styles of playing, there still seems to be some distinction of style between them; and this has come down to the present day, both in playing and in settings. The MacCrimmon style at the present day has descended chiefly through the pupils of Calum Macpherson of Badenoch (father of Angus Macpherson, composer of 'The Cairn at Boreraig' above mentioned) and of Donald Cameron, Seaforth's piper, and his sons and pupils, including the noteworthy piper John MacDougall Gillies. John MacDonald of Inverness, a great teacher and a piper whose playing became a famed tradition towards the end of his life, was a pupil of Calum Macpherson, and through him, an exponent of the Mac-Crimmon tradition.

It may be of interest to set down the line of teaching of a distinguished player of piobaireachd, the late Pipe Major William MacLean, whose playing the writer extensively recorded some years ago—recordings which are among the most precious of the archives of the School of Scottish Studies. As he recounted it, this was as follows:

Patrick Og MacCrimmon

Malcolm MacCrimmon (son)

Iain Dubh MacCrimmon (son)   Donald Ruadh MacCrimmon (son)

John Mackay, Raasay (pupil)

Angus Mackay (son)   John Ban Mackenzie (pupil)

Alexander Cameron (pupil of both)

Malcolm MacPherson, Badenoch (pupil)

William MacLean (pupil)
(Pipe-major 8th Cameron Highlanders)
(recorded by the writer)

Note. John Mackay, Raasay, (above) reached back to the MacCrimmons also through John Dall Mackay, Gairloch (Am Pìobaire Dall—whom we met in an earlier chapter) and his son Angus, with both of whom Angus Mackay, Raasay, studied. John Dall Mackay was a pupil of Patrick Og MacCrimmon.

THE ANCIENT NOTATION: CANNTAIREACHD

The ancient notation of the pipes was one in which the notes and figurations of the piobaireachd were represented by vocables, in a system having some type-resemblance to the present sol-fa notation.[1]

---

[1] The writer has twice come across the tradition that the idea of sol-fa notation came to its inventor through this ancient pipe notation. The late pipe-major William Mac-Lean told the writer of a tradition of a lady unnamed who had learned of and heard

Its use seems to have been a close secret of the initiated few of the piping schools, for we read an intriguing story in Dalyell's *Musical Memoirs*, of a competitor, at a piping competition in Edinburgh in 1816, John Campbell, who produced a folio volume of canntaireachd which he said contained bagpipe compositions written out by his father. Not one of the judges had ever heard of canntaireachd, and the contents of the volume appeared to them to be some strange writing in a completely unknown language, bearing no relation either to Gaelic or any other language within their knowledge. The volume proved completely unintelligible to them, and it occurred to none of them that it could be a musical notation. The competitor, John Campbell, declared that there were three volumes of this writing in all, belonging to his father. In the *Kilberry Book of Ceòl-Mor* the author, Archibald Campbell of Kilberry, tells us that these volumes, now known as *The Campbell Canntaireachd*, a rare piobaireachd manuscript, were the work of Colin Campbell (Cailein Mór) of whom we read above. The father of Cailein Mór, as we have stated, was a pupil of Patrick Og MacCrimmon, and it is fully possible that these are a legacy of the MacCrimmons and their music.

The volume produced by John Campbell at the Edinburgh competition in 1816 subsequently became lost, but the other two volumes are now in the National Library of Scotland. It is stated in the preface to the Society's published volumes that these two volumes of canntaireachd contain the notation of a hundred and sixty-eight 'tunes' (i.e. piobaireachd) of which sixty-four are completely unknown elsewhere.

There were apparently three systems of canntaireachd in use, that of the MacCrimmons, who may possibly have been the inventors of it; that of the MacArthurs, and the system known as the Nether Lorn canntaireachd as used by the Campbell pipers. The code of the Nether Lorn system has been successfully 'cracked' largely with the help of the volumes above mentioned, which contain many piobaireachd already known. It is in regular use by the Piobaireachd Society. Authenticated examples of the MacArthur system of canntaireachd do not seem to have survived.

---

the *canntaireachd* from the last of the MacCrimmon pipers while on a visit to Skye, and from it had helped to evolve the tonic sol-fa system. The system was perfected and developed by John Curwen, founder of the present firm of music publishers of that name, from the idea of the daughter of a Norwich clergyman, Miss Sarah Ann Glover (1785–1867). It would be interesting to know if it could have been this Miss Glover who was the lady of the above tradition and if she was ever in Skye. It is an acknowledged fact that the sol-fa system seems to come naturally to the Scottish Highlander, and is the one almost in sole use for choir training throughout the Highlands.

The MacCrimmon system, though it has been claimed to have been used by the older pipers of the MacCrimmon school of playing in the days of their instruction, is not fully understood. It was expounded to the writer by William MacLean who has his exposition on a tape recording; but as will be seen, it has its unsolved difficulties which require further explanation, explanations which William MacLean is no longer here to give.

The following examples show the two systems in comparison, first in the plain scale and then in the chief figurations of the piobaireachd. Both systems are as given to the writer by William MacLean.

THE PLAIN SCALE

Canntaireachd:

Nether Lorn	Em	en	o	o	a	e	ve	di	I
				or	or	or	dhe	vi	
				ho	da	de	he	hi	
MacCrimmon	Hum	hin	ho	ho	ha	hee	hae	hue	di
	or								
	him								

Dithis

etc.

Nether Lorn	hin - en	hio - en	ho - en	ha - en
MacCrimmon	hin - din	ho - din	ho - din	ha - din

Siubhal

etc.

Nether Lorn	hin - to	hin - do	hin - da	hin - de
MacCrimmon	hin - do	hin - do	hin - da	hin - di

Taorluath

etc.

Nether Lorn	hin-dar-id	hio-dar-id	ho-dar-id	ha-dar-id	che-dar-id
MacCrimmon	hin-dir-it	ho-dar-it	ho-dar-it	ha-dar-it	hie-dar-it

191

Crunluath

| Nether Lorn | hin - ban - dre | hio - ban - dre |
| MacCrimmon | hin - da - tri | ho - da - tri |

| ho - ban - dre | ha - ban - dre | che - ban - dre |
| ho - da - tri | ha - da - tri | hie - da - tri |

The difficulty of the MacCrimmon system as it appears in writing is that there is nothing to distinguish the vowel 'O' of the note B from the same letter for the note C sharp. In the Lorn Canntaireachd, the inevitable high G grace-note qualifies the B as 'hio' instead of 'ho' while the C sharp is simply 'ho'. In the MacCrimmon system there is no such distinction. The plausible suggestion has been made by R. L. C. Lorimer of Edinburgh that one of the two O vowels in the Mac-Crimmon system may have borne the short vowel sound as in 'hop', 'top', etc., and the other by the long vowel as in 'show' 'flow', etc. These would normally be distinguished by a grave or acute accent; but if this was so, the distinction has been lost in transmission down the ages, and from the tape recording which the writer made of William Mac-Lean,[1] he obviously makes no difference between the two.[2]

The editors of the Piobaireachd Society publications confess that their use of canntaireachd has been 'a matter of some anxiety' as they admittedly have not yet got sufficient information on many points. It seems that neither system has fully yielded up its secrets!

Up till comparatively recently, pipers were all taught exclusively by canntaireachd, the master singing over the phrase to be learned or studied by its means and the pupil repeating it on his practice chanter.

[1] Now in the archives of the School of Scottish Studies.

[2] Since writing this, the writer has been given a different version of the scale of the MacCrimmon Canntaireachd by Mr Angus Macpherson. This is as follows:

Low G	Low A	B	C	D	E	F	High G	High A
Hum	Hin	Ha	Ho	Hae	Hee	He	Hu	Di

Later still, Calum Johnston, Barra, has recorded about a dozen complete pibrochs in *canntaireachd* for the School of Scottish Studies. His system of vocables is slightly different from those previously recorded. He is said to have learnt *canntaireachd* in his boyhood by hearing his elders sing whole pibrochs in this way.

Pipe-Major Maclean told the writer that he never saw pipe-music in staff notation in all the years of his tuition under Calum Macpherson of Badenoch, but learned his piobaireachd entirely by the MacCrimmon notation in this way.

Captain Macleod of Gesto took down or copied from manuscripts not now available, a number of piobaireachd in the MacCrimmon canntaireachd, of which he published twenty in 1828. The full title, which is interesting, runs as follows:

> A Collection of twenty Piobaireachd or Pipe tunes as verbally taught by the M'Crummen Pipers in the Isle of Skye to their apprentices. Taken from John M'Crummen, Piper to the Old Laird of Macleod and his grandson, the late General Macleod of Macleod, by Captain Neil MacLeod of Gesto, 'In the hope that these ancient relics may be thus preserved for future generations, and tend to keep up and foster that spirit which they have in former times, and are still so well calculated to excite.'

An interesting description of this Captain Macleod of Gesto exists in a letter by a fellow enthusiast on piobaireachd of the same era, Alexander MacGregor—'Alasdair Ruadh'—who says:

> I was in Edinburgh during the winters of 1831, 1832, 1834, and 1835, and almost all these years Captain Neil Macleod of Gesto. in Skye, resided in Edinburgh.

Captain Macleod of Gesto

He was a tall, thin-faced man, with long nose, grey hair, white hat, tartan trousers and plaid. He was known as the 'Parliament House Ghost', and at times as the 'Advocates' Library Ghost', as he frequented these places day and night. I saw him daily, or almost so. He was crazy about 'Piobaireachd' but did not play himself. He knew, I believe, almost every 'piobaireachd' in existence—their name, their composer, their origin, and the causes for composing them. When strolling to and from the Advocates Library, he very frequently called on and sat for hours with, old John MacDonald the father of Donald MacDonald, Pipe-Major to the Highland Society. He would make MacDonald (then about 80 years old, while his father, then alive, was upwards of 100) play 'piobaireachds' to him, all of which he himself could articulate with his pliant lips in the MacCrimmon noting style. He had a large manuscript collection of the MacCrimmon 'piobaireachds', as noted by themselves, and part of it was apparently very old and yellow in the paper from age, with some of the writing getting dim. Other parts were evidently more modern, and on different paper. Donald Ban MacCrimmon, who was killed at the rout of Moy the day before the battle of Culloden, was (Gesto said) one of the best of the MacCrimmon performers; but *the best of them all was Padruig Mór MacCrimmon*.[1]

For many years these pipers noted down their 'piobaireachd', and Padruig Mór had a daughter who was very expert at noting, and could play herself when asked as a favour to do so. I should think that the manuscript I saw with him would contain upwards of two hundred 'piobaireachds' from the bulk of it; and out of that manuscript he selected twenty or so, which he published as specimens. The MacArthurs, pipers to the Clan MacDonald of the Isles, noted their 'piobaireachd' also, but with different vocables. Gesto had one very old-looking leaf of their noting, on which the vocables appeared very faint, but I did not look much at it.

A number of piobaireachd in the MacCrimmon notation were said to have been noted down direct from one of the later MacCrimmons by a Simon Fraser,[2] who subsequently went to Australia. Copies of these which the writer saw some years ago, were brought back to this country by one of Fraser's descendants. They show considerable differences in a number of the vocable sounds of the canntaireachd as evidently taken down by Fraser phonetically, differences applying not only to the notes B and C sharp as discussed above. A study of this, as well as some of the piobaireachd is now published in *Some Piobaireachd Studies* by G. F. Ross (Glasgow, 1926).

The master pipers of the old days used to have a boy attendant or gillie whose duty it was to carry the pipes for him. When the player came to the end of a piobaireachd, he used, according to William Maclean, to throw the pipes disdainfully away from him—generally over his shoulder—as showing that the music lay in the soul and

---

[1] The writer's italics. [2] Or possibly his father. This is not clear.

fingers of the piper rather than in the instrument. It was the boy's duty to catch the pipes (and as William Maclean said to the writer, 'God help him if he let them fall!') and to lay them by with more care than his master showed, at least in public! To this day, if a piper feels that the reeds of his instrument have let down his performance, he will often end a piobaireachd, earnest though his performance may have been, with a skirl of derision at the pipes themselves for failing him.

The great players and composers of piobaireachd thought it beneath them to play the lighter bagpipe music, i.e. *ceòl beag*, at any time.

The chief collections for the study of this fascinating subject of piobaireachd are, *The Kilberry Book of Ceòl Mor* (Glasgow, 1953); the nine books of piobaireachd published by the Piobaireachd Society (Glasgow, recent, non-dated) and the now rare *Ceòl Mór* by General C. S. Thomason containing about two hundred and seventy-eight piobaireachd (London, 1900). Of the older 'source collections' there may be mentioned *A Collection of the Ancient Martial Music of Caledonia called Piobaireachd*, by Donald MacDonald, Edinburgh, 1822; and the essential collection of its period, *A Collection of Ancient Piobaireachd*, by Angus Mackay (Edinburgh, 1838). Other collections are those by Donald MacPhee, *A Collection of Pibrochs* (37 tunes) (Glasgow, 1880), and Glen's *Collection of Ancient Piobaireachd*, 1880–99. An exceedingly interesting account of the MacCrimmon canntaireachd as taken to Australia by Simon Fraser is to be found in *Some Piobaireachd Studies*, by G. F. Ross above mentioned. Not the least interesting of the statements it contains is that Simon Fraser knew two systems of canntaireachd, 'what he calls the old system, given in Gesto, and a *newer system*, said by him to have been *perfected by Patrick Mór MacCrimmon*'.

The Pibroch Songs
Though the pibroch songs are, as their title indicates, *songs*, it is more appropriate to treat of them here than in the chapters on Gaelic vocal music; for they are in fact word-settings to the tune of the ground or other movement of a piobaireachd, and may be said to occupy a sort of musical common-ground to both song and bagpipe. Some, like 'MacCrimmon's Lament' are better known as songs than as piobaireachd; with others, the reverse is true; some, like *Cholla mo rùin*, are equally well known, to the Gael at least, in either form.

We have already seen one example of the pibroch song in Patrick Mór MacCrimmon's '*Tog Orm mo Phìob*' (see page 64), of which the piobaireachd itself may be found in Angus Mackay's collection. Another MacCrimmon pibroch song of the same type is Donald Ban

MacCrimmon's 'Cha Till mi Tuille' (MacCrimmon will never return) better known as 'MacCrimmon's Lament'. It was said to have been composed in a premonition of his own death at the 'Rout of Moy' in the 1745 Rising, where the piper Donald Ban was the sole casualty of the battle.

Other examples of the setting of words to the ground or *Urlar* of the piobaireachd are given by Angus Mackay, though some of these are fragmentary.

Many of the actual piobaireachd originals of the pibroch songs have become lost and the tunes exist solely in the songs themselves. 'Ceann Tràigh Ghruineard' (a piece on the Battle of Gruinard), 'Fàilte Dhruim Fionn's sinn a falbh', 'Fraoch a Rònaigh', 'Théid mi Dhachaidh Chrò Chinn t-sàile' and 'Iain Shomaltaich e ho ró' (the musical celebration of a cattle raid) are a few of these.

Some of the pibrochs songs bear the names of well-known piobaireachd in the present-day repertory of the piper, but have no resemblance to them in their tune, such as 'An Tarbh Breac Dearg' (The Red-speckled Bull) which the writer helped to record in the Isle of Vatersay.

Uamh an Oir, the song of the piper who entered a cave and met his death far underground in a struggle with the 'monster of the cave' with the agonizing cry from the piper of *O that I had three hands, two for the bagpipe and one for the sword*, has long been thought to be one of the lost piobaireachd, though well known as a song; but Simon Fraser of Melbourne provides a version of the piobaireachd of that name in his collection of piobaireachd communicated to and published by G. F. Ross.[1] Three versions of this pibroch song with its striking melody are given in the Tolmie Collection, but these are all dissimilar to the tune of the piobaireachd as published, and the song must therefore be included in the same category as 'An Tarbh Breac Dearg', of which the tune of the song differs from that of the piobaireachd.

Another and quite different species of pibroch song is that of the poem composed and sung in a form imitative of the structure of a piobaireachd. This usually opens with a verse in stately slow metre and tempo, entitled *Urlar*, and the poem or song continues with verses in quicker tempo alternating with the 'urlar', entitled 'Siubhal' and 'Crunluath', roughly representative or imitative of these movements of the piobaireachd. This type of 'pibroch song' is purely the musical setting of a poem for singing, and is not performable on the pipes. The best known example is the famous long poem by Duncan Ban Macintyre

[1] *Op. cit.* William Matheson says he knows a version of the pibroch song 'Au Tarbh Breac Dearg' of which the tune does resemble that of the piobaireachd.

(1724–1812), 'Moladh Beinn-Dorain' (In Praise of Beinn Dorain),[1] of which the writer has recorded a traditional version to its own tune.

CEÒL BEAG (*The Small Music*)

This is the music of the pipes which most people understand and know, the music of the march, strathspey and reel, of the quickstep, the jig and the livelier of the Highland (and even of the Lowland) song tunes. It is the music we hear from the pipe-band, by whose agency the national instrument and its music has become known wherever Scottish Regiments have marched—which means in most countries of the world.

Ceòl Beag, like *Ceòl Mor*, seems to have depended upon oral transmission for its survival until a surprisingly late date; for apart from a few very isolated examples printed as addenda to collections of piobaireachd or of vocal airs—perhaps not two dozen in all—the first collection of *ceòl beag* to be printed did not appear until 1829. This was *A Collection of Quicksteps, Strathspeys, Reels and Jigs* published by the Edinburgh bagpipe maker Donald Macdonald, a little oblong volume beautifully engraved in the manner of the period, containing a hundred and twenty tunes, of which there is a copy in the National Library ot Scotland.

No more than half a dozen similar collections of *ceòl beag* found their way into print before the last quarter of the nineteenth century, when what had been a trickle suddenly became a flood with the issue of the now well-known *Collection for the Great Highland Bagpipe* by the Glen family of bagpipe makers in Edinburgh, which contained a thousand tunes. Part I of this collection, which has now become something of a collectors' piece, has by way of introduction to the series, a remarkably well-written short history of the bagpipe, both in its Highland and Lowland form. This first book of the series is of interest also in giving the old Gaelic names for the tunes as well as their better-known Lowland Scots titles, a practice which regrettably was not continued throughout the series.

The student of Scots music will find much of interest in many of these collections of *ceòl beag*, including tunes which will not readily be found elsewhere—pipe tunes *pur sang* which for one reason or another have not found their way also into the fiddle books. The reader must always remember in reading these, to supply mentally the key signature

---

[1] Kurt Wittig in his *The Scottish Tradition in Literature* makes the observation that this form of a theme and variations in Scottish poetry was anticipated by some centuries in the fifteenth-century poem of 'Cockelbie's Sow' (p. 106, op. cit.).

of two sharps, as they all follow the general practice of omitting the key signature.

In discussing *ceòl beag*, pipers will often use a species of canntaireachd to demonstrate a tune vocally. No historical record of a system of canntaireachd for the playing of *ceòl beag* has been discovered, and the modern piper's use of it for this purpose is probably improvisatory. The point is however open to further research.

Later collections of bagpipe music issued during the present century tend to become more and more associated with the music of the pipe bands of the Scottish Regiments. Modern tunes with the names of their composers (many of these, Regimental officers with musical ambitions) begin to appear, to the displacement of a corresponding number of the anonymous traditional tunes to make room for them. 'Standard settings' of pipe tunes according to the usage of particular regiments, e.g. The Scots Guards, The Seaforth Highlanders, etc., are in circulation, many of their pages filled by such comparative innovations as Routine Pipe Calls, Ceremonial military slow marches, and 'Retreats', in which numerous tunes not of bagpipe or even of Scottish origin such as 'The Green Hills of Tyrol' (borrowed from Rossini's 'William Tell'[1]) have been pressed into service, and the extremely doubtful practice introduced of playing in 'seconds', i.e. in two-part harmony, something for which the instrument was never intended, and for which its characteristic scale is quite unsuited.

Nevertheless it is the old—sometimes perhaps even *ancient—Ceòl Beag* which we still hear everywhere. This is the music, played upon the ancient instrument, that thrills the Scottish exile, and of which the Scottish ear never tires, even with a surfeit. *Ceòl Beag*, played upon its proper instrument the pipes, is, for most, the Music of Scotland *par excellence*, even if it be the *Ceòl Mór* that takes first place with the initiated!

[1] Rossini is supposed to have derived the tune from an actual Tyrolean song.

CHAPTER VII

The Fiddle

STRINGED instruments of different sorts and styles played with a bow
have existed in Scotland from a very early period. Henry Farmer,
in his *A History of Music in Scotland* points out a reference to two of
these in a poem by Thomas the Rhymer,[1] the *fedyl* (fiddle) and the
rybid (rebec):[2]

> Harp and *fedyl* both he fande,
> The *getern* and the *sawtry*
> *Lut* and *rybid* ther gon gan,
> Thair was al maner of mynstralsy.

Both the fedyl and the rybid or rybybe (rebec) were played by the bow;
the other instruments mentioned were either plucked with the fingers
or played with the plectrum.

A third bowed instrument, the *croud*, or rather the player of it, is also
quoted by Dr Farmer from the fourteenth-century tale of *Orfeo and
Heurodis*, a Celtic version of the tale of *Orpheus and Euridice*:[3]

> There were *trompours* and *tabourers*,
> *Harpers* fele and *crouders*

The *croud* is important in Scottish musical history, as it may well have
been the only indigenous instrument of the three.

Dr Farmer is of the opinion that the fiddle and the rebec, as well as
the psaltery and the gittern were imported from the East by returning
Crusaders. (Farmer, op. cit., p. 50) As the Crusades went on from 1096
till 1291, this would provide the possibility of a very early date indeed
for these instruments in Britain, though it might not necessarily date
their introduction into Scotland.

[1] The poem in full may be found in the Appendix to Part I of Thomas the Rhymer:
Minstrely of the Scottish Border: Sir Walter Scott, Vol. IV (1833 Edition).

[2] The spelling of the instrument differs in the version of this poem as quoted by
Dr Farmer, namely *fethill* and *rybybe*. According to him *rybybe* is the Scots version of
Rebec, though Scott gives this as *rybid*, above.

[3] Auchinleck Manuscript.

Melrose Abbey (commenced 1136) provides a carving of the rebec, which was a pear-shaped instrument somewhat resembling a mandoline in shape. Some of these had a belly of parchment, and some, according to Grove, of a thin table of pine. The Melrose Abbey carving is of a female figure playing the rebec with a bow. Of the early representation of the fiddle, a manuscript said by Dalyell to have belonged to the Abbey of Dunfermline, of date 1400–1500 shows a fiddle-like instrument of apparently two strings being played with a bow by a female (?) musician, together with a player of a *timbrel* or tambourine, and a female tumbler (not at all suitably dressed for her act in long skirts) turning a somersault.

The *croud*, mentioned in *Orfeo and Heurodis* above, may well have been a native Celtic instrument. There are various spellings of it, as, *crot, cruit, cruth Gue* or *Goe* (Shetland) and (the commonest) *crwth* (Wales). The instrument was of a shallow rectangular box-like shape about not quite two feet in length by not quite one foot in width and about two inches in depth. The earliest examples were strung with two strings of horsehair and played with a bow. There was a hole near the top of the rectangular sound-box body through which the fingers of the left hand were thrust from the back in order to stop the strings.

The same instrument is known in Finland as the *Jouhikantele*, and among the Swedish inhabitants of Esthonia as the *Talharpa*. The Finnish authority Professor Otto Andersson gives these instruments the name of the *Bowed Harp* and shows them to have from two to four strings. The tessitura of the instrument would seem to have been of the tenor range.

The Crwth was in use in Wales until as recently as the middle of last century (Grove). Here it has six strings; four on the fingerboard, played with the bow; and two placed to one side of the fingerboard to be either bowed or plucked with the left hand, at will.

As regards the country of origin of the instrument, Professor Otto Andersson in his monograph 'The Shetland Gue, the Welsh Crwth, and the Northern Bowed Harp' (*The Budkavlen*, Abo, 1956) thinks that two alternatives are possible—either that it was indigenous to the British Isles and migrated thence to Norway and so towards the East; or that its first home was in the Scandinavian North and it moved in the contrary direction. Most of the evidence, according to Professor Andersson, is in favour of the former alternative, i.e. that it was indigenous to the British Isles. Indeed he considers that this is the only possible origin if the 'bowed harp' represents the conjecturally bowed instrument of the older Celtic sources—unless indeed it existed in

Ireland even before the coming of the Celts. If on the other hand the date of its origin were in the period just before the Vikings, he continues, it might be an importation from Scandinavia into the British Isles. It was long thought that the Crwth in its earliest form had been a plucked instrument which had later been adapted to the use of the bow. Professor Andersson rejects this theory however and maintains that the instrument was played with a bow from the first.[1]

Of the fiddle, Grattan Flood states that the Irish of the sixth century were acquainted with the instrument (the fidil), which is named in an account of the *Fair of Carnan* as one of the instruments played there. Though this may in fact have been the Crwth, it shows that the name fidil was early in use in Ireland, and so probably also in Scotland. Dalyell is of the opinion, from the representation of the instrument in iconography, that the early instruments of the 'fithel' type had only two strings. It is difficult however to be certain of this from the limitations of detail in stone carvings, particularly where they have been subject to weather conditions in exterior sites.

Brantôme, the French historian and soldier who came to Scotland with the court of Mary Queen of Scots, made the important observation, writing in 1560, that 'There came under her window (i.e. at Holyrood) five or six hundred citizens of the town who gave her a concert of the vilest fiddles and *little rebecs*, which are as bad as they can be in that country. Ah! what melody it was! What a lullaby for the night!' John Knox on the other hand, writing of that same night's music-making, speaks of the musicians as 'a company of honest men, who with instruments of music, gave their salutation at her chamber window'; and adds, 'the melody, as she alleged, *liked her well*, and she willed the same to be continued'. Nevertheless she is said to have changed her apartment forthwith to a quieter part of the house!

Dr Farmer is of the opinion that by that time the fiddles were probably the four-stringed instruments that we know today, although not of such delicate manufacture; to which one must add that they would probably be flat in the body and not arched like the modern violin.

At this point, we have to chronicle the arrival of another species of stringed instruments, the *Viols*. These are said to have been invented in the fifteenth century, and Dr Farmer thinks that they may have been introduced into Scotland by James V on his return from his marriage to the daughter of the King of France in Paris in 1537.

[1] Nevertheless the references to the *cruit* in the Heroic Ballads, Arthurian and Ossianic are such as make it hard to believe that it was not a *plucked harp* that was meant. Nowhere in the ballads is there any suggestion of a bow being used.

The viol, to quote from Grove, 'differs from the violin (i.e. the Italianate instrument) in having deeper ribs and a flat back. The shoulders of the viol curve upwards, joining the neck at a tangent instead of at right-angles as with the violin. The normal number of strings is six.'

The viols were the instruments of the Court and of polite musical society. They were made in three principal sizes, the *viola da gamba* in the bass register; the *viola da braccio* in the tenor register; and the *treble* or *descant viol* as the upper member of the group. There were four viols in use at the Court of James V.[1] According to Dalyell, four violers played upon the stage at the Cross in Edinburgh 'on the day of His Majesty's solemnite, that is, his Coronation in 1660'. Charles II to whom this obviously refers, was however crowned at *Scone* nine years previously, in 1651, and the occasion referred to must have been that of his *proclamation* at the Restoration on the 8th of May 1660.

Dalyell goes on to observe that for some time following, viols are mentioned a good deal more frequently than fiddles; and they seem to have been the more usually accepted instruments, at least in musical society. A 'Chest of Viols' was the popular term for a set of instruments used for playing in concert. It was so called because the set referred to was often kept in a wooden chest specially made to receive them. This *chest of viols* consisted of six instruments, 'two basses, two tenors, and two trebles' (Grove). A 'Consort of Viols' was another name for such a set of the instruments. This combination was a standard one somewhat similar to our string quartet of today.

Much fine music was composed in Scotland for the viol, most of which has only been rediscovered in the present century, mostly in the privately owned Panmure Collection of musical manuscripts.[2] A few consorts for strings from this collection are included in *Music of Scotland* edited by Kenneth Elliott and Helena Mennie Shire,[3] and doubtless a lot more still awaits publication. It may be remembered too that much of the concerted vocal music of the period was described as 'apt for voices or viols', as for example the songs in three, four and five parts in Forbes's *Cantus*, before mentioned. This may of course be rightly included in the category of 'native music of Scotland', though it cannot be classed as either traditional or national in the sense of the terms as applied to the music of this book.

Collections of Scots airs in our sense of the term do exist however for

[1] In the year 1538 or 1539, Dalyell, p. 204.
[2] Now on loan to the National Library of Scotland.
[3] *Musica Britannica Series*, Vol. XV. Published Stainer and Bell, 1957.

several instruments of the viol family. The Guthrie Manuscript at Edinburgh University is in tablature for the *viola da braccio;* the Leyden (instrumental) Manuscript and the Scone Manuscript, both containing Scots airs, are in the tablature of the *Lyra-viol,* and the Blaikie Manuscript in tablature for the *viola da Gamba.*

Although viols were obviously in use in Scotland in 1660 (the date of 'His Majesty's solemnitie') as referred to by Dalyell, he states that they had really gone out of fashion before the Restoration, being supplanted by the violin. This was of course not the *fithel* or fiddle as previously known in the country, but the violin proper as perfected in Italy by the Amatis and their successors (1520–1684).[1]

It is impossible to say exactly when the first of the perfected violins of the Italian makers reached Scotland. Dalyell cautiously puts it that 'the quality of Cremona violins . . . was recognized in Scotland at the commencement and during the progress of the preceding (i.e. eighteenth) century; and he goes on to say that 'two Cremona violins were offered for sale in Edinburgh, along with a parcel of fine music books' in 1708. Though this was the first observed occasion however, it is to be remembered that the Amatis had been in business since the sixteenth century, and it is therefore quite possible that Italian violins may have reached Scotland long before. A manuscript of 'violin' music of estimated date 1680 is amongst the Panmure collection.

Whenever it was that the violin arrived, the Scottish traditional fiddlers were quick to see its possibilities as an instrument for their native folk music in its flexibility and incisive tone quality. Scots fiddle-makers were equally quick to supply home-made copies of them. A long line of Scottish fiddle-makers, avowedly copying the Italian models, sprang into being and founded a craft that still flourishes today. Each fiddle-maker tended to stick to one particular model, and openly advertised his violins as copies of Guarnerius, Amati and so on; and eventually a particular fiddle-maker would come to be known as 'the Scottish Stradivarius' or whatever Italian maker he based his models upon. The most famous of these Scottish violin or fiddle-makers were the members of the long line of the family of Hardie. The subject of the Scottish fiddle-makers is a study in itself, which has been ably written up by William C. Honeyman in his *Scottish Violin Makers, Past and Present* (1898) and by A. G. Murdoch in *The Fiddle in Scotland* (1888).

[1] Expenditure accounts at Dunvegan show however that it was not until 1740 that payments were made to a *fiddler* which had formerly been entered as to a *violer*, referred to as 'Macleod's violer'. For the record, the violer's name was James Glass (entry of 1706) and the fiddler's name, Munro (1740). Cf. I. F. Grant, *The Macleods.*

The writer had the good fortune to know one of Scotland's native fiddle-makers, Charles Milne of Dufftown, by trade a shoemaker, aged eighty odd, who had been making violins all his life since the age of sixteen. He took for his model the celebrated Austrian violin maker Stainer (1621–83) on account of the penetrating tone quality of his violins. In the course of his life he made eighty-one violins, of which the later ones possessed a beauty and finish which made them virtually impossible to detect as being 'home-made' except perhaps by the expert.

To sum up the story of Scotland's stringed instruments played with the bow: one can say that one of them, the *cruit* or *crwth*, may have been indigenous to the Celt, or if not, certainly to the Northern countries—in which case it probably came to Scotland with the Norse invaders. Two other stringed instruments, the *rybybe* (rebec) and the later viol, came and went—the rebec probably appearing as early as the fiddle, or at least as early as its first reference in literature by Thomas the Rhymer in the thirteenth century, the viols coming comparatively late—say sixteenth century. Percy Scholes in his *Oxford Companion to Music* says that the rebec remained 'in some degree of vulgar use' in certain parts of Europe right into the eighteenth century. No Scottish collection of music for the *rybybe* or *rebec* or for the *croud* or *cruth* has survived.

The viol family on the other hand, though it has gone out of general use, has never become *totally* obsolete; and indeed it has seen a considerable revival in Scotland during the present century with the growing interest in the old Scottish court music, stimulated by the researches of Kenneth Elliott. It went out of general use in Scotland however, in the eighteenth century.

The fiddle, which appeared as early on the Scottish scene as the *rybybe*, if not earlier, has survived to become, with the bagpipes, one of the two national instruments. In its own particular territory of northeast Scotland, and particularly in the Strathspey district which gave the characteristic music of that title its name, the fiddle holds supremacy over the pipes. The strathspey, it should be added, though played now as often on the pipes, is essentially *fiddle music*, depending for its full effect upon the characteristic up-bow stroke of the Scottish traditional fiddler, and the capacity of the instrument to stop the sound abruptly after the essential reversed dotted rhythm figure, particularly in the old 'slow strathspey'.

THE FIDDLE MANUSCRIPTS

Unlike the other Scots musical manuscripts, manuscript collections of fiddle music abound in great numbers. It has been an established practice from the early days of the coming of the violin proper into Scotland, i.e. the beginning of the eighteenth century or thereabouts, for fiddlers to write out their own repertoire of tunes in a manuscript music book. The writer has half a dozen or more of these in his possession. These fiddlers' tune-books are of a characteristic small oblong format, of an average size of about eight inches by six.

Possibly the earliest known of these is one owned by the writer, which can be dated to at least as early as 1705, from a statement written on the fly-leaf, '*At Edinburgh the iith day of October 1705, J.G.B. grants me to have borrowed from M.M. ye soume of 12 pounds Scots of which I justly owe to ye said M.M.*' Possibly J.G.B. is George Bowie, a name which also appears on the stub of another torn off fly-leaf. One song, the only song with words in the whole collection, helps to date it. This is, 'Though you make no return to my passion', which is a song by Henry Purcell in his cantata 'The Maid's Last Prayer', first published in 1693; and the inclusion of the song sets this as the earliest possible date of the book. The book contains, among a number of minuets, Scots measures, bourees, jigs, chaconnes, etc., twenty-six song airs, some of them with variations typical of the earlier instrumental collections. These include such well-known tunes as 'Allan Water', 'Catherine Logie', 'Katie Bairdie', 'When she cam ben she bobbit', 'Tibbie Fowler in the Glen', 'Old Lang Syne', 'Over the Moor to Maggie', and others.

Another such book, undated, but probably of equally early date, is in the Panmure Collection, similarly containing a mixture of instrumental pieces and song airs, including 'Green grow the rashes' and others, several of these also being followed by variations.

Fiddlers' tune-books of more recent date are common, and the writer's collection includes a representative sprinkling of dates spread over the middle of the nineteenth century. The earliest of such books, now mostly in library manuscript collections, provide the first sources for some of our song airs. They often also contain dance measures of the more formal type such as the bouree, courante, minuet, etc., but the typical Scots strathspey for the fiddle does not appear until the later printed collections of the eighteenth century.

THE EARLY PRINTED FIDDLE COLLECTIONS

As with the manuscript tune-books, the early printed collections of fiddle music were mostly of Scots song airs adapted for the fiddle, in many of which the air is followed by one or more variations. This is more important than may meet the eye, for it continues the practice of the variation form in Scots traditional music which had already been established in the early lute and viol books, and in pibroch, and is probably of greater antiquity than the existing records of it. It points to the variation form as an accepted and established form in all kinds of Scots traditional instrumental music from an early date.

The first printed collections of Scots tunes for the fiddle were, like the early song collections, published in England following the Union of the Crowns (1603), in such collections as John Playford's *Apollo's Banquet* (1669) which is the first collection in which 'Scotch tunes' are mentioned as such; and the first printed collections consisting entirely of Scots fiddle tunes, Henry Playford's *Collection of Original Scotch Tunes (Full of the Highland Humours) for the Violin* (1700); and a similarly titled collection by John Young, London, *A Collection of Original Scotch Tunes for the Violin, the whole Pleasant and Comicall being full of the Highland Humour* (undated). It should be observed however that though these have the undoubted characteristics of Scots tunes, there is nothing particularly distinctively 'Highland' about them as their title would lead us to expect.

The first purely instrumental collection of Scots tunes to be published within the borders of Scotland can only by courtesy be called fiddle music, for it was Adam Craig's *Collection of the Choicest Scots Tunes adapted for the Harpsichord or Spinnet and within the compass of the Voices, Violin and German Flute* (1730). James Oswald seems to have been the first Scots publisher to set down the violin as the first instrument in the catch-title, though with the German flute as an alternative. This was *A Curious Collection of Scots Tunes for a violin, Bass Viol, or German Flute, with a thorough Bass for the Harpsichord*, etc. (Edinburgh, non-dated but probably about 1740). Similar collections, in which the tunes *qua* 'Scotch Tunes' were projected as of greater importance than the instrument on which they were to be played, appeared up to the middle of the century, the *hautboy* appearing as another of the instruments on which the tunes might also appropriately be performed. Such for instance is the fine collection of Scots tunes (i.e. song airs), *A Collection of Scots Tunes for the violin or German Flute, and a bass for the Violoncello or*

Harpsichord by William McGibbon (1768). These, though they are of considerable value for the study of Scots song airs, cannot be described as true fiddle music except that many of them have a variation or two of instrumental character added to them.

So far therefore, no *essentially fiddle-music* had as yet been published; and the first which could properly be so described was the collection of *Scots Reels or Country Dances* published in Edinburgh by Robert Bremner (undated, circa 1757). Here appears the first mention of Scots reels in the title. This is an important collection, and many of our Highland reel and strathspey tunes make their first appearance in it. Other early collections in which Scots reels and strathspeys appear are *A Collection of the newest and best Reels or Country Dances*, Neil Stewart, Edinburgh, 1761–4; and *Thirty-seven New Reels and Strathspeys for the Violin, Harpsichord, Pianoforte or German Flute*, composed by Daniel Dow, Edinburgh (c. 1776); also *A Collection of the Newest and Best Reels and Minuets with improvements, adapted for the Violin or German Flute*, by Joshua Campbell,[1] Glasgow (1778) and *A Collection of Strathspeys or Old Highland Reels* by Angus Cumming of Grantown in Strathspey, Edinburgh, 1780. Here for the first time is the real fiddle music of the Strathspey country, compiled or composed by one of the important names for fiddle music in Strathspey, as we shall see presently.

It may be stated here that though the reel belongs equally to the Scottish Bagpipe, and probably was first heard on that instrument, the Strathspey is essentially music of the fiddle, though it is of course played nowadays as often on the one instrument as on the other.

This is also the appropriate place to mention John Riddell, the amateur fiddle-composer of Ayr (born 1718, died 1795) who published in circa 1776 *A Collection of Scots Reels, Minuets, etc. for the Violin, Harpsichord or German Flute*. His slow air of 'Finlayston House' was set to a rather indifferent lyric 'Fate gave the word—the arrow sped' by Robert Burns. Though many of Riddell's tunes don't quite hit the mark, he deserves to be remembered for his still popular reel 'The Merry Lads of Ayr' and his jig 'Dumfries House' (the better tune of the two to the writer's mind). Riddell has been credited with being the composer of the air of 'Jenny's Bawbee' (an exceedingly doubtful assertion), and the good reel tune of 'Stewarton Lasses', an interesting study in the so-called 'double tonic' (here D major and C major):

[1] The Joshua Campbell collection is interesting as containing the first appearance of the very well known Country Dance tune 'Soldier's Joy'. This has been attributed to Campbell himself, but as the melody is also a well-known folk-dance tune in other countries of Europe, it is hardly likely to be his composition.

STEWARTON LASSES: A Reel

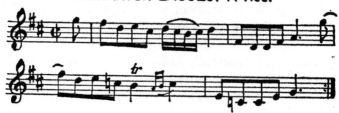

At this point the interest shifts more to the fiddlers than to the collections, and as so far we have not dealt with the personalities of the instrument themselves, it is necessary to retrace our steps a little.

THE FIDDLERS

A number of individual Scots fiddlers are mentioned by name in early records; notably, in 1489, James Widderspune, 'the fitheler that told tales and brocht fowles to the King', i.e. James IV (Dalyell); Anton, *fydlar* in 1526, and 'Cabroch fidlar' in 1530–3. If, as seems likely, 'Cabroch' refers to the district of The Cabrach in Aberdeenshire, this is of some interest as being the first mention of that long line of fiddle players of north-east Scotland which was later to include such notable names as Gow and Marshall, Isaac Cooper of Banff and Daniel Dow of 'Moneymusk' fame.

In Fife there was Patrick ('Patie') Birnie, a celebrated fiddler of Kinghorn born about 1635, the reputed composer of both words and music of the song, 'The Auld man's mare's dead'. Though this is best known as a song (and one of capital pawky Scots humour it is) the wide leaps of a tenth and a ninth in the sixth and seventh bars point clearly to its fiddle origin:

THE AULD MAN'S MEER'S DEAD

Words and tune attributed to
Patrick Birnie

The auld man's meer's dead,
The puir man's meer's dead,
The puir man's meer's dead,
A mile aboon Dundee.
She was cut luggit, painch lippit,
Steel waimit, staincher fitit,
Chanler chaftit, lang neckit,
Yet the brute did dee!

Patie Birnie also gained fame for having, it is said, *run* all the way home to Kinghorn from the Battle of Bothwell Bridge, a distance which must be all of seventy miles! According to David Baptie a painting of him exists, by William Aikman, probably painted about 1705 or 1710, but he does not say where.

Down in the Border country there was Nichol Burne ('Burne the violer' or 'Minstrel Burne') said to be the author and composer of the song 'Leader Haughs and Yarrow'.[1] This, though it is a pleasant and innocuous song air has no special instrumental characteristics which could classify it as fiddle music. It has the plaintive sound of a Border air. Though some of the words are but a string of place-names, these fall as music on the Border ear—'Wanton-wa's', 'Whitslaid Shaws', 'Braidwoodshiel', 'Kaidslie Birks', etc. There is said to have once been a portrait of him in Thirlestane Castle, but it is not now to be found.

There was also a fiddler of the sixteenth century named Muckhart frequently referred to in the old Scottish chap-books.

It is in the north-east of Scotland however, the home of the Strathspey, that the chief interest in the fiddle lies. Thomas Newte in his *Tour* (1791) writes:

With regard to the first composers, or even performers of strathspey reels, there are not any certain accounts. According to the tradition of the country, the first who played them were the Browns of Kincardine, to whom are ascribed a few of the most ancient tunes. After those men, the Cummings of Freuchie (now Castle Grant) were in the highest estimation for their knowledge and execution in strathspey music, and most of the tunes handed down to us are certainly of their composing. A successive race of musicians . . . followed each other for many generations. The last of that name made famous for his skill in music was John Roy Cumming.

Newte also makes the interesting if somewhat cryptic remark that 'The Strathspey is to the common Scotch Reel what a Spanish Fandango is to a French Cotillon'.

[1] Stenhouse dates Burne as mid-sixteenth century, but Laing puts him a century later. Cf. *The Scots Musical Museum.*

The most colourful of the early Strathspey fiddlers was undoubtedly the notorious James Macpherson, freebooter, fiddler and composer of fiddle tunes. His story is worth the telling. He was the illegitimate son of Macpherson, Laird of Invereshie, born about 1675. His mother was a gipsy woman, red-haired and said to be of great beauty. The Laird reared the child as long as he was alive, but at his death the boy seems to have been taken by the gipsy mother to lead the life of the gipsies. He was said to be of great intelligence, and became famed for his skill on the fiddle. He turned reiver and became the leader of a band of robbers, though it is said that, Robin Hood wise, he 'never committed any cruel or atrocious deed, and many of his actions were characterized by great kindness and brotherly love towards the poor and oppressed'.[1] Among the band were Peter and Donald Brown who may well have been the fiddlers of that name mentioned by Newte.[2]

Macpherson and his band became wanted men, and as might be expected, were in the end apprehended. They seem to have been taken first at Aberdeen (cf. *Romantic Strathspey* by James Alan Rennie). They were condemned to be hanged, but an Aberdeen serving maid of one of the Aberdeen magistrates who may have been enamoured of him, sent word to his friends. The Browns, with Donald Macpherson, a cousin of James, contrived a most daring rescue, in which they managed to snatch James from the condemned cell—manacled for execution as he was—and after a ferocious fight outside the prison, to force their way through the crowd already assembled to witness the execution. They made their way to an inn, where they freed Macpherson from his fetters and where horses were waiting. They eluded the guard at the city gates and got clean away to the hills. After a spell of freedom however Macpherson and his band were at last apprehended in Keith Market by Duff, the Laird of Braco, having it is said been betrayed by an enemy. The reivers made a desperate resistance, and Duff had a narrow escape with his life. Macpherson carried an enormous two-handed claymore, so heavy that only a very powerful man could wield it. This weapon is said to be still in the possession of the Duff family. Macpherson and the Browns were brought to trial before the sheriff of Banffshire, Nicholas

[1] Cf. 'Strathspeys and Reels', a paper read to the Banffshire Field Club by Dr Alexander Grant of Dufftown (the late father-in-law of the writer and an authority on the subject) in 1921.

[2] See the account of the trial of James Macpherson in *Miscellany of the Spalding Club*, Vol. 3 (Aberdeen, 1846), where the evidence states that 'Peter Brown went some-tymes to Elchies, and played on the wiol' (sic). See also the informative article on Macpherson by Hamish Henderson in the folksong magazine *Spin*, Vol. 3, No. 7, 1964.

Dunbar. The two Browns, and possibly Macpherson also, had a powerful protector in the person of the Laird of Grant, who applied to have the Browns tried in the court of his own regality, as they lived within his bounds; and offered *culreach* or pledge for their appearance. The sheriff refused the plea, on the grounds that 'they were known by habit and repute as "Wagabonds, soroners and Egyptians".' Macpherson was sentenced to be hanged at the Cross of Banff on 16 November 1700. (The Browns were later sentenced to be hanged also, but the sentence was never carried out, and it is thought that they may have escaped from jail.)

In the final hours before his execution, Macpherson composed the famous rant by which he is to this day remembered. The story goes that as a last boon he was granted leave to play this last composition at the scaffold itself, and that after playing it he offered his fiddle to anyone in the crowd who would have it. No one was bold enough to come forward however, and Macpherson thereupon broke the fiddle over his knee and threw the pieces among the crowd. A man picked up the pieces of the broken instrument and sent the neck of it to Macpherson's cousin Donald. He passed it on to his clan chief, Cluny Macpherson, by whom it was preserved.[1]

There is a final twist to the story, which though not widely known, is said to be true. This is that a last-minute reprieve was known by the magistrates of Banff to be on its way, possibly through the representations of the Laird of Grant, or perhaps, of Macpherson's own chief Cluny. The magistrates were however determined to be rid of their troublesome prisoner once and for all, and they gave orders that the town clock, by which the time of the execution was to be fixed should be advanced. Tradition has it that the bearer of the reprieve came into sight over the brow of the hill just as Macpherson was 'launched into eternity' as the phrase of the time had it. To this day the taunt of 'Wha hing't Macpherson?' is a popular reproach to the folk of the town of Banff.

Macpherson's Rant, as we would expect of a tune aurally transmitted, exists in a number of different variants. The best known is the version set to words by Robert Burns, based on a broadside ballad entitled *McPherson's Rant; or the last words of James Macpherson, murderer. To its own proper tune.* The tune appears first in the Margaret Sinkler manuscript (National Library of Scotland) and in a number of printed collections including the *Caledonian Pocket Companion*. There are also

[1] The remains of James Macpherson's fiddle are now in the Macpherson Clan House Museum at Newtonmore, Inverness-shire. See plate 18.

several traditional versions, one of which is published by Scott Skinner the violinist, from 'a very old manuscript copy'. The following is a version in a fiddlers' tune book in pencil manuscript in the possession of the writer.[1]

McPHERSON'S FAREWELL

From a fiddler's M.S. tune book, circa 1823 in the possession of the writer

(Allegro moderato)

*The ending is doubtful; possibly the last two notes should be tied.

It has been generally accepted that the 'rant' or as it is sometimes called 'Farewell' is the sole surviving composition of Macpherson; but the writer was recently informed by Mr Alan Rennie, author of *Romantic Strathspey* (Robert Hale, 1956) that he once heard a tinker pearl-fisher, camping on the banks of the Spey at Dalvey, play another tune which he claimed was composed by Macpherson. This clue is being followed up, and it is to be hoped that the tune may yet fall into the net.

Though emphasis has been placed on the north-east of Scotland as the cradle of the fiddle and Scots fiddle-playing, it must be said that the West of Scotland was not without its share of it, and particularly the Isle of Skye, which may almost be said to have possessed a school of fiddlers of its own. Lachlan McKinnon (Lachlunn Mac Thearlaich Oig) seventeenth-century bard, is mentioned by John Mackenzie in *Sar Obair* as an excellent musician, and is described with rather amusing snobbishness as carrying his violin about with him from place to place—'more for recreation and amusement than for *any sordid consideration of pecuniary remuneration*'. (The writer's italics.)

[1] Mention must also be made of versions of text and tune of Macpherson's Rant recorded by Hamish Henderson from the singing of Jimmy MacBeath and Davie Stewart, preserved in the archives of the School of Scottish Studies.

Mary Macleod, the seventeenth-century Gaelic poetess alludes to 'the music of the fiddle lulling me to sleep'. Martin Martin (seventeenth century) says that to his knowledge eighteen men played well on the violin in Lewis. Mention has already been made of records of *violers* being attached to the household of the MacLeods of Dunvegan.

Other notable Skye Fiddlers have been Neil Campbell Macintyre of Sleat, known as Neil Mór; Alexander McDonald of Stonefield, Skye, born circa 1795, and his son James; and Neil McKinnon of Strath, born *c.* 1795.[1]

From personal observation the writer would aver that the West of Scotland fiddlers differ in playing style from those of the Strathspey country, being somewhat less aggressive in accentuation, and with musical ornamentation more closely modelled on that of the pipes.

The long line of fiddle composers which followed Macpherson is too numerous to give in anything like entirety, for there is hardly a fiddler of note to the end of the nineteenth century who did not leave his quota, large or small, of reels and strathspeys of his own composing, many of them in publications now virtually unobtainable.

One such, Johnny McGill of Girvan (born circa 1707) deserves mention as the reputed composer of the tune bearing his name 'Johnny McGill' to which the words of the well-known song 'Come under my plaidie' were written.[2] Robert Burns used the air for his lyric of Tibbie Dunbar ('O, wilt thou go wi' me, sweet Tibbie Dunbar'). It is a splendid jig tune.

Another fiddler of about the same period is also mentioned by Robert Burns. This is John Bruce, born in Braemar some time between 1700 and 1720. Bruce was 'out' in the 1745 rising, was taken prisoner by the Government forces, and confined in Edinburgh Castle. He afterwards lived at Dumfries, where Burns may have become acquainted with him, and where he died in 1785. He was the reputed composer of the airs of the songs, 'Whistle o'er the lave o't' and 'Whistle and I'll come to you my lad'. Of the latter air Burns writes, 'The music is said to be by a John Bruce, a celebrated violin player in Dumfries about the beginning of the [eighteenth] century. This I know, Bruce, who was *an honest man, though a red-wud Highlandman* (!) constantly claimed it; and by all the old musical people here is believed to be the author of it.' (The italics and exclamation mark are the writer's.)[3]

[1] Baptie, *Musical Scotland*.
[2] The words of 'Come under my plaidie' were written by Hector Macneil of near Roslin, Midlothian.
[3] Burns to George Thomson, 19 October 1794.

We now arrive at the greatest of all Scotland's fiddlers, Niel Gow—
'famous Niel' as he was everywhere known. (He always spelt his name
Niel, with the i before the e.) Niel Gow was the son of a plaid weaver.
He was born at the village of Inver in Perthshire in 1727, where he lived
all his life, and where his son Nathaniel was born. Principal Baird of
Edinburgh gives Strathbaan in Perthshire as his birthplace, and this
account supposes that he was brought to Inver in his early infancy, but
this does not seem to be substantiated.

Niel Gow started playing the fiddle at nine years of age, and was
largely self-taught, except for a few lessons at the age of thirteen from
one John Cameron, a retainer of the Laird of Grandtully. In the fateful
year for Scotland of 1745, presumably before the country was thrown
into a ferment by the raising of the standard by Prince Charles at
Glenfinnan on 19 August, he won a prize for fiddle playing open to all
Scotland—in which one of the competitors was his former teacher John
Cameron. Young Niel was apparently already well known in the
locality, for the judge, who was a blind man (as often in musical contests
in Scotland) declared that 'he could distinguish the stroke of Niel's bow
among a hundred players'.

Gow's fame as a fiddler spread all over Scotland. He became in
demand to play at all the important balls and great parties in all the
principal cities of Scotland, so much so that it was often inquired of
Niel what evening he was free to play before fixing the date on which a
ball was to be held.

Besides being famed as a fiddler, he became a considerable composer
of tunes for the instrument, and has left some seventy tunes of his composing. These included not only dance tunes such as strathspey, reel, jig,
hornpipes, etc., but also tunes to be listened to for their own sake.
Among these are the *slow strathspeys*—a species of tune in strathspey
rhythm, but played at a slower tempo than now used for dancing, as
purely exhibition pieces and in a characteristic and peculiarly detached
staccato fashion. Niel Gow's repertoire of other exhibition pieces include
such types of tune as the 'Lament for Abercairney' and 'Niel Gow's
lament for the death of his second wife', and a number of pieces known
as 'So-and-so's Favourite', some of these being lively and some slow
airs.

Nathaniel Gow, the fourth and youngest son of Niel was in his day
even better known as a composer than his father. He was rather more
sophisticated, both in musical and personal outlook. His first teacher
was his father Niel at the family home at Inver. Then he was sent to
Edinburgh to continue his studies under 'Red Rob' Mackintosh, a

celebrated fiddler-composer who later went to London. Nathaniel Gow also studied with Alexander McGlashan—'*King*' *McGlashan*, said to be so-called from his stately and rather dressy appearance. He studied the 'cello as a second instrument under Joseph Reinagle, an academic musician who later became Professor of Music at Oxford, and commenced his professional career by playing the 'cello in McGlashan's band in Edinburgh. On the death of McGlashan, the leadership of the band went to Nathaniel Gow's elder brother William, said to be a player of 'bold and spirited style'. William died at the age of forty, when Nathaniel took his place and maintained it for nearly forty years. Nathaniel also played the trumpet, and became one of His Majesty's Trumpeters for Scotland, his duties being to officiate at Royal proclamations, and to herald the Scottish judges on circuit.

Nathaniel Gow came to be in even greater demand as a fiddler than his father, and went frequently to London to play at Almack's Club,[1] and often at the private parties given by King George IV. He was, like his father, the leading musical figure at the Caledonian Hunt Balls and at most of the parties of fashionable Edinburgh.

In 1796 Nathaniel Gow started an extensive music-publishing business in Edinburgh in company with William Shepherd. He had already in 1784–92 helped his father to prepare and publish at Dunkeld three collections of Strathspey reels, but he now commenced to publish extensively sheet music of a general kind, though he also continued the publication of the music of his father, his brothers and himself. The business continued with breaks and vicissitudes, including a bankruptcy, until the death of his son, Neil Gow junior, in 1823. Nathaniel Gow himself died in 1831.

Nathaniel Gow's best known composition is undoubtedly 'Caller Herrin' ' the descriptive piece for pianoforte or harpsichord which Lady Nairne later turned into an eternally popular Scots song by supplying words to it. Gow's harpsichord piece was however one for the fashionable ladies of the day in Edinburgh to play as a party piece, and is out of the mainstream of the contributions of the Gows to Scottish traditional music, which lies rather, like his father's, in reels and strathspeys, such as his 'Loch Earn' and the 'Largo's Fairy Dance', a tune for the eightsome reel which is as popular today as the day it was written.

Niel's eldest son William was the composer of some well-known fiddle tunes including 'The Fife Hunt', 'Lady Loudon's Strathspey' and

[1] J. C. Dick in his *Songs of Burns* says that Niel himself played at Almacks, but it seems likely that he mistook Nathaniel for Niel.

'Mrs Dundas of Arniston' (reel). Of his other two sons, Andrew, his second, wrote two good pieces, 'Lady Baird's Strathspey' and 'Major Moll's Reel'. His third son John composed a number of pieces including the reels 'Tullymet Hall' and 'Ayr Races', and the 'The Hon. Mrs John Ramsay's Strathspey'.

Nathaniel's son Neil Gow junior (who spelt his first name in the conventional way), entered the medical profession, but was a keen amateur musician. Although he died at the early age of twenty-eight, he left behind him some tuneful music, including the two songs set to words by James Hogg—'The Ettrick Shepherd', 'Bonny Prince Charlie' and 'Flora MacDonald's Lament'. He also contributed to the family output of reels and strathspeys with such tunes as 'The Marchioness of Huntly's Favourite' and 'Miss Hay of Hayston's Reel'.

The Gows held place in the Scottish scene for nearly a hundred years, and as might be expected, their music displays an illuminating cross section of fiddle writing style over this period. Niel Gow's tunes have a ruggedness about them which does not appear in the writing of his sons. It is obvious from their music that the Gows from first to last thoroughly understood the use of the Scottish gapped scales and diatonic modes, and the trick of ending a tune on a note other than the implied final of the mode. This is most evident in the first strain of the tune, while the second strain, probably from the ingrained tradition of the use of variation, more often than not dilutes the potency of the mode by filling in one or both of the gaps. This is often filled in with an unaccented and therefore 'weak' note arising out of the ornamentation of the writing, which however allows only the *flavour* of the mode to remain. A good example of this is to be seen in Niel Gow's 'Mr Graham of Orchill's Strathspey', where the first strain is in the pentatonic scale on F in its basic or first position FGA-CD. In the second strain it will be seen that the seventh degree (E) appears as an unaccented note. The tune is also interesting as a consciously composed tune which ends on another note than the keynote or 'final' of the mode. If the last note of the tune (G) were accepted as the 'final' of the mode, it would of course require the tune to be classified as being in the *second* position of the pentatonic scale.

Mr Graham of Orchill's Strathspey
Niel Gow

*7th degree, intrusive to the mode

Similarly, in Niel Gow's 'Lamentation for James Moray of Aber-carney' the first strain is in the hexatonic scale on G with gap at the seventh degree, while in the second strain the gap is filled with an unaccented note:

Niel Gow's Lamentation for Jas. Moray Esq. of Abercarney
Niel Gow

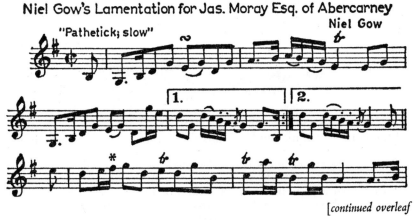

[*continued overleaf*

217

*F♯ in the second strain fills in the hexatonic gap of the first strain.

This 'dilution' of the mode in the *second strain* of a tune by filling in the gap or gaps in the scale will be found in very many of the song airs of Scotland.[1] It is thought that many of these second strains in the song airs have been added subsequently to what was originally a single-strain tune, though this must have been done at an early date, for these second strains are found in collections as early as the beginning of the eighteenth century.[2] Other positions of the pentatonic and hexatonic scales are also freely used by the Gows. 'Mrs Wright of Laton's Strathspey' is an interesting example of the hexatonic scale on the sixth degree of the scale according to the key signature:

Mrs Wright of Laton's Strathspey

Niel Gow.

Scale

1   2   3   4   5   6

The Marquis of Tullibardine's Jig, also by Niel Gow, is another example of the same hexatonic mode. 'Dunkeld House' is another, though here

[1] Lowland Scots song airs of two strains which are also common to Gaelic song sometimes appear in the Gaelic song culture as of only one strain.

[2] The second strain to the air of 'Mary Scott of Yarrow' appears in the fiddler's tune book of about 1705 owned by the writer, described above.

an unaccented major sixth degree gives it the flavour of the Dorian mode:

DUNKELD HOUSE A Jig

Niel Gow.

Niel's use of the *Mixolydian* mode may be seen in 'Mrs Baird of New Byth's Strathspey', though towards the end of the tune there is an intrusive major seventh instead of the modal flat seventh degree. In 'Miss Stewart of Grandtully's Strathspey', which is also in the Mixolydian mode, we find both the fourth and seventh degrees thus varied chromatically in the course of the tune.

Niel was particularly fond of the effect of the Scottish 'double-tonic' so-called, and indeed uses it so often as to make it almost a cliché in his writing. In his earlier tunes he was content to plunge from the one major triad straight to the other on the tone below, as in 'Mrs Moray of Abercairny's Strathspey' quoted on page 25. Later he tended to use modulatory chromatic notes which do not belong to the mode, as in 'The Dutchess of Buccleugh's Strathspey':

The Dutchess of Buccleugh's Strathspey

"Slowish"   (a)   Niel Gow
etc.

(a) modulatory note
* So spelt in the printed copy.

Nathaniel Gow, whose music was more sophisticated than that of his father, practically never uses this effect of contrasting major triads, though he does do so as a sly allusion to his father's style in his strathspey 'Niel Gow's Fiddle'. When he does use the progression on his own account, it is with a rather self-conscious show of modulatory dexterity and cleverness, as in 'Miss Nisbet of Dirleton's Reel':

219

Miss Nisbet of Dirleton's Reel

Nathaniel Gow

Nathaniel Gow does often use the altogether smoother and less rugged but much more ordinary progression however of proceeding from a *minor* triad to the major triad a tone below, e.g. 'Miss Eleanora Robertson's Favourite':

Miss Eleanora Robertson's Favourite

Slow

Nathaniel Gow

etc.

(bar 9)

etc.

Gradually, throughout the progress of the Gow family's writing we see a progressive loosening of the strict confines of the old modes and gapped scales, until in their sixth and last *Collection of Strathspey Reels* (published in 1822) we find such passages as:

220

Sir Alex.ʳ Don's Medley (Reel)

Nathaniel Gow

and this rather un-Scottish passage from a tune by John Gow, Nathaniel's elder brother:

Jnᵒ Gow's compliments to the Minstrels of Scotland

John Gow

This modal freedom, which ultimately developed into chromaticism of a sort, continued to grow among the fiddle composers, so that in the composition of the last of the great Scots fiddle composers, J. Scott Skinner we may find such passages as:

which certainly seems to be a bursting at the seams of the old Scottish modes!

The stroke of Niel Gow's bow has been remarked upon, and it was his *up-bow* stroke that was particularly meant; for it is the trick of the up-bow that is the distinguishing mark of the traditional Scots strathspey player. It is done with a jerk of the wrist on the up-stroke of the bow and it gives the characteristic accent to the strathspey rhythm—the Scot's snap *par excellence*. It is a trick of technique unknown to the classically trained violinist, or for that matter to the traditional fiddler south of the Border, as for instance the players for the English Morris or English sword dances, etc. Whether Niel Gow invented the stroke it is impossible now to say; probably it is as old as the strathspey itself and was used by the Cummings and Macphersons and Browns of Speyside. Certain it is that every Scots fiddler since Niel Gow's time has been judged on the power and agility of his up-bow stroke.

The knack still survives in players whose teaching descends from the

Gows and allied schools of playing. Probably the best exponent of it today is Hector MacAndrew of Aberdeen, whose (great?) grandfather learnt from a pupil of Niel Gow. Harvey Webb, a schoolmaster now living in England who played the part of the blind fiddler in Dylan Thomas's play about Burke and Hare, *The Doctor and the Devils* at the Edinburgh Festival,[1] has the accomplishment of this style through a line of teaching that descends from Geordie McLeish, who played along with the Gows. Geordie also played with James Hogg 'The Ettrick Shepherd' (who was a keen fiddler as well as a poet) and who also knew and probably played with 'Pate' Baillie, the fiddler from Liberton near Edinburgh of whom we shall have more to relate presently.

We have dealt with the Gow family at rather great length because, extending from the mid-eighteenth century to the near mid-nineteenth, it presents a fair picture of Scots fiddle playing and fiddle music over its most important and interesting period. For a systematic chronological study however it is necessary to retrace our steps to the important fiddler-composers whose dates of birth follow in order after Niel Gow.

The first of these and undoubtedly the greatest was William Marshall, whom Robert Burns styles 'The first composer of strathspeys of the age'. William Marshall was born at Fochabers, Morayshire, in 1748, that is, twenty-one years after Niel Gow. Marshall was the son of poor parents, and had to face the world at an early age but poorly equipped, for he had by way of education only six months at school. Yet he rose to be butler and house-steward to the Duke of Gordon, whose service he entered at the age of twelve; and he travelled with the Duke and Duchess between their various residences in different parts of Scotland and England. In spite of his lack of education he became skilled in mechanics, a good mathematician, an able astronomer, a tolerable architect and a famous composer of Scottish melodies. In the last he found ready encouragement from the Duke, who was himself the author of the words of the well-known song 'Cauld Kail in Aberdeen'.

Marshall published *A Collection of Strathspey Reels* in 1781.[2] In 1822, at the entreaty of his friends he published by subscription his *Scottish Airs, Melodies, Strathspeys, Reels, etc.* for the pianoforte, harp, violin and violoncello. This consists of a hundred and seventy-six tunes in all. There was also a posthumous collection published in 1847. In all, he published two hundred and eighty-seven tunes of his own composing. Next to Scott Skinner with six hundred tunes this makes him Scotland's second most prolific composer of national airs.

[1] The music for the play was selected by the writer.
[2] Published: Neil Stewart, Edinburgh.

Marshall as a composer is the doyen of all Scots fiddle players, much more so than the Gows or the later Scott Skinner; yet it must be stated that in the use of the Scottish gapped modes and scales he is unadventurous. A few such there are certainly, but the great number of his tunes are in the ordinary major mode. His best-known tune is 'Miss Admiral Gordon's Strathspey', but this is partly for the reason that Robert Burns used it for his 'Of a' the airts the wind can blaw'. Of his other tunes, the best, in the opinion of the writer are, 'The Marquis of Huntly's Farewell' (a slow strathspey) 'The Duchess of Manchester's Farewell to the Highlands of Scotland', 'Knockando House', 'Miss Stronach of Marnoch's Strathspey', and 'Craigellachie Bridge'.

Marshall did not often use the effect of the 'double tonic', as Niel Gow did, but when he did do so he used it with great effect, as in his strathspeys of 'Craigellachie Bridge' and 'The Fiddichside Lasses', both of which must also be included amongst his best tunes ('Craigellachie Bridge' is outstanding!). It may be worth setting down here his 'The Marquis of Huntly's Farewell' as an example of his melodic grace and power:

The Marquis of Huntly's Farewell

"Slow when not danced"   William Marshall

It will be noticed that here again the tune ends on another note than the keynote or tonic.

Angus Cumming of Grantown in Strathspey, thought to have been born about 1750 is the next in date of birth to Marshall. He published about 1778 a *Collection of Strathspeys or Old Highland Reels.* This is worth a mention for the obvious authenticity of its Strathspey tradition; on account of its author's locale; and particularly emanating as it does from a Cumming in Strathspey, a name we find mentioned by Thomas Newte as being '*in the highest estimation for their knowledge and execution in strathspey music, most of the tunes handed down being certainly of their composing'.* The inference in the title of his collection that the strathspey was an old form of highland *reel* is interesting, for the strathspey is generally considered to be essentially fiddle music, and as such, to date from the introduction of the violin into Scotland at the beginning of the century, which is almost certainly later than the reel.

Isaac Cooper of Banff, thought to have been born about 1755, published in 1783 *Thirty New Strathspey Reels* stated to be composed by himself; and about 1806, a further *Collection of Slow Airs, Strathspeys, Reels and Jigs.*[1] Isaac Cooper composed some good tunes, including the air 'Miss Forbes of Banff' and the strathspeys 'Lord Banff', 'Banff Castle' and 'Mrs Colquhoun Grant's Strathspey'.

John Bowie, a Perth fiddler who comes next on the scene, (being born in 1759), is of interest not only for his *Collection of Strathspey Reels* published by himself at Perth in 1789, but because of his publication at the end of this collection, of a number of airs for the harp. This is the only Scottish harp music published as such, and even in this case it is obviously adapted for the fiddle from the older harp pieces.

Robert Petrie, born at Kirkmichael, Perthshire, in 1767, was a talented fiddler who gained the prize of the 'silver bow' at Edinburgh. He was a fine composer of fiddle music, and his splendid strathspey 'Mrs Garden of Troup' has found its way into the permanent repertory. He published in all, four collections of *Strathspeys, Reels, and Country Dances,* the dates of publication being 1790 and 1796, the third and fourth collections being undated. He is credited as being the composer of the very well-known strathspey 'The Braes of Tullymet'. This is disputed however, and Petrie himself did not claim it as his.

We now come to a man who, though essentially interested in fiddle music and himself a good fiddler, is best known for his collection of

[1] Despite Cooper's own statement in the title of his collection, Baptie limits Cooper's own compositions, though without stating his authority, to twenty-five pieces.

Highland folk melodies. This is Captain Fraser of Knockie,[1] whose great work *The airs and melodies Peculiar to the Highlands of Scotland* forms one of the source books for the study of Gaelic music. It contains two hundred and thirty tunes consisting of traditional Gaelic song airs without words, and instrumental tunes in form for the fiddle but one or two of which are acknowledged pipe-tunes. The collection is also besprinkled with a number of fiddle tunes thought to be by Fraser himself, a few of which indeed he claims in his notes. These include the strathspeys 'Caledonia's Wail for Niel Gow', 'Niel Gow's style' (which is actually rather a poor parody of its inspirer) 'Killachassy', 'Huntly's Wedding Medley' and the reels 'Merry Lads and Bonny Lasses', and 'Lasses of Inverness', 'The Editor's Thanks to Mr Nathaniel Gow', and other airs. Every air in the collection appears under a Gaelic title, but one cannot be certain that in every case these are the original titles of the airs and that in some cases Fraser may not have rendered a Lowland Scots title into Gaelic. English translations of the Gaelic titles appear side by side with them, but some of these appear to be rather freely translated and do not always convey the literal meaning of the Gaelic. Nathaniel Gow is reported to have declared, 'The musical world is much indebted to this gentleman for his successful labours in rescuing from oblivion many beautiful native airs that must be ever dear to the Scot and the Highlander'. The flaw in the collection is that Fraser evidently interpreted the task of editor as including the 'improvement' of the old airs by altering their modal characteristics to the major-minor modes of the nineteenth-century musical fashion, particularly in their cadences. Fortunately it is generally possible for anyone with even a slight knowledge of Scottish modes and scales to hazard a conjectural reading of the original form of the air.

A second volume, prepared for publication by Simon Fraser's son Angus but never published, exists in manuscript of which only one out of five parts was published.[2] The manuscript was discovered in the 1950s in a second-hand bookshop in Edinburgh by Professor S. T. M. Newman, Dean of the Faculty of Music at Edinburgh, and presented by him to the University Library.

Peter ('Pate') Baillie of Liberton, Edinburgh, born 1774, was an immensely popular fiddler at the balls at Edinburgh and the Borders. He published a set of original fiddle tunes in 1825, now an extremely rare book. He was said to have been irascible and overweening in temperament and noted for 'extinguishing' lesser fiddlers when he

[1] Baptie sets down Simon Fraser as 'of Ardachie' (*Musical Scotland*, Baptie).
[2] Published by Hugh Mackenzie, Inverness, 1874.

came on the scene. He met his match however in William Thomson of Auchindenny, an amateur fiddler whose forte was the playing of strathspeys, and who more than held his own at one ball at Auchindenny at which Peter Bailie was also playing. 'Pate' got so enraged at last that he threw his own fiddle on the floor and jumped on it! The incident is indeed his chief claim to fame. It is said also that he once tried to take Niel Gow's fiddle from him in a fracas in Leith Walk near Edinburgh late one night after a ball, but that old Niel proved more than a match for him!

Robert ('Red Rob') Mackintosh was another outstanding Scottish fiddler, of whose birth however the date does not seem to be ascertainable with certainty. (Both John Glen and Grove evade the question.) Baptie puts his date of birth as about 1745, which would place him between Niel Gow and William Marshall, but Baptie is not always accurate. Doubtless from his nickname of 'Red Rob' he must have had red hair. He has left behind a tremendous reputation as a player, while as a composer his music, as John Glen says, 'stamps him as a musician of the first order in Scottish music'. He published four collections of Scottish dance music, of which his best tunes are, the reels 'Miss Katy Trotter', and 'Miss Stewart's'; the strathspeys 'Lady Charlotte Campbell's', 'Mrs Menzies of Culdair's', and 'Miss Margaret Graham of Gartmore's'.

Red Rob's son Abraham Mackintosh was also a fiddler and composer of ability. He published three sets of dance tunes of his own composing, amongst which is his notable strathspey 'Athole Brose', which also goes under the alternative titles of both 'Buckingham House' and 'Niel Gow's Favourite'. On account of its later title it has often been attributed to 'Famous Niel' himself, but he never claimed it. Others of Abraham Mackintosh's tunes which are well known are the strathspeys 'The Bridge of (or 'Brig' o') Dee', and 'Springfield'; and the reels 'Mordington House' and 'Kelso House'; also the hornpipes 'Miss Jessie Scales' and 'Miss Mary Lee's Delight'.

The host of lesser fiddler-composers is so great that one could not even set down their names here. Suffice it to say that they pave the way for the most prolific of all the Scots fiddle composers James Scott Skinner, born at Banchory in 1843, died at Aberdeen 1927. He began, as so many of the famous fiddlers did, by playing the violoncello accompaniment, first to his elder brother Sandy and later to the celebrated Aberdeen fiddler and teacher Peter Milne (born in the village of Kincardine-O'Neil, Aberdeenshire, 1824).[1] Scott Skinner could claim

[1] An aunt of the writer's by marriage, Miss Grant of Balvenie House, Dufftown,

the enormous number of six hundred pieces in print, besides the many that may still be in manuscript. By virtue of this alone his self-assumed title of 'The Strathspey King' was justified, though it was a token also of the healthy 'guid conceit' he had of himself. His best pieces such as 'The Miller o' Hirn', and 'The Laird of Drumblair' and the ever popular air of 'The Bonnie Lass o' Bon-accord'[1] are rightly popular favourites, and will remain so for as long as Scots music is played.

Scott Skinner was the last of the famous Scots fiddle composers.

ACCORDATURA TUNING OF THE FIDDLE

The device of *accordatura*, i.e. the altering of the tuning of the strings for some particular effect, was often used by the older Scottish fiddlers, and the writer has heard it himself on several occasions. It is of course an artifice known and used in other countries beside Scotland, and is to be found particularly in the Hardanger fiddle music of Norway.

In Scottish music, *accordatura* is often used for the purpose of playing a bagpipe-drone effect on the open string so altered, on a note consonant with the key of the piece. A frequent example is in the tuning of the G string up to A, so that the note A on the now open string may be used as a drone, by means of 'double stopping' (an unsatisfactory conventional musical term when one of the strings is open and therefore not stopped). This drone on A can be used either as a drone on the tonic in the key of A, or on the dominant in the key of D (as in the bagpipe itself in either key). The reel tune *Greig's Pipes* was usually played in this way; and to avoid the obvious inconvenience of restoring the tuning to normal for the rest of the programme, this piece was, according to the information of Charles Milne of Dufftown (q.v.) to the writer, usually played as the last item of the evening.

Sometimes the other strings were altered as well. James Oswald, in his *Caledonian Pocket Companion*, gives a group of six tunes for which the strings of the fiddle are directed to be tuned—G to A, D to E, A left unaltered, and the E string to be tuned *down* to C sharp, thus making on all four strings the chord A, E, A, C sharp. Directions for *accordatura* tuning rarely appear in the printed collections (it does not appear anywhere in Gow) and it seems to have been largely an idiosyncratic trick of individual fiddlers.

---

[1] 'Bon-accord' is the accepted nickname for the city of Aberdeen.

---

remembers this characteristic 'cello accompaniment to the fiddle or fiddles at the dances in Banffshire in her youth. She describes it as 'a kind of accented drone'.

CHAPTER VIII

The Harp

O F Scotland's three national instruments—the harp, the pipes and the fiddle—the harp or clarsach is undoubtedly the oldest. The instrument appears on stone carvings in Scotland from the early ninth century onwards. Some of these are to be found on stone crosses as at Dupplin in Perthshire (mid to late ninth century) and on a cross of tenth-century date now in the National Museum of Antiquities of Scotland, formerly at Monifieth, Forfarshire; and on 'cross slabs' at Nigg, Ross-shire (early ninth century) and at Auldbar, Forfarshire (late ninth to tenth century). Later examples of from early fifteenth- to early sixteenth-century date are to be seen at Keills, Argyll, and at Iona.[1]

The finest of these is the example at Dupplin, now much weathered, which also shows the harper, seated on a chair or 'throne'. Dr H. G. Farmer, in his *History of Music in Scotland* makes the apt observation that it reminds one of the 'throned bard' (*bardd cadeiriog*) mentioned in the Welsh Laws of Hywel Dda (tenth century).

The one-time common use of the harp in Scotland is commemorated in Scottish place-names, such as The Harper's Pass, in Mull, and in The Harper's Field, *Fàn-mór nan Clàrsairean* on the estate of Torloisk, (also in Mull), held as part of their fee by the harpers attached to the family of Torloisk. There is also a Harper's Field in the parish of Urray in Ross and Cromarty called *Cruiteach*, though the name might more accurately refer to the *cruit* or *crowd* than the harp. The record continues in the old castles of the Highlands with such features as The Harper's Window at Duntulm Castle in Skye, and The Harper's Gallery at Castlelachan in Argyll. A few such names occur in the Lowlands also, such as Harpersland near Eglintoun Castle in Ayrshire.

The Harper's Pass in Mull referred to is the place of a folk tale of how a harper broke up his harp and made a fire with it to save his wife from

---

[1] I have to thank Mr Robert Stevenson, Keeper of the National Museum of Antiquities of Scotland, for these dates. Cf. his article in *Proceedings of the Society of Antiquaries of Scotland*, 1958, p. 55.

perishing with cold while they were on a journey in the midst of winter. The wife turned out to be faithless to him—a faithlessness that gave rise to the harper's agonized cry, ' 'S mairg a loisgeadh a thiompan rithe', 'Fool that I was to burn my harp for her', an exclamation that became a proverbial reproach in Mull for ingratitude.[1]

References to the harp by early writers are numerous. The first is by the twelfth-century Welsh monk and scholar Giraldus Cambrensis, who writes glowingly in Latin of the harpers of Wales, Ireland and Scotland. Beginning with the Irish harpers, in a passage which, because of its continuation, is worth quoting in full—he writes, in a well-known translation:[2]

> The cultivation of instrumental music by this people [i.e. the Irish[3]] I find worthy of commendation; in this their skill is, *beyond all comparison*, superior to that of any nation I have ever seen; for their music is not slow and solemn, as in the instrumental music of Britain, to which we are accustomed; but the sounds are rapid and articulate, yet at the same time, sweet and pleasing. It is wonderful how, in such precipitate rapidity of the fingers, the musical proportions are preserved, and by their art, faultless throughout, in the midst of the most complicated modulation, and the most intricate arrangement of notes; by a velocity so pleasing, a regularity so diversified, a concord so dicordant, the melody is preserved harmonious and perfect; and whether a passage or transition is performed in a sequence of fourths or fifths,[4] it is always begun in a soft and delicate manner, and ended in the same, so that all may be perfected in the sweetness of delicious sounds. They enter on, and again leave, their modulations with so much subtlety, and the vibrations of the smaller strings of the treble sport with so much articulation and brilliancy, along with the deep notes of the bass; they delight with so much delicacy, and sooth so charmingly, that the great excellence of their art appears to lie in their accomplishing all this with the least appearance of effort or art.

Giraldus then goes on to extend his remarks to the harpers of Scotland with which we are more concerned, and of Wales:

[1] Cf. *Tour to the Hebrides*, Dr Garnet, 1800.

[2] John Gunn gives the passage in Latin in full in his historical enquiry respecting the performance of the harp in Scotland (Edinburgh, 1807).

[3] Alan J. Bruford, Research Archivist, School of Scottish Studies comments: 'Instrumentalists—harpers and players of the *Timpanum*, which was certainly a plucked string instrument.'

[4] 'Per diatesseron seu diapente.' Mr Bruford adds: 'Cf. English version by *J. J. O'Meara* (*The First Version of the Topography of Ireland, by Giraldus Cambreusis*), Dundalk, 1951, p. 87, which gives a very different reading (e.g. "Bb" for "a soft and delicate manner!").'

It is to be observed however that both Scotland and Wales, the former from intercourse and affinity of blood, the latter from instruction derived from the Irish, exert themselves with the greatest emulation to rival Ireland in musical excellence. In the opinion of many however, Scotland has not only attained to the excellence of Ireland, but has even, in musical science and ability, *far surpassed it*; insomuch, that it is to that country [Scotland] 'they' [i.e. the harpers of all three countries] now resort, as to the genuine source of the art.

John Major, the Scottish historian, in his *Annals of Scotland* published in 1521, says (also in Latin) that 'for instrumental music and the accompaniment of the voice they make use of the Harp, which instead of strings made of the intestines of animals, they strung with brass wire, and on which they perform most sweetly'. Even the king, James I, was a performer on the harp, and indeed the historian Fordun, according to his continuator Bower, said that he touched it 'like another Orpheus', while Major comments that, 'on the harp he excelled the Irish or the Highland Scots, who are esteemed the best performers on that instrument.'

A few years later, in 1565, we have an informative account of the instrument by George Buchanan, in his *History of Scotland*. Writing of the people and customs of the Western Isles, he says, 'They delight very much in music, especially in harps of their own sort, of which some are strung with brass wire, others with intestines of animals. They play on them either with their nails grown long or with a plectrum. Their only ambition seems to be to ornament their harps with silver and precious stones. The lower ranks, instead of gems, deck theirs with crystal.' George Buchanan came from near Ben Lomond and presumably knew what he was talking about as regards things Highland.

Another account, which follows George Buchanan's remarkably closely, particularly in its opening sentence, but which is nevertheless worth quoting, is by an anonymous writer on *Certain Matters concerning the Realme of Scotland as they were A.D. 1597*. This is of some importance as enlarging on this difference between wire and gut stringing, and the nomenclature arising from it. Dealing like Buchanan also with 'the Ysles of Scotland' the account reads, 'They delight in musicke, but chiefly in Harpes, and *Clairschoes* after their fashion. The strings of their Clairschoes are made of brasse wyar, and the strings of the Harpes of sinews, which strings they strike either with their nayles growing long, or else with an instrument appointed for that use.'

Lacking the distinction between the two varieties of the instrument indicated in this account, one would naturally take it that the word *clarsach* in its various spellings was merely the Gaelic for harp;[1] but this writer speaks of Harpes *and* (not *or*) clarsachs, and his statement would plainly infer that the two instruments were different—the clarsach strung with wire, and the harp strung with gut.

Major, in his description above quoted, of the playing of James I excelling that of the Highland Scots, infers that he regarded King James as a Lowlander, and that the harp was consequently popular in the Lowlands as well as in the Highlands. Dauney in his *Ancient Music of Scotland*, evidently subscribes to this view when he says:

> That the Irish introduced their national harp or Clarseach into this country is probable. Indeed, considering the extent of their early settlements in Argyll and Galloway, it is scarcely possible that it could have been otherwise. But there was a large portion of Scotland which was never occupied by the Scoto-Irish and here it is equally probable that the early inhabitants [i.e. of the Lowlands] possessed an instrument of this nature to which *the Irish could lay no claim.*

That there was harping and professional harpers in the Border counties is evinced by the allusions to it in the Border ballads, which may be dated as sixteenth- to seventeenth-century. The Lochmaben Harper of whom the ballad goes:

> And aye he harpit and aye he carpit[2]
> Till a' the nobles were sound asleep, etc.[3]

(whereupon he crept quietly to the stables and stole the king's horse)

must surely have been a player of high technical, if not moral standards. Sir Walter Scott observes that this ballad of 'The Lochmaben Harper' is the most modern in which the harp, as a Border instrument of music, is found to occur.

In the ballad of 'Thomas the Rhymer', the Queen of Elfland invites Thomas to '*harp and carp along wi' me*'.[2]

[1] The earliest literary reference to the *clarsach* occurs in the mid-fifteenth century poem of 'The Houlate', by Richard Holland in the passage:

> The Chenachy, The Clarsach,
> The Bebeschene, The Ballach,
> The Crekry, The Corach,
> Scho kens yame ilk ane.

[2] The Scottish dictionary gives the word *carp* as meaning to recite or to sing *minstrel fashion.*

[3] The theme of lulling an adversary to sleep by the music of the harp is common also in the Gaelic Heroic ballads. In the story of Caoilte's Urn is described the harp of three strings; one of silver named *Geantarghléas*, one of 'bright brass', *Goltarghleas*, and one *Suantarghleas* of iron. If the string of bright brass were played it made its hearers full of sorrow and mournfulness; if the silver string were played, its hearers would dissolve in laughter, while the string of iron had the power of putting its hearers into a deep sleep.

As Buchanan and, later, Dauney seem to indicate, there was a school of thought which would have it that the harp of the Highlands was the wire-strung Clarsach, and that the harp with the gut strings was the harp of the Lowlands. On the other hand John Leyden thought[1] that 'The Irish Clarsach strung with wire (sic) rather than the Welch harp strung with hair was that with which the Lowlanders were acquainted'. Dalyell probably is nearer the truth of the matter when he says of the two varieties.

> Two species of the instrument were evidently in use by our pro-genitors—one denominated the harp, the other the clarsha. But I enter-tain little doubt that they were often confused in common speech and that both passed under the usual appellative the *harp;* 'I apprehend that the true distinction was gradually obliterated or lost, or that their names were employed synonymously at a period comparatively recent.'[2]

Dalyell's opinion seems to be borne out by the fact that in the official records of payments to players of the instrument the terms harp and 'clarscha' seem to be used indiscriminately, as (14 April 1502):

> To Pate, harper on the harp xiiij s.
> To Pate, harper on the clarscha xiiij s.[3]

On the whole, we know more about the use of the harp in the Highlands than in the Lowlands. This is partly because the harper was one of the normal regular members of the establishment of the Highland Chief. We have already read of the Chief of Macleod having 'a harper, a piper, a bard and a fool in his train'. Maclean of Coll had a harper whose name, Murdoch Macdonald, is known to us. Dalyell gives references also to The Laird of Balnagown's harper, the Thane of Calder's (Cawdor's) harper, Lord Sempill's harper and the Countess of Craw-ford's harper. Not all these of course are Highland.

That the Earl of Argyll took his harper with him to the Battle of Strathaven, fought on 3 October 1594, is known from an account of the alleged prophecy of a witch (who was also apparently on the strength of the Earl's establishment) that on the morrow of the battle his harp should be played in Buchan—which it was, but in the possession of the enemy, the Earl of Errol, who was the victor!

Of the instruments themselves, two examples survive in the Cale-donian or Lamont Harp (*Clarsach Lumanach*) and the Queen Mary

---

[1] Introduction to *The Complaynt of Scotland*, John Leyden, 1801. Horse hair as used in Wales (and in Shetland) was an alternative to sinews or catgut.
[2] *Musical Memoirs of Scotland*, Sir J. G. Dalyell (Edinburgh, 1849), pp. 235 and 232.
[3] Dalyell, op. cit., p. 233.

Harp, both in the National Museum of Antiquities of Scotland. Tradition dates the Lamont Harp (*Clarsach Lumanach*) to be at least as old as 1464, when it was said to have been brought from Argyll by a daughter of the Lamont family of Argyll who married into the family of Lude in Perthshire. Into the possession of this family of Lude came also the Queen Mary Harp or Clarsach. Of this second acquisition to the family the tradition is that it was presented to a later member of the Lude family, Beatrix Gardyn, about a hundred years after the other harp by Mary Queen of Scots when she was on a hunting expedition to Athol. This harp, of obviously Celtic design, is said to resemble closely the Harp of Brian Boru, reputed to have belonged to the King of Ireland of the name who was slain in 1014, though this is now disputed.

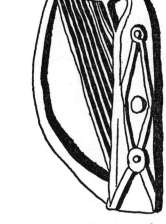

Detail of stone-carving of a harp from a 15th-16th century cross-slab at Keills, Knapdale, Argyll. The similarity of ornamentation to that of the Queen Mary Harp is remarkable.

The *Clarsach Lumanach* or Lamont Harp is thirty-eight and a half inches in height and sixteen inches wide at the broadest part of the sounding board (the lowest part). The tuning pins, thirty in number, which are nearly four inches in length, were evidently originally of brass but have been replaced at some time by iron pins. As the harp was almost certainly tuned diatonically, this gives a compass of four octaves and one note. (John Gunn.)[1]

The Queen Mary Harp, which is more lightly and finely made than the Lamont Harp, is thirty-one inches in height as compared with the

[1] John Gunn in his *Historical Enquiry* is obscure in his specification of the actual octaves of its compass and it would be misleading to quote his statement on the subject.

thirty-eight and a half inches of the Lamont Harp, while the breadth of sounding board at its widest part is only eleven inches as against the sixteen of the Lamont. It has twenty-eight tuning pins as against the Lamont's thirty, giving one note short of four octaves if diatonically tuned.

The Queen Mary Harp was re-strung by John Gunn at the request of the Highland Society of Scotland about 1806. Strings of brass were first tried, but these were abandoned after trial for gut strings, for the wire strings had to be plucked with the finger-nails, which would have had to be grown long for the purpose. (The convenient and accepted form of punishment of a harper for misdemeanour was said to be, though with doubtful authority, to cut his finger-nails short so that he was unable to play until the nails grew again—though of course this had also the disadvantage of denying to the chief himself the music for which he was paying the harper.)[1]

When the Queen Mary Harp was re-strung it was played upon by a professional harpist of the day, Elouis, to the members of the Highland Society. The harp was tuned to the following compass, diatonically:[2]

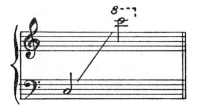

Some time in the nineteenth century the Lamont and Queen Mary Harps passed from the Lude family by another marriage into the possession of the Stuarts of Dalguise. From Dalguise they came in the 1880's to the Museum of Antiquities in Edinburgh where they now are.

Unless, as is now very unlikely, another genuine old instrument should still come to light, these two ancient clarsachs must be regarded as the only examples remaining in existence of Scotland's oldest and once popular instrument. But for the care taken of them for *over four centuries* by the Robertson family of Lude, and later by the Stuarts of Dalguise, Scotland would have been without a single specimen of its clarsach from which to know just what it was like and to base its later revival on a proper historical footing. One could only have guessed at the design

[1] Cf. Gunn, p. 19.

[2] This is Gunn's account (p. 22) but it must be pointed out that this compass requires twenty-nine strings, which does not tally with the number of tuning pins, which, as has been stated, is only twenty-eight.

and size of the instrument by analogy with the Irish harps. Having these two ancient instruments for comparison, we can in fact say that there was little difference between the Scottish and Irish harps *at that period*. Considering the similarity of the Queen Mary Harp to the Brian Boru Harp (now in Trinity College, Dublin), we cannot indeed be sure that the two Scottish harps may not have been made by the Irish harp makers.

For the study of the development of the small harp in Ireland, as well as for fine pictures of the Scottish clarsachs, the reader is recommended to see the magnificent collection of photographs of harps of all countries by Miss Russell Fergusson at the Mitchell Library in Glasgow.

THE HARPERS

We are woefully lacking in details of the names of the ancient Scottish Harpers as compared with those of the great pipers. The early public accounts of the Royal Household of Scotland show payments to harpers in their Christian names such as, Martyn clareshaw (1490), Alexander harper (1505), Pate harper (before mentioned) (1505), and Roland clarschaar (1507). Doubtless in some cases the description *harper* would become a surname later on. Some true surnames do however also occur, as, Hew Brabanar (1503), James Mytson or Mylsoun the harper (1496), Sowles the harper (1496), Bragman harper and Henry Philip (1506).

Highland names occur amongst them, such as McBretane clarschaw (1492), MacBerty the clarscha (1505);[1] while Dalyell mentions a Donald Mclean, harper to the Earl of Sutherland, who perished in the Glen of Loth in a snowstorm (1602).[2]

Strange to relate, only one player of this one-time national instrument has come down to us in name as a musician of magnitude in a sense comparable to the MacCrimmons on the pipes. This is Roderick Morison, better known as Rory Dall (Blind Rory) and as *An Clàrsair Dall* (The Blind Harper). Though some of his poetry has survived (for he was bard as well as harper) his reputation as a harper rests upon tradition alone, for none of his harp music has survived, at least in recognizable form.

Roderick Morison, Rory Dall, was born in the Isle of Lewis *circa* 1660. The son of a well-to-do tacksman, he was intended, along with his two brothers, for the Church. While yet a student at Inverness, however, he contracted smallpox, from the effects of which he lost his sight. He had to give up further thoughts of the Church as a career. He had a gift

---

[1] Cf. Dalyell, op. cit., p. 234.   [2] Ibid., p. 238.

for music, and as music was the recognized profession for the blind at that period, both in Scotland and Ireland, he turned to it for a living.

The harp had always been his favourite instrument, though Mackenzie tells us that he was 'no mean performer on other instruments' as well. He presumably studied first with one of the established Scottish harpers, a course of study which, if analogy with the tradition of the piping schools means anything, would be doubtless long and rigorous. His natural gifts as a musician, again according to Mackenzie, 'soon served him as a passport to the best circles in the North'. He decided however to perfect his art further by going to Ireland for further instruction.

He returned from Ireland in 1681, that is at the age of about twenty-one, and travelled home to Scotland via Edinburgh.[1] There he met in with the Chief of Macleod, Iain Breac (the nineteenth chief) who shortly afterwards offered him the post of family harper to himself.

While in Edinburgh Rory Dall evidently sojourned with the Macleods, for it was at their Edinburgh residence that there occurred the loss of a harp key for tuning the instrument which was to give rise to a famous song. It should be added that such harp keys were objects of value, being often of silver and gold, and ornamented with precious stones. The story goes that the Lady of Macleod one morning came down to find Rory searching among the ashes of the kitchen fire with his fingers. She asked of one of the maids, '*Ciod e tha dhith air Ruairidh?*' (What is Rory missing?) '*Mhuire! tha a chrann; chaill e san luath e*' (Mary Mother! it is the harp key; he has lost it among the ashes). '*Ma ta feumair crann eile 'cheannach do Ruairidh*' (Well, we'll have to buy another 'crann' for Rory) continued the Lady of Macleod; and Rory forthwith composed the beautiful melody of '*Feill nan Crann*', clothing it with words of side-splitting humour and representing the kitchen maids as ransacking every shop in the town for a replacement of the lost key.[2]

Roderick Morison stayed on as harper to the Macleod at Dunvegan until the death of Iain Breac in 1693. The succeeding (nineteenth) chief, Rory Og, who was consumptive,[3] lived chiefly at Fortrose, possibly as Dr I. F. Grant suggests, for health reasons; and he dispensed with the

[1] I am indebted for these and other particulars (including corrections to John MacKenzie's account), to William Matheson of the Celtic Department of Edinburgh University, who is at present engaged on writing a book on Roderick Morison, and who has most kindly put much valuable information arising from his researches at my disposal.

[2] The story is related by Mackenzie in *Sar-obair nam Bard Gaelach*. William Matheson states however that the incident happened at Dunvegan.

[3] *The Macleods*. I. F. Grant (London, 1959), p. 330.

services of a harper, though the records show that he was not neglectful of the poets and pipers, and was certainly not economically minded.[1] The Clarsair Dall had to leave his 'harpers land' of the farm of Claggan.[2] He went for a time to the farm of Genelg and finally returned to his native Lewis, where he lived out the remainder of his days. Mackenzie gives the date of his death as 1725, but William Matheson has found evidence to show that it was twelve or thirteen years earlier, in 1712–13.

On the death of his patron Iain Breac, he wrote two poems, 'Creach-na-ciadain' and 'Oran Mór Mhic-Leoid', which not only sing the praises of Iain Breac, but the dispraises of his heir—and that in no small measure. John Mackenzie describes these in *Sar-obair* as 'pathetic, plaintive and heart touching productions ... that finely harmonize with the poignacy of our poet's grief'. Dr I. F. Grant on the other hand crisply alludes to them as 'two very spiteful poems', which certainly gives the reader a wide latitude of choice.

Five of Rory Dall's song-poems in all appear without their tunes in Mackenzie's *Sar-obair*, and others still exist orally.

Another harper of whom we have mention, this time an amateur, was the Laird of Coll, John Garve Maclean, who was esteemed both an excellent performer and a good composer. According to Gunn, he lived in the latter end of the reign of James the Sixth and during that of Charles the First—in other words the period about and before 1649, the date of Charles the First's execution. Gunn says that two of his compositions have been handed down—one called '*Toum Muran*' (The Hill of the Bents) and another, '*Caoineadh Rioghail*' (The Royal Lament) thought to have been composed by him in memory of King Charles. '*Toum Muran*' cannot be located, but the writer has found the melody of '*Caoineadh Rioghail*' in a musical manuscript in Edinburgh University Library, though in what is probably reconstructed form (see p. 238).[3]

The family of Maclean of Coll evidently continued the tradition of employing a family harper until well into the eighteenth century, for the family accounts show a payment made to their harper in 1734. This was Murdoch Macdonald known as *Murchadh Clarsair* (Murdoch the harper). The entry has long been thought to have been the last payment of a family harper on record, but Dr I. F. Grant mentions, in the accounts of Macleod of Dunvegan, a tailor's bill of 1755, which, in addition to the making of clothes for Macleod and his family, contains the item 'to making a frok to the harper'. The date is in the time of the

---

[1] Ibid., p. 330.   [2] Information from William Matheson.
[3] *A Collection of the Vocal Airs of the Highlands of Scotland ... as formerly played on the harp*, by Angus Fraser.

AN COINEADH RIOGHAL
The Royal Lament or Keening

Consisting of ground and two variations; said to be composed
c. 1649 by John Garve Maclean, Laird of Coll, possibly on the
execution of Charles I.

(As given in the Angus Fraser M.S., Edinburgh University)

Note: The M.S. gives only the melody as here, without any sustaining
harmony.

By courtesy of Edinburgh University Library.

238

twenty-second chief, Norman (1706–72). (It will be remembered that Iain Breac, who employed the Clarsair Dall, was eighteenth chief.)

The entry is an important one for the history of the harp, for if we allow, at a conservative estimate, say five more years for the employment of the harper referred to, this protracts the last-known date of the inclusion of a harper in a Highland Chief's establishment by no less than twenty-one years—a crucial period in the history of the instrument, as we shall see.

It is not known how long 'Murdoch the Harper' lived (he retired to Quinish in Mull in his old age). It can be fairly certain however that the harp disappeared from use in Scotland about the middle of the eighteenth century—a good deal later than is generally imagined—until its revival under its old name of the clarsach in the 1930s, to be presently described.

THE HARP MUSIC

Before trying to piece together a picture of what the now extinct harp music of Scotland was like, it is necessary first to clear up a major confusion which has arisen between Roderick Morison, 'Rory Dall' who has regrettably left no harp music we can identify,[1] and an Irish harper of similar cognomen who lived immediately before him, spent much of his time in Scotland, and who left quite a number of compositions for the harp. This was Roger or Rory O'Cathain, who, because he too was blind, was also known as Rory Dall. He composed a number of tunes with Scottish titles which still survive and which are often wrongly ascribed to Rory Dall Morison.

The precise dates of Rory O'Cathain's birth and death are not known, but he is stated by Bunting, the Irish musical historian and folk-music collector, to have been born about 1550. He is said to have lived to a hundred years of age, which would put the date of his death about 1650, before Roderick Morison was born. One cannot do better than quote the description of him, in spite of its palpable exaggerations, by Arthur O'Neill, an Irish harper who dictated his memoirs to Bunting— with due allowance for the fact that it was a full hundred and sixty years after O'Cathain's death (i.e. in 1810) that O'Neill's memoirs were written.[2] He says in his racy style:

'Rory Dall O'Cathain (Blind Roger O'Kane) was born in the County of Derry, a gentleman of large property and heir to an entire barony in

[1] Angus Fraser Manuscript gives several of the airs of Rory Dall's songs.
[2] This extract from the *Memoirs of Arthur O'Neill* is taken by kind permission of Dr Donal O'Sullivan of Dublin from his *Carolan, The Life, Times and Music of an Irish Harper* (Routledge and Kegan Paul, London, 1958).

that county. He was titled by O'Neill *Oireachtaidhe O Cathain* (Chief O'Cathain) before he inherited his estate, which was Coleraine, Garvagh, Newtown-Limavaddy, Kilreagh, and several others. He showed a strong inclination for the harp, and at the time he came to his estate he was an excellent performer and lived in a splendid style in them days (James the First's reign). He took a fancy to visit Scotland, where there were great harpers. He took his retinue (or suite) with him. Amongst other visits in the style of an Irish chieftain he paid one to a Lady Eglintoun, and she (not knowing his rank) in a peremptory manner demanded a tune, which he declined as he only came to play to amuse her, and in an irritable manner left the house. However when she was informed of his consequence, she eagerly contrived a reconciliation and made an apology, and the result was that he composed a tune for her ladyship, the handsome tune of 'Da mihi manum'[1] (Give me your hand) for which his fame reached through Scotland and came to the ears of the Gunpowder Plot prophet James the First of England (then the Sixth of Scotland). O'Keane delighted him so very much that the crabbit monarch walked towards him and laid a hand upon his shoulder as a token of approbation, which one of the courtiers then present observed to Roger. 'What!' says O'Keane, somewhat nettled, 'A greater man than ever James was, laid his hand upon my shoulder.' 'Who is that?' says the King. O'Neill my liege' says he, standing up.

He composed several fine tunes in Scotland, particularly 'Port Atholl', 'Port Gordon'[2] (*port* means a lesson in music) and several others. The Ports are uncommon fine tunes. I played them once but now forget them. Roger died in Scotland in a nobleman's house, where he left his harp and silver key to tune it. About forty years ago a blind harper named Echlin Keane, a scholar of Lyons whom I often met and an excellent performer, went over to Scotland and called at the house where Roger's harp and key were, and the heir of the nobleman took a liking to Echlin and made him a present of the silver key, he being namesake to its first owner. But the dissipated rascal sold it in Edinburgh and drank the money.'

There can be very little doubt that the harp key referred to is the one mentioned by Boswell in his *Journal of a Tour to the Hebrides* with Dr Johnson in 1773 where, in his entry for 15 October he writes concerning a certain '*penurious gentleman of our acquaintance*', 'Col[3] told us, that O'Kane, the famous Irish harper, was once at that gentleman's house. He could not find it in his heart to give him any money, but gave him a

[1] The tune, with a bass, of 'Da Mihi Manum' is to be found in Dow's *Ancient Scots Music* (n.d., *c.* 1775).

[2] Both tunes are to be found in *A Collection of Strathspey Reels*, etc. by John Bowie.

[3] i.e. the Laird of Coll. William Matheson adds: 'Boswell is here referring to Sir Alexander (later Lord) MacDonald of Sleat, a good performer on the violin.'

key for a harp, which was finely ornamented with gold and silver, and with a precious stone, and was worth eighty or a hundred guineas. He did not know the value of it; and when he came to know it, he would fain have had it back; but O'Kane took care that he should not,' etc.

This Echlin O'Kane or Keane is of course easily mistaken for his namesake Rory O'Cathain, and so has added further to the confusion with the Scots Rory Morison, though the latter had by this time been dead for some fifty years, and the Irish Rory Dall for some hundred and twenty years.

Of the tunes with Scottish names almost certainly composed by the Irish Rory Dall when in Scotland (generally for some particular member of the Scottish aristocracy) O'Neill has mentioned 'Port Atholl', 'Port Gordon' and 'Da Mihi Manum'. Four other 'ports' of a similar type exist, namely Rory Dall's Port, the tune to which Robert Burns wrote his song 'Ae fond Kiss';[1] and a different tune with the same title, 'Rory Dall's Port', in the Straloch Manuscript, reproduced in the notes to Johnson's 'Scots Musical Museum'. (This latter air appears also in the Skene Manuscript under the title of 'Port Ballangowne'.) Two more, 'Jean Lindsay's Port' and another nameless 'port' are also published in the notes to the Musical Museum and make up the four mentioned. 'Port Lennox' is to be found in John Bowie's and Daniel Dow's collections.

One would like to think that even one of these tunes could be claimed for the Scots Rory Dall as a genuine specimen of a Scottish harp melody; but internal evidence of form and style point to the strong probability that they all emanate from the same hand, that of the Irish Rory O'Cathain. They all have the same characteristically unsymmetrical phrase construction, with a second strain several bars longer than the first. In this respect they bear a resemblance to the Irish 'Planxty'. Petrie, the Irish musical historian characterizes this as a piece of music:

> not being bound, as the Jig necessarily is, to an equality in the number of bars or beats in its parts; for the Planxty though in some instances it presents such an equality, is more usually remarkable for a want of it, the second part being extended to various degrees of length beyond that of the first, so that it would be equally unfitted for a dancing movement as, from the irregularity of its cadences and the unlicensed compass of its scale, it would be unadaptable to a singing one.

The description fits all these 'ports' pretty closely and points to an Irish rather than a Scottish origin. Nevertheless a surprising number of

[1] William Matheson observes: 'This is why Hì ho ró 's na hó ro eile (a variant of this "port") has been attributed to Rory Dall.'

able musical historians have confused the two Rory Dalls and their music. David Laing, in his commentaries on Stenhouses' notes to the *Scots Musical Museum*, writes of these ports that:

> they exhibit along with the vigorous and strongly marked features of a bygone age, not a little of the master's hand and the poet's fire for which Scotland was anciently so renowned. As showing that the 'land of the mountain and flood' at one time possessed a style of harp minstrelsy peculiarly its own, and different from that of Ireland and Wales, these remains are not only interesting but instructive. (!)

Even John Gunn in his specialist *Historical Enquiry on the Harp in Scotland* confuses the two Rorys, for he relates that Roderick Morison (sic) accompanied the Marquis of Huntly on a visit to Lude about the year 1650, when he composed a port called 'Suiper Chiurn na[1] Leod' (Lude's Supper). The Scottish Roderick Morison was however not yet born. On the other hand if O'Cathain was born in 1550 as he was said to be, he would then be a hundred years of age. Perhaps they were tougher in those days!

The tune of 'Lude's Supper' is to be found in Dow's *Ancient Scots Music*. In that Collection may also be found a 'Lament for Rory Dall's sister'. Here again it could not refer to the Scottish Rory Dall, for according to William Matheson, Roderick Morison had only one sister who *outlived* him. It follows that this lament too must almost certainly have been composed by O'Cathain. The disposal of this last hope therefore leaves nothing among all these tunes which can with any reasonableness be claimed for Roderick Morison, but must with a fair probability be ascribed to Roger O'Cathain. Strictly speaking these tunes should thus be accounted as of Irish provenance. Perhaps however by the circumstances of their composition, written as they were for the Scottish nobility whom Rory O'Cathain visited, possibly to be looked upon by the families concerned as a sort of private 'signature tune', they may be regarded as *in a sense* Scottish harp music; certainly the Irish do not seem to have laid claim to them as part of their national musical corpus.

What then, we may ask, has become of all the *true* harp music of Scotland? It is most unlikely, and indeed hardly possible, that the—doubtlessly numerous—melodies composed by some hundreds of Scots harpers down the ages have simply ceased to exist, for tunes in quantity don't disappear in this way, as we may see by the Ossianic tunes still in existence after at least seven centuries, and still being sung in the Hebrides

---

[1] 'Chiurn na'; this is an attempt at *Tighearna*, (Laird) William Matheson.

as these words are written. Rather the probability is that other musical instruments have fallen heir to them. Not even O'Cathain's tunes have come down to us *in proper form for the harp*. 'Port Gordon', 'Port Atholl' and 'Port Lennox' were recovered by being taken down by John Bowie, a music publisher in Perth[1] of the eighteenth century, from the fiddle-playing of the contemporary representative of the family of Lude, who had acquired them from long aural tradition within the family over many generations; originating, it would seem, with those two ladies who brought their harps and harp tunes with them when they married into the family of Robertson of Lude in the fifteenth and sixteenth centuries respectively. Doubtless other harp tunes too had been acquired since by this musical family. Other tunes of O'Cathain exist in early Scottish collections for the lute as we have seen, and later, for the German flute, such as in Oswald's *Caledonian Companion*.

One may fairly reasonably hazard a guess that among the Scottish harp music the *variation* form must have found place, as it had done in every other form of Scottish instrumental music—in the lute collections of folk-tunes such as the Skene and Straloch Manuscript, in the early manuscript fiddle books and printed collections for the fiddle by Bremner and others; most important of all, in the ancient piobaireachd, a form of theme and variations for a folk instrument found nowhere else but in Scotland; for though the variation form exists of course in plenty in the music of other countries, it is mostly in the *art music* of academic composers, as in the Fitzwilliam *Virginal Book*, rather than in the music of the folk.[2] Matthew Locke, it is true, refers in the preface to his *Little Consort for Viols or Violin*, to 'the tearing of a Consort in pieces with divisions'—an old custom of our (English) country fiddlers; but this kind of division seems to have consisted of variation *in the course of a tune* rather than a series of separate variations following a given tune or ground. It is noteworthy that amongst the music of Carolan the famous Irish harper and a prolific composer for the instrument, the only pieces in variation form are two which are *based upon Scottish themes*, i.e.

---

[1] This is as recounted by Gunn. Alan Bruford rightly points out however that Ports 'Gordon' and 'Lennox' appear in Dow's *Ancient Scottish Music*, an earlier publication by some years than Bowie's.

[2] Some of the writer's colleagues will not allow this antithesis, on the ground that *piobaireachd* and its probable predecessor the ancient Scots harp music was not 'folk' music, but the work of professional composers. One must of course concede that they were professional in that music (sometimes mixed with the composing of song) was their sole profession; but they were musicians composing for a native instrument, and composing by ear guided by *traditional native formula* (which is the writer's point) and not on paper, with the style and heritage of the 'paper music' of the outside world to influence them.

'When she cam ben she bobbit' and 'Cock up your Beaver'.[1] These are interesting further in that the variations consist not so much in mere meanderings around the melody as we find in much eighteenth-century variation, but in the manipulation of a series of musical figures, which almost appear to be a kind of groping by this Irish composer for the piobaireachd—or could it be the Scottish harp-music?—form.[2]

Patrick Macdonald, who published his *Collection of Highland Airs* in 1784, i.e. from thirty to fifty years after the last known record of a professional harper in Scotland[3] (though he says in his introduction that the harp had ceased to be the favourite instrument for *upwards of a century*—the encouragement of the people having been transferred to the bagpipe) says that some of the airs in his collection, and others of similar structure, are valuable as probably the most genuine remains of the ancient harp-music in the Highlands. The writer of the *Dissertation* following Macdonald's preface (which is by another hand than his own) says of the *luinneags* or work songs, 'the greater part of them appear to be adapted to the harp, an instrument which was once in high estimation here.'[4] The same writer adds of the *dirge* or *coronach*—'In the days of Ossian, the dirge appears to have been accompanied by the harp, but after it had lost its credit, the piper would doubtless attempt to catch the spirit of the dirge as far as it could be accommodated to the bagpipe.' He also adds the remark worthy of notice that 'the contrast between the *pipe* and *harp* tunes is so striking that one could hardly imagine them to be the music of the same people', a statement which the writer proposes to challenge.[5]

It is important to remember that the time which elapsed between the

[1] Cf. *Carolan* by Donal O'Sullivan (Routledge and Kegan Paul, 1958).

[2] The variation form seems however to have been (and obviously still is) a favourite device of the Welsh traditional harpers, *vide* the performance of Nansi Richards Jones, the only surviving player of the triple harp, in a B.B.C. Third Programme lecture-broadcast by Joan Rimmer on 21 September 1963, when she played a number of interesting variations of astonishing technical virtuosity of her own composing, to Welsh hymn tunes.

[3] Cf. p. 237.

[4] This requires some elucidation. The Gaelic dictionary gives the meaning of a *luinneag* as 'a song, a ditty, or a chorus'; and in that sense many luinneags might be said to be 'adapted to' (i.e. suitable for playing on) the harp. The usual meaning of luinneag however is a *work song*, and it is *here used in that sense*. It is extremely doubtful if the harp was ever used in the performance of work songs, though it is impossible to say that some of the work-song tunes may not have been taken from the harpists' repertoire.

[5] This whole statement by the writer of the Dissertation in Patrick Macdonald's collection is characterized by William Matheson as 'nonsense'; an opinion with which the writer is inclined to agree. Mr Matheson states that the writer was (John) Ramsay of Ochtertyre, an interesting fact which had escaped the writer.

last known harper and the publication of Patrick Macdonald's collection, perhaps about twenty years, is a lot less than the period during which the bagpipe and its music was suppressed following the 1745 Rising (which indeed overlapped this period). This is much too short a time for melodies to become forgotten and disappear, as the consequent resurgence of the pipe music after the '45 itself shows. The probability is that the harp melodies lived on in song airs, in the repertoire of the fiddle (as we have seen) and of the lute, the flute *and the bagpipe*.

Here one may mention a musical manuscript in the library of Edinburgh University which may have an important bearing on this question of what happened to the harp music. This is the manuscript of a second volume (of which only one out of five parts was published) of Simon Fraser's *Highland Airs*, which was edited and prepared for publication by his natural son Angus Fraser.[1] The manuscript includes, besides a large number of fiddle tunes, what purports to be a number of specimens of the ancient harp music *reconstructed for the piano*, on the lines of information supplied by persons *who remembered them as they were played on the harp*. The relevant title of this part of the collection is: *A Collection / of the / Vocal Airs / of the Highlands of Scotland / communicated as sung by the people / and formerly played on the harp / Arranged for the Pianoforte / by / Angus Fraser*. The title is misleading, for the airs are not in vocal form, but in the form of instrumental variations which are plainly meant to relate to the old harp style.

These variations are very much after the manner of piobaireachd, but in simpler patterns and musical figures. Among the tunes, as has been mentioned, is '*Caoineadh Rioghail*', 'The Royal Lament', the piece composed for the harp by the Laird of Coll, probably about 1649. What is even more interesting is what purports to be a harp version of the well-known piobaireachd '*Cumha Craobh nan Teud*'.

CRAOBH NAN TEUD
Lament for the Harp Tree (or harp key?)

As given for the harp in the Angus Fraser M S., Edinburgh University.

Slow

[continued overleaf

---

[1] This is the same manuscript referred to under fiddle music on page 225.

By courtesy of Edinburgh University Library.

Pipe version of the same tune

(from Angus Mackay's Ancient Piobaireachd)

Urlar - Adagio

This piobaireachd, which is in the standard repertory of piping, is usually translated as 'The Lament for the Harp Tree'. John Mackenzie, as may be remembered, tells in 'Sar-Obair nam Bard Gaelach the story of Roderick Morison's loss of a harp *key*, in the words 'Tha a chrann—chaill e san luath e' (It is the harp key—he has lost it in the ashes). Another meaning of the word *crann* however is a *tree*, for which we likewise find the word *craobh*. William Matheson suggests that *craobh*, which does not possess the secondary meaning of a key, as *crann* does, may have been an accidental substitution, thus changing the meaning of the title 'The Lament for the Harp-key', which makes sense, to 'The Lament for the Harp-*tree*' (which does not). The importance of the proper title (if such it be) is that it suggests the possibility, if indeed one may not use a stronger term, that the lament may have been originally composed not by a piper but a harper—perhaps even by Roderick Morison himself —perhaps about the very harp key of the story.

If all this be indeed the case, it lets in a flood of light upon the whole subject. It means that a specific piece of harp music, which, according to Fraser, was in variation form, was taken over by the pipers and adapted to the technique of their own instrument as a piobaireachd. And if one piobaireachd could originate in this way, others could of course have done so also. It raises the possibility that a number of the earlier piobaireachd, not identifiable as the known compositions of named pipers, may similarly have been originally composed for the harp. Early writers like Buchanan, as we have seen, have stated that the harp was supplanted by the bagpipes; it seems to be by no means impossible that some of the harp music was taken over in the process, both as to its melodic themes and its variation form. This would of course offer an explanation of the always puzzling fact that piobaireachd seems to have come into existence fully fledged, without any of the rudimentary experiments which one could expect in the development of so perfected a form. It could be that the form had already been perfected, or had gone some way towards being so by the harp composers.

All this is admittedly pure supposition; and as it arises from the single evidence of Angus Fraser's manuscript, much depends on the worth of that evidence. Simon Fraser the father of Angus died in 1852, less than a hundred years after the last records of the harpers. According to a note on the manuscript by a later hand, his son Angus died 'in or prior to 1874'. This may seem a very long stretch of time for tradition to be accurately transmitted. On the other hand, Simon Fraser's grandfathers on each side of the family both lived in the time of the harpers, and both were, as Simon says in his notes, amateur musicians and keen acquirers of songs and tunes, to whom he declares his indebtedness for many of the airs he published. References to the harp by Simon Fraser himself are rather vague, being confined to that of 'accompanying a sweet female voice, or round the festive board', which does not tell us much.[1]

[1] Cf. his note to air No. 3, 'Grant of Sheuglie's contest betwixt his violin, his pipes and his harp.'

Some slight confirmation of the possible similarity of form between piobaireachd and the ancient harp music may perhaps be allowed in the fact that in Bunting's table of harp nomenclature in his *Ancient Music of Ireland* gleaned from the *Irish* harpers, we find a number of terms, including *Siubhal, Canntaireachd,*[1] *Barluadh* and *Barluadh fosgailte*, which are the same as those of the movements of piobaireachd.[2] On the other hand piobaireachd is not known in Irish music. Probably the most that can be said, until more evidence turns up, is that the theory is not impossible, while Angus Fraser's evidence does seem to lend it some feasibility.

It is not likely in any case that *all*, if any, of the harp music would be cast in the same heroic mould as piobaireachd. As hinted in Patrick Macdonald,[3] the lighter *luinneags* may also doubtless have found place; while we know from countless sources that the harp was used to accompany song both grave and gay. The three musical categories could very well be covered by the existing pipe-music terms of *Ceòl Mór* (great music), *Ceòl Beag* (small or light music, i.e. dance music) and *Ceòl Meadhonach* (middle music, which could include the accompaniment of songs, heroic and otherwise). There is nothing in these terms themselves to suggest that they must necessarily always have been restricted to the music of the pipes.

As a final word on the subject it might be added that if the pattern suggested by Angus Fraser *can* be accepted as one of the possible forms of the ancient harp music of Scotland, it should be within the powers of a composer of imagination to re-create such music for the instrument, again happily in use, either on existing or on original themes.

THE REVIVAL OF THE CLARSACH

Except for a small harp of somewhat curious shape, thought to be of nineteenth-century make, which was formerly owned by Lady John Scott (1810–1900) of Spottiswoode in Berwickshire (the composer of 'Annie Laurie') we do not hear of the small harp in Scotland again until the Clarsach Revival of the end of the nineteenth century.

[1] It must be confessed that it is difficult to see how *canntaireachd*, which requires a different vocable syllable for each note, could ever have been applied to the thirty strings of the harp. It may however have been used for the melody of the air only.

[2] *Barluadh* and *Barluadh fosgailte* are terms for pibroch figures now gone out of use. They are set down by Joseph MacDonald in his *Compleat Theory of the Scots Highland Bagpipe*.

[3] According to William Matheson as stated above however, the writer was Ramsay of Ochtertyre, and Mr Matheson holds that Ramsay is in error in connecting the tunes of the *luinneags* with the harp. The writer accepts his opinion.

The first tentative step towards this revival was taken by Lord Archibald Campbell, father of the late Duke of Argyll, who, in 1891 or thereabouts, asked the firm of Glen, bagpipe makers in Edinburgh, to make three clarsachs. Later he had six others made by Robert Buchanan, a Glasgow piano maker. These were modelled on the Queen Mary Harp, with its carvings reproduced; but whereas the soundbox of the ancient clarsach was rectangular in section (probably a legacy of the *cruit*) those made by Buchanan were rounded on the outside face, giving the instrument the appearance of a concert harp in miniature.

In addition to the three made for Lord Campbell, Glen's made at the same time a number of clarsachs for other customers who were interested, and for members of the Glen family. These were made of old wood, and were carved and decorated with semi-precious stones or pieces of rock-crystal on the fore-pillar, in the manner of the ancient Scots harps as described by Buchanan.

It takes the expert to distinguish these Glen clarsachs from the ancient models, and they have frequently been mistaken for antique instruments. One of these was presented to the Folk Museum at Kingussie by Miss Russell-Fergusson and is on view there. Opinion has been divided as to whether indeed this harp may not be an ancient one, but the fact of the polished stone ornaments being affixed to the nose-piece with small nuts and screws almost certainly confirms it as a reproduction, according to the experts. Another similar Glen harp is in private ownership at Banchory, Kincardineshire.

Lord Archibald Campbell was the first President of *An Comunn Gàidhealach*, and he instituted a competition for the playing of the clarsach at the first Gaelic Mod in 1892, for which, until 1902 he gave yearly money prizes. In 1907 and 1908, the prizes were given by that picturesque Jacobite personality Theodore Napier, whose tall kilted figure was a familiar one in Edinburgh in the early years of the century. The clarsach competitions were popular for the first few years; but towards 1909 they seem to have languished through lack of competitors; and for the next five years or so, little seems to have been heard of the instrument.

The person who seems to have done more than anyone to save the clarsach from a second demise at this critical period, and who is acknowledged to have inspired others afresh to play it, was Miss Patuffa Kennedy Fraser, daughter of Marjory Kennedy Fraser, who, in 1914 took up the instrument for the purpose of accompanying her mother's songs. For this she used a small Celtic harp made by George Morley of London. The firm of Morley, who have been established as makers of harps since 1816, had commenced making the small Celtic harp for the Irish market about 1890. George Morley did not copy any particular model but made his own design. The nearest similar instrument to his was the Irish harp made by John Egan, harp maker in Dublin until about 1820; but there were considerable variations between the Egan harp and the Morley Celtic harp, in length of strings and in overall dimensions. Miss Kennedy Fraser has said that Morley's Celtic harps were then all painted green and decorated with Irish Shamrocks, and she had to wait some time to get one in plain wood which might be considered as more suitable for Scottish use!

Later, Miss Kennedy Fraser sang the Songs of the Hebrides to her own clarsach accompaniments arranged by herself. She sang and played the clarsach to the troops in France during the 1914–18 war, and afterwards played the instrument to her own singing in concert tours in the United States and then in most of the capitals of Europe, as well as in this country.

Miss Patuffa Kennedy Fraser's enthusiasm inspired others, as has been said. In the early 1920's, Duncan Macleod of Skeabost, Mrs Hilda Campbell of Airds, the Royal Celtic Society and others assisted the revival by the further giving of prizes for the competitions. Mrs Campbell of Airds played the instrument extensively herself at concerts and recitals in the 1920's amidst a growing enthusiasm, and interest.

In 1931, at the suggestion of Mrs Duncan Macleod of Skeabost, the Clarsach Society, *Comunn na Clàrsaich*, was formed. Under the presidency of Mrs Campbell of Airds, the fortunes of the Society and of its ancient instrument advanced steadily, until it could be said that once again the clarsach had become part of the musical life of Scotland. On the retirement of Mrs Campbell as President in 1954, when she was made Honorary Life President, the Society was fortunate enough to have as her successor General Sir Philip Christison, a man of strong musical interests in whose energetic hands *Comunn na Clàrsaich* continues to advance, with a steadily growing membership of some four hundred both in this country and abroad.

Concerning the clarsachs themselves, these have been obtained from several sources. Those of Morley have already been mentioned. The Irish harps of John Egan, though becoming increasingly rare, are still to be had, and are much sought after for their beauty of tone. The development of the harp in Ireland however as seen in the Egan harps, shows that the instrument had grown away somewhat from the pattern of the ancient Scottish one with which it once had such a close identity.

In 1932 Henry Briggs, a Yorkshire-born violin maker living in Scotland, was asked by Mrs Campbell to try his hand at the making of a clarsach. For his first attempt he and his father cut down a large harp and made of it a small one of the Irish pattern. Later he incorporated the distinctive and musically important feature of the Scottish clarsach known as 'The Highland Hump'. This is an upward curve or hump in the crosspiece, rising over the narrow treble end of the harp towards the top of the sound-box, which gives a greater length of string in the upper compass of the instrument, and is acknowledged to improve the tone-quality.

Henry Briggs died in 1963 after making clarsachs for thirty-four years. His clarsachs are highly prized for their fine tone and superb craftsmanship, as well as for the beauty of their carving. They will doubtless become more and more sought after.

Arnold Dolmetsch also made several small clarsachs based on antique Irish models in the Dublin museum, which he strung with wire, to be played with the finger-nails after the old fashion. (The modern clarsach is strung with gut.) Miss Edith Taylor, the first Honorary Secretary of *Comunn na Clàrsaich*, has one of these on which she once played for the writer at a B.B.C. 'Country Magazine' programme from Lochaline, Morvern. Dolmetsch also made a number of larger gut-strung harps based, though freely, on the Queen Mary Harp. The wire-strung clarsach has an incisive tone-colour interestingly different from that of the gut strings played with the pads of the fingers.

In addition to proving the ideal accompaniment for the singing of Gaelic song, the clarsach has of recent years shown its usefulness for special effects in the theatre and in plays on radio. Playgoers may remember Miss Jean Campbell's playing of the clarsach in J. M. Barrie's *The Boy David*; in Alexander Reid's *The Lass wi' the Muckle Mou*; and in Robert Kemp's play, with music by the writer, *The Man among the Roses*, at the Gateway Theatre.

CHAPTER IX

The Music of Orkney and Shetland

THE island communities of Orkney and Shetland are of course of Norwegian racial origin. The indigenous music of both—or what is left of it—is therefore of Scandinavian provenance, and culturally speaking should not be included with the music of Scotland. However as both island groups have formed a part of Scotland politically for five centuries, a book on Scottish music would hardly be complete without reference to them, for their music is full of colour and interest.

Who the original inhabitants of the islands were, is a question for the ethnologists. All that concerns us is that *Hjaltland* (Shetland) was conquered by the Norwegian Harald Fairhair about A.D. 890.[1] The islands remained Norwegian until 1468, when they were put in pledge to Scotland pending payment of the final portion of the promised dowry of Margaret, daughter of Christian I, king of Norway, on her marriage to James III of Scotland. The pledge was never redeemed, and the islands were annexed to Scotland in lieu in 1612.

The Norn language continued to be the ordinary speech of Orkney until the end of the seventeenth century, and of Shetland to the middle of the eighteenth.[2]

All the signs of a rich musical culture exist. Unfortunately the collecting of it was not done in time, and most of it has been lost. The songs largely perished as the Norn ceased to be the spoken language,[3] and while in Shetland a large number of instrumental tunes survive for the fiddle—some of them perhaps originally composed for the *Gue* (the Shetland version of the *croud*, which apparently survived as late as Sir Walter

---

[1] Hume Brown, *A History of Scotland* (Cambridge, 1911).
[2] *County Folk Lore*, Series Vol. III, 'Orkney and Shetland Islands', Preface, p. vi (London, 1903).
[3] Gunn in his *Orkney: The Magnetic North* (London, 1927), says that Norse songs and ballads were current in North Ronaldsay as late as the last quarter of the eighteenth century and that 'Probably such songs were sung in Orkney as in Shetland at the beginning of the nineteenth century as well.' The latter part of his statement at least however must be treated with considerable reserve.

Scott's day); in Orkney even the instrumental music seems to have gone.

The stringed instrument played with the bow seems always to have been popular in Shetland, as it is in Norway in the Hardanger fiddle. Writing in 1809, A. E. Edmonstone says 'Music is very generally cultivated as an amusement of the Zetlanders of all ranks, and some of them have, at different times, attained no inconsiderable degree of excellence in several departments. Many of both sexes have voices of great modulation, but they are seldom improved; and among the peasantry almost *one in ten*[1] can play on the violin.(!) There are still a few native airs to be met with in some parts of the country which may be considered as peculiar, and much resemble the wild and plaintive strains of the Norwegian music.' Edmonstone however considered that the violin itself was then of comparatively recent importation.

Writing of the more ancient stringed instrument, the *Gue*, the predecessor of the violin in Shetland, Samuel Hibbert says,[2] 'Before violins were introduced, the musicians performed on an instrument called a Gue, which appears to have some similarity to a violin, but had only two strings of horsehair, and was played upon in the same manner as a violoncello.'

The *Gue* is mentioned by Sir Walter Scott in his novel of *The Pirate* (Chapter XV) where he refers to the sound of the *Gue* and the *Langspiel*. Scott visited the islands in 1814. The Welsh instrument of comparable type, the *crwth*, is known to have been in use in Wales as late as *the end of the nineteenth century* (Grove), and it therefore seems fully possible that its Shetland equivalent may have been in use at the time of Sir Walter Scott's visit. His mention of the Langspiel, an Icelandic instrument said by Professor Otto Andersson to be related to the Norwegian *Langeleik* and the Swedish *Hummel*, seems however to be the only reference to its use in Shetland, and must be regarded as questionable.

Hibbert says further: 'When the Gue . . . was aiding the conviviality of Yule, then would a number of the happy sons and daughters of Hjaltland take each other by the hand, and while one of them sang a Norn *viseck*, they would perform a circular dance, their steps continually changing with the tune.' The description of this *viseck* dance seems

---

[1] The writer's italics: The writer is informed by Mr Tom Anderson of Lerwick that a hundred years ago a fiddle could be bought for one and sixpence (which happily accords with the old nursery rhyme: 'I bought a fiddle for eighteen pence!'). The fiddles came in ship-cargoes from Germany.

[2] *A Description of the Shetland Islands*, Samuel Hibbert (Edinburgh, 1822).

very similar to the circular sung-dances ('ballads') of Iceland and the Faroe Islands, which the writer has seen performed.

Of the *viseck* above mentioned, the Danish scholar J. J. A. Worsaae wrote following a visit to Orkney and Shetland in 1846 that the young people used to dance to *songs* (Visecks) and *ballads* (in Danish, *Qvad*), a custom once prevalent all over the North and still to be found in the Faroe Islands.

More recently, in 1932, Mrs Jessie Saxby writes that some of the old rhymes called 'Veesiks' (which she herself remembered) were in an *unknown tongue*, and that these must be of Scandinavian origin.[1] Professor Otto Andersson sums up the situation by saying that 'We now know that the Scandinavian settlers in the Shetland islands brought over songs, tunes, and the ballad-dance to their new land in early times. Consequently they presumably also brought with them the musical instruments used in the old country.'

Considering that most of the traditional and national fiddle music of Scotland itself has come into being since the seventeenth century at earliest, it might be expected that a large new corpus of native music might by this time have arisen in the northern islands also; yet the creation of the Shetland fiddle tunes seems to be of comparatively recent date, much of it having been composed within living memory, and indeed being composed today. In Orkney there seems to be as yet no comparable creative activity, although it now has a flourishing reel and strathspey society, which may perhaps provide a first step for its emergence.

Following this general summary, we may now consider the music of Orkney and Shetland separately in greater detail.

THE MUSIC OF ORKNEY

A few Orkney ballads without their tunes are given in *County Folklore*, Vol. III, including the verse play, presumably once sung, of 'Lady Odivere'. This also gives 'The Finfolk's Foy Song'. Unfortunately this has been 'improved' in the fashion of Bishop Percy, by W. T. Dennison, who frankly admits that he could not remember afterwards which were the original lines and which were the result of his 'tinkering' (he uses the actual word).

The Balfour Collection of *Ancient Orkney Melodies*[2] was a praise-

---

[1] *Shetland Traditional Lore* (Edinburgh, 1932). See also 'Scandinavian Folk Music— A Survey', by Erik Dal, *International Folk Music Council Journal*, Vol. VIII, 1956.

[2] *Ancient Orkney Melodies*, Colonel David Balfour of Balfour, Edinburgh, 1885 (privately printed).

worthy though scarcely successful attempt to capture the songs of Orkney in 1885, by Colonel David Balfour of Balfour Castle in the island of Shapensay. It consists of thirty-six of the song airs which were being sung in the islands at that time. He describes these as the native airs of his childhood, as heard round the kitchen fire at his home, songs sung by the young women at their spinning, and the men and lads at the mending of their nets or harness.

Unfortunately it is well nigh impossible to guess which, if any, of the tunes are of native Orkney origin and which are importations, as he has not been able to remember the words of any except two, and neither of these is of Orkney subject or locale. The forgotten song words have been replaced by a series of verses of Victorian flavour, mostly by the collector himself, which are of no value as a contribution to the subject. Two of the airs bear Orkney titles—'Sigurd' and 'Alorelo', the latter thought to be from the Norse interjection of sorrow 'Ylur' still then common in Orkney as 'Aloor'! A few bear the titles of the great Scots ('Child') ballads such as 'The Cruel Mother', 'Johnny Armstrong', 'Chevy Chase', etc. Some have palpably Scots titles like 'My Bonny Boy' and the well-known 'Oh my love's in Germany'. Some are recognizably English folk-song airs like 'I wish in vain' ('Died for Love'), 'Rings on her Hand', 'The false lover', and the good old English favourite 'When Stormy Winds do Blow'. Many of the airs are unnamed, but these follow the general pattern of the others. There are a number of genuinely beautiful airs in the collection, but one must sum it up regretfully as contributing little to our knowledge of the real, indigenous Orkney music.

Much more important is the find of Professor Otto Andersson of Finland who visited Orkney in 1938 to search for songs and tunes. He publishes thirty of these,[1] most of them, like the songs of the Balfour Collection, folk-songs of Scots or English provenance. In the island of Flotta however he found a pearl of great price. This was no less than the tune of the great Orkney ballad of 'The Great Selchie'[2] of Sule Skerry (Child 113):

[1] Cf. *Ballad Hunting in the Orkney Islands, The Budkavlen* (Abo, 1956).
[2] Selchie = a seal.

Arranged for voice and piano in 1952 by the writer with Professor Otto Andersson's permission. Cf. *Songs from Country Magazine* (Paxton and Co.).

Professor Andersson's Collection also includes a tune with the title of 'Wedding March in Orkney', about which however one would require to know more before one could accept it as of true Orkney tradition. It is strongly reminiscent of the style of 'Scots marches' composed in numbers in the eighteenth century by James Oswald, General Reid, the Gows and others.

Summing up, it must be concluded as already stated that most of the native music of Orkney has failed to survive. Some of the tunes of the ancient *visecks* may perhaps exist in the circular song-dances of Iceland and the Faroes if one could identify them.

One can understand the songs dying out with the change of language from Norn to Scots; but why the instrumental music died out also is not so easy to explain.[1]

THE MUSIC OF SHETLAND

In Shetland the Norn language lingered, as we have seen, into the middle of the eighteenth century.[2] Though this was only a half century

[1] The statement of non-survival of folk-music in a particular locality is of course one which has been proved wrong again and again by practically everyone who has ever been rash enough to make it, from Patrick Macdonald in 1781 onwards, and the writer would be happy to be proved wrong in his turn. (To be exact it is the unnamed author of the *Dissertation* in the Patrick Macdonald Collection who makes the comment.) One must add however that such a sad statement of Orkney music seems to be in accordance with the evidence—or lack of it—at present available—discounting some recent 'finds' by undiscriminating collectors, which are either of Scottish (or English) mainland origin, or for other reasons valueless in this connotation.

[2] *Country Folk Lore*, Vol. III.

later than the generally accepted date for its survival in Orkney, it was evidently in some ways a vital period for its preservation, for more of the Norn tongue has survived in both song and folk-tale in Shetland than is the case in the less northerly group; and Norn words as well as many of the characteristics of pronunciation of the dialect are still in use in everyday speech.

As in Orkney, a number of the Norn words of the older songs have survived while the tunes have become lost. The tradition of preserving words and ignoring tunes has held sway in Shetland as elsewhere. Specimens of these may be seen in *County Folklore*, Vol. III, such as the following:

> Saina poba wer-a
> Leetra mavie, Leetra mavie,
> Saina poba wer-a
> Letra mavie drengie, etc.
> (three verses given).

The same volume gives the tune without the words of 'an ancient Scandinavian Air preserved in Shetland' from Hibbert's *Shetland*. The air is an interesting one. There is also the well-known New Year's Even Song, 'We're a' Queen Mary's Men' which is still sung by the children.

WE'RE A' QUEEN MARY'S MEN

Singer: Kitty Anderson, Yell, Shetland.　　Recorded and transcribed by Francis Collinson

This is good New Year's ev-en night　Sant Ma-ry's men are we, an, we've come here to craa wir rights a-fore wir la - - die.＿＿ Op-en your kist an' shak' yir fead-ders Sant Ma-ry's men are we an' din-na think 'hat we ir' beg-gars a - fore wir la - die.＿

↑ = sung sharper than written.

Shetland is fortunate in having a flourishing Folk Society, which has recovered much genuine folk material of Shetland both musical and non-musical, such as the charming lullaby 'Hurr hurr dee noo' (partly reconstructed) and an attractive spinning song 'De Norrowa Wheel'.

The best known of the instrumental tunes is the Foula Reel, which may be found both in the Folk Lore Society's volume and in the *Shetland Folk Book*.

The most striking of the older Shetland songs is the Unst Boat-song, published by the Viking Society from the notation of William Ratter and reprinted in the *Shetland Folk Book*. The words are in Norn, of which the first verse is:

> Starka virna vestilie,
> Obadeea! Obadeea!
> Starka virna vestilie,
> Obadeea monye!

Obadeea might perhaps be translated as 'abide ye!' or 'put yourself to the task!'[1]

Another interesting song with its Norn refrain of ' *Skowan ürla grun* is the ballad of King Orfeo. This is the Celtic version of the story of Orpheus and Euridice, in which Orfeo successfully rescues Heurodis (Euridice) from Elfland to which she was carried off by the king of the fairies. (The word 'trow' is not here used.) The ballad, with some stanzas lacking, is published by Child (No. 19). The earliest version of the text[2] is in the fourteenth-century Auchinleck Manuscript. With our preceding chapter on the harp in mind it is interesting to note that at the end of the Auchinleck text it says that 'harpers in Britain heard this marvel, and made a lay thereof, which they called ' *Lay Orfeo*' (this agrees with the Gaelic nomenclature in ' *Laoidh Fhraoich*', *Laoidh Chaoilte*', etc.). The tune of ' *King Orfeo*' was noted down by Patrick Shuldham Shaw in 1947. Mr Shuldham Shaw has done much valuable work in collecting the music of Shetland, and his articles in the *Journal of the English Folk Dance and Song Society* are useful contributions to the subject.[3]

A number of old Shetland song melodies have, like those of the Balfour Collection in Orkney, had new words written for them to replace lost originals, such as 'The Galley Song', sung at the New Year Festival of Up-Helli-'A; and 'De Hümin' (the evening).[4]

---

[1] Cf. also, 'Suggested glossary by Wm. Ratter' in *Shetland Folk Book*.
[2] Printed by David Laing in *Select Remains of the Ancient Popular Poetry of Scotland*.
[3] *Journal E.F.D.S.S.*, Vol. V, No. 2, Vol. VI, No. 1 and Vol. IX, No. 3.
[4] Many of the older Shetland fiddle tunes have until recently existed only in the memories of the older fiddlers, among whom special mention must be made of the

Shetland, like the Hebrides, has its fairy tunes, there called 'Trow' tunes. They are said, like those of the Hebrides, to have been heard issuing from the fairy mounds or in other ways heard from the playing of the 'trows', and to have been picked up and remembered by the passing wayfarer. Among the more attractive of these is the '*Aith Rant*'.[1]

The favourite musical instrument of Shetland, as we have seen, is the fiddle, and today it flourishes as healthily—probably more so—than ever before. The old fiddle tunes have been preserved, and so many new ones composed, that Shetland fiddle music has become a *genre* of its own, with characteristics that are distinctive. The Shetlander has been acquisitive too of the tunes which have come his way from other countries, mostly brought by the large foreign floating population from whaling and other fishing vessels. The 'Muckle Reel of Finnigarth'[2] for instance has been identified as a Norwegian 'Halling' or country dance; similarly the 'Shetland Bride's March'[3], played to accompany the bridal party to the church, is of everyday occurrence in Norway, where the instrument is of course the Hardanger Fiddle. The Wedding tune '*Da farder ben da Welcomer*'[4] is also said to follow the Scandinavian idiom. The air of 'The Merry Boys o' Greenland'[5] bears a strong resemblance to a country dance tune from North Jutland; 'The Shaalds o' Foula' (Foula Reel)[6] is said to be known as a Swedish country dance.

The Greenland whaling ships all carried a fiddler to entertain the crews at work. The fiddler might be from Shetland, Holland, or from Greenland itself. Sometimes the fiddlers from different ships would meet and exchange tunes, and these have found their way into the Shetland repertoire.[7]

Mr Tom Anderson of Lerwick informs the writer that a number of the fiddle tunes of Shetland are of Irish origin, and he recounted that on a recent visit to Ireland he was able to join in with the Irish fiddlers in a number of the airs which he knew already as Shetland tunes. One

[1] *Shetland Folk Book*, Vol. II. [2] Ibid., p. 38.
[3] Ibid., Vol. III, p. 50.   [4] Ibid., Vol. I, p. 37.   [5] Ibid., Vol. II, p. 39.
[6] Although the Shaalds o' Foula is now known as the 'Foula Reel' the latter was a different dance altogether and was danced to a Scots tune.
[7] The writer has heard one of these Greenland-Shetland tunes played at a folk-music conference in Canada as a French-Canadian tune.

late John Stickle (1875–1957) whose repertoire has been extensively noted down by Patrick Shuldham Shaw; and the veteran fiddle player and friend of the writer, Peter Fraser.

must add that Mr Anderson himself and his fellow fiddle-players are composing new and good fiddle tunes in numbers and of a quality that makes it possible to say that, whereas the classic days of the composition of fiddle tunes in Scotland were those of the eighteenth century, in Shetland they are those of today. A number of these Shetland fiddle tunes, old and new, are available on disc.[1]

The fiddle tunes of Shetland have an altogether different sound from those of Scotland itself. This is probably chiefly due to the fact that the fiddle music of Shetland has been quite uninfluenced by the scale of the bagpipe, which is to the Shetlander a foreign instrument—though Scots fiddle music itself is popular enough in Shetland. The characteristically Scottish effect of the progression of figures on major triads a tone apart is not by any means unknown in Shetland, but it is managed with a smoothness and neatness that is quite unlike the rugged and somewhat brusque effect of the 'double tonic' of the Scots fiddlers.

[1] Issued by Waverley Records, Edinburgh.

CHAPTER X

The Gaelic Long Tunes for the Psalms

THOUGH church music in the ordinary sense can hardly be classed as folk or traditional music, there is a species of unaccompanied unison psalm singing among the Gaelic-speaking congregations of the West Highlands of Scotland which is of interest to the student of Scottish folk tradition because it is in fact a folk embellishment of the Scottish psalm tunes originally introduced at the Reformation. It is a style of singing directly derived from the Scottish musical tradition— the same tradition of melodic variation and ornament which we see in piobaireachd.

At the time of the Reformation, the tunes of the psalters were composed, some at Geneva by French composers like Louis Bourgeois, and some by Scotsmen in Scotland, like Andrew Blackhall, David Peebles, John Angus, etc. The psalms were printed in English *with their tunes* by Robert Lekprevik of Edinburgh in 1564, that is, five years after the commencement of the Reformation in Scotland with John Knox's famous and catastrophic sermon at Perth on 11 May 1559, a sermon which as one might say, 'lit a beacon' for the people—of which unfortunately much of the combustible material was to be provided in the physical form of the manuscript music books of the older church![1]

The psalms were not printed in metre in *Gaelic* however until 1659— *a hundred years later* (and then only the first fifty). The Highlanders had no means of acquiring the tunes of the psalms but that of oral transmission; in the course of which all the processes of ornamentation and variation which invariably goes with the oral transmission of tunes, began to operate. The tunes were of course completely foreign to the Highland musical style to begin with—an alien quality of idiom to which the Highlanders soon evolved their own solution. Commencing probably with the ornamentation of the tune with grace-notes to bring

[1] For a full account of the Scottish psalm tunes, the reader is referred to a series of eight weekly articles by the writer in *The Scotsman* commencing 1 October 1960, commissioned for the 400th anniversary of the Reformation in Scotland.

it more into line with native practice, they gradually came to accept these embellishments as the normal form of the tune. Eventually ornamentation accumulated to such an extent that each individual syllable of the words of the psalms were made to carry a whole *roulade* of notes. The tunes gradually grew both in complexity and in length until they became quite unrecognizable as the printed Common Tunes of the Lowland psalter in English from which they had started, except to the skilled musicologist.

In addition to this, each line of the psalm was interspersed with a musical 'reading of the line' before it was sung, by a percentor, (as it is in Gaelic congregations today), to a conventionalized curious, almost oriental-sounding cantillation which owes nothing to the tune of the psalm at all.

In time, the origin of the tunes as those of the psalter became forgotten, and the psalm tunes as sung in the Highlands came eventually to be regarded as tunes of unknown and rather mysterious origin in their own right. They were known as the *Long Tunes*, a not inappropriate term, as each tune had eventually grown to three or four times the length of its printed original. There were six of these 'Long Tunes' in use, and they bore the names of well-known Common Tunes of the (Lowland) Scottish Psalter—'French', 'Martyrs', 'Stilt', 'Elgin', 'Dundee' and 'Old London'.

Ingenious suggestions appeared from time to time as to the origin of the Long Tunes. Even in a comparatively recent publication authorized by the Free Church of Scotland, we find the following introduction to a printed transcription of the Long Tunes:

> It may be stated as a possible origin of these Long Tunes that they are Swedish airs picked up from fellow soldiers by the Highlanders who served in the army of the seventeenth century.[1] The fact that the tunes were confined entirely to those districts of the Highlands from which the soldiers were recruited makes the conjecture of this origin almost a certainty.

Needless to say it is hardly possible for the musical historian and student to agree with any such reasoning.

The first person to investigate the Long Tunes systematically was Joseph Mainzer, a German musician who came to Scotland in 1842 and lived here for five years. Mainzer demonstrated in a painstaking study of the tunes that they were in fact merely profusely ornamented and

[1] This must certainly mean the army of Gustavus Adolphus (1594-1632) in which there were many Scots volunteers, including David Leslie (of 'Leslie's March' tune) the victor of Philiphaugh.

extended versions of the psalter tunes bearing the same names. He found that each note of the original psalter tune had lengthened into as many as ten notes in the Long Tune, all ten notes being sung to one single syllable of the words of the psalm—the melody twining around the notes of its Psalter original like a Celtic knot-pattern. Mainzer showed that the two sets of tunes corresponded, inasmuch that (a) the notes of the Psalter tune could be found among the notes of the Long Tune (though this was not a strong argument; (b) wherever the Psalter tune rose and fell the Long Tune did likewise; (c) the first notes of each phrase of the two tunes nearly always corresponded—an important point. It may be observed further that the end-notes of each phrase or line of the psalm significantly *only fail to correspond* in both tunes where the last note of the Psalter tune is one which the Highland ear, with its partiality for its own gapped scales, finds ungrateful and difficult of acceptance. Finally the two sets of tunes bear the same names in the Highlands as in the Lowlands—and these are in *English* and not Gaelic, which points further to their Lowland origin.

Mainzer arranged one of the Gaelic Long Tunes, 'French' for voices in four-part harmony; a proceeding which though of dubious propriety to the folk-musician, paradoxically now probably provides the only survival of the Long Tunes in actual congregational performance, being sung by the massed choirs at the closing concert of the annual National Gaelic Mod; for the Long Tunes went out of general use towards the end of last century, possibly being looked upon at last as having become impracticably ornate. Fortunately this most interesting form of folk-singing still survives in the memories of those who heard their parents sing the tunes in their old accustomed way, and the writer has been able to record examples of the singing of them. These have since been supplemented by remarkable recordings made by Dr Thorkild Knudsen for the School of Scottish Studies, of the singing of the Psalms in home family worship—a singing in which the overlapping of the precenting and answering of each line of the Psalm by two or three solo singers displays an astonishing species of free and musically uninhibited counterpoint.

Though the full flowering of the Scottish Highland genius for musical decoration may have gone from the singing of the psalms with the passing of the Long Tunes however, the process which evolved them is still very much alive, in the singing of newer tunes such as 'Torwood', 'Martyrdom', 'St David's',' Stornoway' and the like. The congregation sing in *unison* unaccompanied, as is the custom of the Gael, but with a profuse ornamentation of the melody with grace-notes, or *slurs* as the highlanders themselves call them in English, each singer *improvising his or her own grace-note decoration of the tune* as the spirit moves him. The result is astonishing, for it creates a shimmering kaleidoscopic harmony of its own, against which the unison of the tune stands out in great strength and dignity. It is, as far as is known, unlike any other singing in the world, being, like *piobaireachd*, apparently unique to Scotland; and it is still to be heard among the church congregations of the Hebrides.[1]

There are signs however that, what with the influence of the more conventional choral singing to be heard on the radio, and the tacit assumption of its being the model for all to copy; what with the conscientious but perhaps to be regretted zeal of musical instructors in the Highlands in attempting to 'reform' the singing of the congregations in their musical charge; and above all perhaps, with the meticulous choir-training of the Mod choirs on non-indigenous methods in the midst of the Highlands themselves, this ages-old grace-noting style of psalm-singing is on its way out.

Fortunately the writer, by courtesy of the Free Church and Church of Scotland in the Hebrides, has been able to record examples of it for posterity.

---

[1] This singing may also be heard in some church congregations of Scots origin in the Dominions (particularly in Canada) and in the United States.

CHAPTER XI

Conclusion: The Reader's Part

THE task of giving a picture of Scotland's traditional music is one of the piecing together of a jigsaw of material available from manuscripts, early printed sources and collected oral tradition. No book about it can ever really be complete until all the material has been recovered; and this is still, as may be gathered from these pages, far from being achieved, if indeed it ever could be.

As far as material in oral tradition is concerned, it will be obvious to the reader that there must be a great deal still to be recovered. Several of the examples which the writer has quoted in this book have only come into his hands, mostly through the courtesy of other collectors, while the writing of it was actually in progress. New material is being brought to light all the time by the devoted members of the School of Scottish Studies. Indeed the writer was present at the recording there of a further variant of one of the ancient Heroic Ballads only three weeks before these words were being penned.

Not so obvious perhaps is it that some of the *manuscript* material necessary for a complete picture may still be expected to come in. Partly this is because so many of the source manuscripts have become lost, of which it is perhaps not too much to hope that some may yet be found again. Some of them may of course have been destroyed; but undoubtedly some must be lying about in private bookshelves, attics or basements, or in second-hand bookshops and even street bookstalls. (It was a *croquet-box* that yielded up the Boswell papers in 1930). Let us consider a few of these lost source-manuscripts.

First there is the Blaikie Manuscript, consisting of two collections of Scots and English airs in tablutare for the viola da gamba, made by Andrew Blaikie, an engraver of Paisley for his own pleasure in 1683, *both* lost. Fortunately transcriptions of most, but not all, of the airs were made, and these are now in the Wighton Library, Dundee; but it would be useful if the originals could be found.

There is also the important Straloch Manuscript, said to be the earliest collection containing Scottish airs.[1] Written in lute tablature for Robert Gordon of Straloch, the manuscript bears the two dates 1627 and 1629. The manuscript disappeared from public ken at the sale of effects of a later owner, James Chalmers, in London.

Then there is 'Mrs Crockat's Manuscript', said to have been dated 1709. This was extensively quoted by Stenhouse in his notes for the 1803 reprint of *The Scots Musical Museum*. Now, lost, no one ever seems to have seen it but Stenhouse. It would be valuable evidence for confirmation of some of his statements concerning many of our Scots songs which are otherwise unsupported.

There is also a 'McFarlane's Manuscript', entitled *A Collection of Scots Airs written for the use of Walter McFarlane of that ilk*, made by a David Young in 1740. One out of its three volumes was lent and never returned. The other two, formerly in the possession of the Society of Antiquaries of Scotland, are now at the National Library.

There is, too, the collection of Scots ballad-tunes made by Mrs Brown of Falkland, which was sent to, and lost by, William Tytler, the father of Lord Tytler of Woodhouselee, mentioned on page 142.

Of the three volumes of the precious 'Colin Campbell Canntaireachd', the source of many of our hitherto unknown piobaireachd, the first went missing soon after it was taken to the famous piping competition of 1818, when it first brought the existence of *canntaireachd* to the knowledge of the general public. It is quite possible that the missing volume may contain unknown piobaireachd.

Various other piobaireachd and other Scots musical manuscripts came into the hands of the Highland Society of London during the first half of the nineteenth century. According to Archibald Campbell of Kilberry, there now seems to be no trace of these. (*Ceòl Mor*, page 11).

So much for the *known* manuscripts which have gone amissing. As an indication of the calibre of manuscript material which may yet turn up, one might mention the remarkable Angus Fraser Manuscript recovered about 1950. This, the most important collection of Scottish Gaelic airs and *Scottish Harp Tunes*, to be recovered in the past hundred years, and the only seemingly authentic Scottish harp-music ever to be recovered, was discovered by Professor S. T. M. Newman, Dean of the Faculty of Music at Edinburgh, in a second-hand bookshop in Edinburgh in 1950 or thereabouts. It has been presented by him to the Library of Edinburgh University.

Regarding fiddlers' tune-books in manuscript, the writer has already described how his late father-in-law Dr Alexander Grant of Dufftown

[1] Frank Kidson; *Grove's Dictionary of Music*, fourth edition.

picked up such a tune-book in a bookshop in Aberdeen bearing the date 1705, which makes it one of the oldest, if not *the* oldest such tune-book for the fiddle known in Scotland.

Other notable manuscript collections gifted in recent years are the Fraser of Mull Manuscript (National Library of Scotland) and Lady D'oyly's Manuscript, now at the School of Scottish Studies

Of hardly a note of Niel Gow's musical manuscripts is the where-abouts known however; and beyond one letter in the National Library and one or two biographical articles about him in print, all records of the personal life of this great Scots fiddler seem to have disappeared.

Here then is where the reader can play a part in the fuller recovery of Scotland's traditional music by keeping his eyes open for any such material, and sending it, or an account of it, to the National Library of Scotland. *Any* musical manuscript of Scottish tunes is worth sending for inspection and evaluation by the experts concerned. Such Scots material may not necessarily of course be in Scotland. It could be in any of the Dominions, or for that matter, in any of the European countries. (Let us not forget, too, that according to Sir John Sinclair, James Macpherson is thought to have lost many of the precious Gaelic originals from which he had composed his *Ossian*, in Florida, U.S.A., when he accompanied Governor Johnstone there as his secretary in 1764.)

In such a way, from New Zealand, came an offer out of the blue to the writer in the summer of 1963 from a descendant of James Hogg the Ettrick Shepherd,[1] to send back to Scotland the Ettrick Shepherd's fiddle. The writer suggested that the donor should place the fiddle under the care of the Faculty of Music, Edinburgh University, where it now is. The same donor is in hopes of recovering some of James Hogg's musical manuscripts, which, if they are found, could be of considerable interest.[2]

As has been said, the equally important task of recording the tradi-tional music still in oral tradition is one of the interests of the School of Scottish Studies, Edinburgh University. The School will always be glad to have the names of informants with knowledge of songs and stories. These pages may have shown the value of the kind of material still to be recovered in this way, both in Gaelic and Lowland Scots, from the *Ossianic* and other Heroic Ballads, to the great Lowland Scots 'Child' Ballads *with their tunes*; from bothy ballads and folk-songs of all sorts (in

[1] The offer came from Mrs E. Parr on behalf of the family of the late Robert Gilkison of Dunedin, grandson of James Hogg, of which she is a member.

[2] Just as this book goes to press, the writer learns that two fiddles belonging to the famous William Marshall have been similarly deposited under the care of the Faculty of Music, Edinburgh University by his descendents.

either of Scotland's two languages) to children's nursery rhymes and game songs. The School of Scottish Studies however only operates at present in Scotland. There must obviously be many tradition-bearers of Scottish folk-material in the Dominions. It is up to collectors there to record them themselves. In Canada, this is already officially organized. Needless to say a copy of all such recordings will always be welcome in Scotland itself.

In conclusion, it is the hope of the writer that he may have been able to show the reader at least something of the tremendous wealth and kaleidoscopic variety of Scotland's traditional and national music, of which there is still so much to be recovered even now. One is tempted to say that the time for its recovery is running out; but this is a statement which has been proved wrong again and again. Let all who love Scotland therefore keep their eyes and ears open in the search.

Index